THE
PROPHET'S
PULPIT

*Commentaries
on the State of Islam*

VOLUME II

THE PROPHET'S PULPIT

Commentaries on the State of Islam

VOLUME II

Khaled Abou El Fadl

EDITED BY JOSEF LINNHOFF

The Prophet's Pulpit: Commentaries on the State of Islam, Volume II

For information about this title or to order other books and/or electronic media, contact the publisher:

Usuli Press
715 Shawan Falls Drive, Suite 662
Dublin, OH 43017
www.usulipress.com
Email: info@usulipress.com

Usuli Press is an imprint of The Institute for Advanced Usuli Studies (The Usuli Institute).
www.usuli.org

Library of Congress Control Number (LCCN): 2022900222

ISBN's:
Hardcover Case Laminate: 978-1-957063-08-9
Hardcover Dust Jacket: 978-1-957063-07-2
Paperback: 978-1-957063-06-5
eBook: 978-1-957063-05-8
Library Bound: 978-1-957063-03-4

Printed in the United States of America

Cover design by Robin Locke Monda
Interior design by 1106 Design

The Arabic Calligraphy on the front cover can be translated as "There is no strength or power except with God."

This book is dedicated to our dear friend, Cameron Lee.
Fiercely honest and passionate about Truth and Justice.

To God we belong and to God we return . . . (Q 2:156)

Contents

· · · · · · · · · · · ·

Contents

Introduction

· · · · · · · · · · · ·

There was a considerable response to Volume I of *The Prophet's Pulpit*. Since its release in April 2022, the work has struck a chord with a wide range of academics, activists, and lay readers, born Muslims and converts, young and old. Many readers have contacted The Usuli Institute to describe the impact the work has had upon them. Many said they found in *The Prophet's Pulpit* the beautiful, ethical, and intelligent Islam that in their hearts they always knew to be true. Converts have described the work as the one book they feel comfortable sharing with their families and non-Muslim friends to explain their reasons for converting to Islam. One reader, so moved by the book, donated a monthly amount for The Usuli Institute to distribute free copies worldwide. Requests soon followed from all over the world. At the time of writing, Volume I of *The Prophet's Pulpit* has reached over 50 countries across the West, the Muslim-majority world, and even farther afield. A major U.S. civil rights advocacy group requested copies for every regional office nationwide. Islamic schools from the U.S. and Canada to Kenya and Nigeria received bulk orders for teachers and students. Several readers have translated excerpts for friends and family into German, Bengali, and Amharic. Nor is the response limited to Muslims. A pleasant surprise has been the warm reception among non-Muslims.

It seems there is a real interest today in hearing a learned, honest, and authoritative insider's account of Islam and the Muslim world. The Islamophobes of today may be vocal and violent, but they are not the full story. For every Abu Lahab, there are many Uthman ibn Talhas.[1]

This response is, of course, hugely encouraging. But it is not a surprise. I was first drawn to Professor Abou El Fadl and the work of The Usuli Institute precisely because of the impact his *khutbah*s (sermons) had upon me. The vision of Islam expressed in his *khutbah*s—at once intelligent and intuitive, rooted in the past but relevant to the present—were a weekly reminder of why I had fallen in love with the faith. I also knew that so many Muslims, like myself, had tired of the dull and uninspiring *khutbah*s they would hear in their local mosques. Yet the response to Volume I should not distract us from a sad truth. *The Prophet's Pulpit* may have resonated with readers around the world, but the book came from the margins, not the mainstream. After almost four decades in the West, Professor Abou El Fadl was forced to give the *khutbah*s that comprise *The Prophet's Pulpit* from outside the context of major Muslim institutions in the U.S. Nor could he have given these *khutbah*s in most Muslim countries. Readers can decide for themselves what this says about our current state.

I have been asked by several readers to explain the method used for selecting *khutbah*s. Professor Abou El Fadl has delivered hundreds of *khutbah*s over the course of his long and distinguished career. He continues to do so each week at The Usuli Institute. How, then, are some *khutbah*s chosen for publication over others? The current

---

1 Abu Lahab was a hostile early opponent to the Prophet Muhammad. For more on the ethics and morality of the then-non-Muslim, Uthman ibn Talha, see Chapter 18: *Who Is the Better Muslim and What Would God Think?* in this volume.

collection of *khutbah*s, twenty-five in total, builds upon many of the themes previously covered in Volume I. Volume II has been organized as a deeper, perhaps more advanced, progression on Volume I. For this reason, readers new to *The Prophet's Pulpit* series are encouraged to read Volume I before turning to the present work.[2] In preparing Volume II, I also considered several other factors.

Since January 2021, Professor Abou El Fadl has embarked upon a major commentary of the Qur'an, *Project Illumine: The Light of the Qur'an*, in which he outlines the core moral message of each Qur'anic chapter. The publication of these lectures is the flagship project of The Usuli Institute. In what follows, I have included several *khutbah*s where Professor Abou El Fadl shares some of his unique insights and reflections on various chapters, including Surah al-Nur (Q 24), al-A'raf (Q 7), and 'Abasa (Q 80), among others. These *khutbah*s give a glimpse of what to expect as we work toward the publication of a multi-volume commentary in the coming years. The Usuli Institute hopes to follow *Project Illumine* with a future project on the *Sira* of the Prophet. In the same vein, I have included several *khutbah*s containing stories from the lives of the Prophet and key Companions such as Salman al-Farsi, Umm Salama, Dihya al-Kalbi, and Thumama ibn Uthal al-Hanafi. This, in turn, led me to include *khutbah*s dealing with the importance of learning from history more generally. Yet history matters not for its own sake but precisely because it shapes our present and future. I have seen firsthand how Professor Abou El Fadl regularly receives correspondence from young Muslims who are confused or in a state of crisis about their faith. Muslim parents also often reach out, concerned for the faith of their children. This

---

2 The Preface and Introduction sections to Volume I also provide useful background information on The Usuli Institute, *The Prophet's Pulpit* series, and the life and scholarship of Professor Abou El Fadl.

lies behind the decision to create an entire section—"On Raising Muslim Youth"—dedicated to the younger and future generations of Muslims. A conscious effort has also been made to include *khutbah*s that directly address some of the major moral issues of our time, such as the murder of George Floyd, Russia's invasion of Ukraine, the status of Jerusalem, and the ongoing genocide against the Uyghur Muslims—the largest internment of a religious minority since World War II. Lastly, in a select few cases, I have included *khutbah*s on account of the reactions they generated online.

Readers may be struck by the breadth of topics covered by Professor Abou El Fadl in the following pages. But this should not distract us from a deeper unity and consistency. The more that I collected, edited, and prepared the current volume, the more I came to realize how each *khutbah* shares the same underlying themes. Each *khutbah* is a call for Muslims to live moral, meaningful, and dignified lives anchored in a relationship with God. Each *khutbah* relates timeless truths from the Qur'an and the Islamic tradition to contemporary challenges. Each *khutbah* affirms how justice, ethics, and beauty are core to what it means to be Muslim—ritual and law are but means to this end.

Yet there is perhaps an even deeper, simpler, and more profound lesson to glean from the following pages: words matter. More precisely, the words of the Qur'an matter. A repeated theme is that when God speaks about justice (*'adl, qist*), truth (*haqq*), or light (*nur*), these are not empty words. When God condemns oppression and injustice (*taghut, zulm*), this is not just rhetoric. These words are, in fact, the very heart and soul of our faith. They are the lens through which a Muslim should see all else. The *khutbah*s that follow, like all his works, are rooted in Professor Abou El Fadl taking these words of the Qur'an seriously. Each *khutbah* is a clarion call for Muslims to do the same.

The responsibility for editing *The Prophet's Pulpit* is both a blessing and a burden. It is a blessing because I get to work closely on material that has deeply enriched my own faith and that I truly believe has the potential to rekindle the love that modern Muslims have for their faith. It is a burden for the same reason. The Usuli Institute aims to leave a legacy of brave, thought-provoking, and inspiring works that are grounded in our rich intellectual tradition and that contain the seeds for a potential revival of Islam in the modern age. But the pages that follow argue clearly that this journey starts by reconnecting with the very basics of our faith. What does it mean to be Muslim? How is Islam meaningful and relevant to the world? In what way does Islam bring people "from darkness to light"? As Muslims, we must be anchored in these basics before all else. It is my hope that by presenting this second volume of *The Prophet's Pulpit*, Muslims will continue to be reminded of all that is beautiful and wonderful about our faith. May the present collection continue to set a new standard for Muslims, a standard worthy of the pulpit of the Prophet. May God accept.

I have followed the same method for editing the *khutbah*s as that used in Volume I. Editing is a highly subjective process. Now, as then, there were inevitable problems in deciding what to keep, delete, and rearrange. Each *khutbah* presented its own challenges. Instances of repetition were typically abridged or deleted or, in a small number of cases, preserved for rhetorical effect. In several *khutbah*s, I restructured the order of paragraphs to fully bring out the ideas conveyed therein. What I have tried to achieve for readers is a clear and accessible text that retains, as much as possible, the very words used by Professor Abou El Fadl and that preserves his authentic style, tone, and voice. The hope is that readers can hear the

Professor and the original *khutbah*s in the text, while still finding the written prose clear, easy to follow, and engaging.

I am thankful to all those who helped in the publication of this volume. Dalia Abou El Fadl, Wietske Merison, Rameen Javadian, and Rami Koujah raised the quality of the finished text and saved me from not a few errors. I am especially grateful to Grace Song, who proofread and carried the work through to final publication, and who has entrusted me with this project and the work of Usuli Press. Finally, I am most thankful to Professor Abou El Fadl himself, for leaving a rich legacy of powerful *khutbah*s that will ensure many future volumes of *The Prophet's Pulpit* in the years to come, God Willing (*Insha'Allah*).

DR. JOSEF LINNHOFF
January 2023

A NOTE ON
PRESENTATION

. . . .

The following is a list of general editorial guidelines that have been followed throughout to impose a degree of structure and uniformity upon the text. Key concerns have included presentation, ease of reading, and preserving the tone and spirit of the original *khutbah*s while assisting readers not familiar with Arabic.

Professor Abou El Fadl often cites from the Qur'an in the original Arabic before explaining or paraphrasing—but not translating—the verse or passage in English. In such cases, translations are largely taken from *The Study Quran* (New York: HarperOne, 2015) and indicated in the text by "SQ." All other instances, such as when Professor Abou El Fadl offers his own translation of the Qur'an, are indicated by "Q."

The intermittent use of Arabic terms is largely preserved but, in most cases, an English translation is inserted in parentheses after the first mention. For example: "*khutbah* (sermon)." Arabic terms that have become part of the English language or that defy simple translation, such as *jihad, Sunna,* or *hijab,* are not followed by parentheses. This involves a degree of subjectivity as to which terms are considered as such. All Arabic terms are included in the Glossary of Terms.

Professor Abou El Fadl occasionally expresses an idea or a turn of phrase in *both* English and Arabic. For ease of reading, in these cases, English has been preferred. In a small number of cases, the corresponding Arabic term has been included in parentheses.

The transliteration system avoids diacritics and includes 'ayn and *hamza*.

Blessings that traditionally accompany the mention of both the Prophet and God, such as "peace be upon him," both in English and Arabic, are omitted.

Anglicized names for the prophets have been chosen, i.e., Abraham, Moses, and Jesus, not Ibrahim, Musa, and 'Isa. In the same vein, the Anglicized "God" has been chosen over *Allah*.

The spellings of the names of scholars or public figures well-known to English language audiences, such as Mohammed bin Salman, Mohamed bin Zayed, Abdel Fattah el-Sisi, or Ali Gomaa, have followed those most used in mainstream media outlets.

Anglicized plurals have been chosen, i.e., *fatwa*s over *fatawa*, also *imam*s, *hadith*s.

Dates are given in the Islamic *Hijri* and then Common Era format. Dates of death are included after the mention of key historical figures from the Islamic intellectual tradition to offer further context.

Footnotes have been deliberately kept to a minimum. The exceptions are to cite *hadith* reports, further explain background context that may elude readers, and provide links to relevant secondary materials.

All Usuli Institute content cited in the footnotes can be found at the Usuli Institute's YouTube page: https://www.youtube.com/c/TheUsuliInstitute.

The spelling of Arabic terms largely follows that found in Professor Abou El Fadl's book, *The Search for Beauty in Islam: A Conference of the Books* (Lanham, Md: Rowman & Littlefield, 2006). The same applies for both the Glossary of Terms and the Selected Biographies.

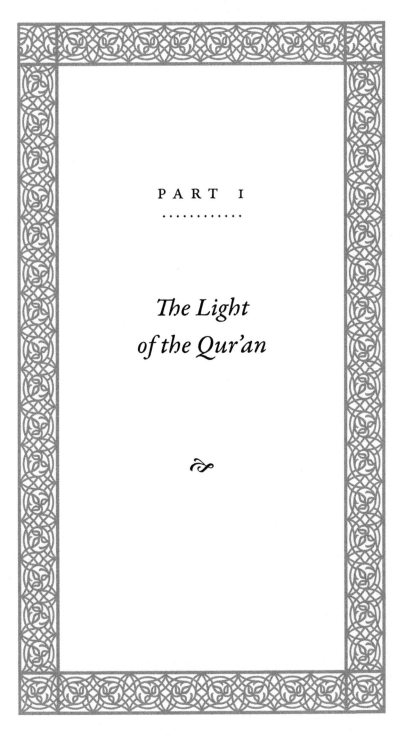

PART I
· · · · · · · · · · · ·

*The Light
of the Qur'an*

1

The Niche for Divine Light

The heart and core of Islam was, is, and always will be the revealed word of God, the Qur'an. It is remarkable that Muslims would ever lose touch with the living word of God, the eternal revelation that speaks to them individually and collectively. We human beings are born into this world in a state of struggle (Q 84:6). God has placed us on this earth to act as God's representatives, inheritors, and vicegerents (*khulafa'*) (Q 2:30; 6:165; 10:14; 27:62; 35:39; 38:26). Every human being, whether they are Muslim or not and whether they realize it or not, is in a de facto state of vicegerency. They bear a trust, and that trust is how they inherit the earth. It is a most honored trust, but it is a heavy responsibility. With this trust comes accountability for how we conduct ourselves on this earth.

The most central theme in the Qur'an, the very heart and core of its message, is the theme of taking people from darkness to light (Q 2:257; 5:16; 14:1, 5; 33:43; 57:9; 65:11) and the idea of God as the light of the heavens and the earth (Q 24:35). This is the central premise that pervades the Qur'an. We see it in the narratives about the life of the Prophet and in the events that unfolded and confronted the Muslim community at the time of the Prophet. We see it in the narratives about previous nations. We see it in the Qur'anic narratives about the laws of nature and creation. We see it in the Qur'anic laws and commandments, the "dos" and "don'ts." It is the foundation of all. If we lose sight of it, then we lose sight of everything. We lose sight of the law. We lose sight of history. We lose sight of the message itself.

This is stated throughout the Qur'an. But it is expressed with particular power in Surah al-Nur.

> *God is the light of the heavens and the earth. The parable*
> *of God's light is as if a niche. In this niche, is a lamp. The*
> *lamp is in a glass. The glass is as if a brilliant star, lit from*
> *a blessed olive tree, neither of East nor West. The oil glows*
> *as if not touched by fire. Light upon light. God guides to*
> *God's light whomever God wills. God sets a parable to*
> *humankind for God is the Knower of all things (Q 24:35).*

How often do we pause to reflect upon what it means for God to say that God is the "light of the heavens and the earth"? If God is the light of the heavens and the earth, what is the nature of creation without God? Is creation itself in darkness, but for God's light? Does light in creation only emanate from God? What is the "niche" wherein there is a "lamp" that is placed in a "glass"? The lamp itself is lit by an oil that is "neither of East nor West," meaning it is a perfectly balanced oil. It has received neither too much nor too little sunlight. It is an oil so pure that it glows by itself. It needs no fire or external agent. The oil, the lamp, and the glass form layers of light. We then have the image of "light upon light." But the verse that follows is no less compelling.

4

> *[It is] in houses* (buyut, *sing.* bayt) *that God has permitted*
> *to be raised and wherein His Name is remembered. He*
> *is therein glorified, morning and evening, (SQ 24:36)*

There are *buyut,* meaning "houses" or "structures," wherein God has ordered that God's name be mentioned fervently in the daytime and evenings. What are these *buyut*? And what is the relation between these *buyut* and the preceding verse that tells us that God is the "light of the heavens and earth" and "light upon light"?

There is an oil that glows by itself and that empowers a lamp within a glass. The oil glows, so the lamp glows, so the glass glows. We are speaking here of a reality that is beyond the laws of rational causation. In our material world, oil does not internally and independently glow. According to the laws of physics, glowing is a function that is produced by a chemical reaction and a discharge of energy. But the properties of the Divine are not dependent on any other. With the Divine, there are levels of illumination that we cannot conceive of rationally.

Most important of all, what is the "niche" wherein the "light upon light" resides? A niche is an enclave in the wall. In pre-modern times, people would place a lamp in a niche for light at night. All homes were built with these niches. In the Qur'anic reference, what is the "niche"? Why is there a reference to a "niche"? We get a better understanding of this from reports in which the Prophet says that the light of God can only be contained by the heart of a believer.[3] The "niche" is, in fact, the heart of a believer. It is reported in a *hadith*

---

3 An allusion to a well-known *hadith qudsi* that states: "Neither My heavens nor My earth contain Me, but the heart of My believing servant contains Me." This *hadith qudsi* is widely cited in Sufi works, including in the chapter "Marvels of the Heart" (*kitab sharh 'aja'ib al-qalb*) in Abu Hamid al-Ghazali, *Ihya' 'Ulum al-Din* (Beirut: Dar al-Kitab al-'Arabi, 2008).

qudsi that God says, "I was a hidden treasure and I wished to be known, so I created creation."[4] It is as if the Divine light wished to be manifest on earth, and the "niche" that can manifest this light is, first and foremost, the heart of the believer.

Understand that this light is layered. It has levels of illumination. Each level leads to another level. But what does all this mean in concrete terms? What does it mean to say that the heart of a believer contains the Divine light? God tells us that there are "*buyut*" (Q 24:36). In Arabic, a *bayt* refers to any home, dwelling, or structure. The *bayt* in Surah al-Nur could be a home. It could be a mosque. It could be a partner or our own heart. The point of the verse is that the *bayt*—whether a home, mosque, heart, or relationship—that is built upon *dhikr* (remembrance of God) becomes the "niche" that contains the "light upon light."

Let us move from theory to practice. As the vicegerents of God on earth, we are charged with a trust. How does the theme of "light upon light" relate to this vicegerency? At a most basic level, if you are in a relationship in which God is not the third partner, meaning you do not strive to bring God into the relationship, then it is a relationship without light. If your heart is constantly distracted by worldly affairs and does not seek the remembrance of God, then your heart is not a niche for "light upon light." The heart is a niche, but it will be filled either by darkness or light. If your home is busy with mundane affairs—paying the bills, taking care of the children, doing chores—but there is no effort to bring *dhikr* or the light of the Divine into the home, then that home is not a niche for light. And a niche without light will bear darkness. The same goes for a

---

4 This "hidden treasure" report is a famous and influential *hadith qudsi* that was developed to great heights in the Sufi tradition, particularly in the works of figures like Muhyiddin Ibn 'Arabi (d. 638/1240) and Jalal al-Din Rumi (d. 672/1273).

mosque. If a mosque is open for the five prayers but, beyond that, is closed, and if people in the mosque do not feel peace, security, or the freedom to explore the "light upon light," then the mosque itself could cease to be a niche for the Divine light.

It requires active effort. Human beings are not like the Divine that can glow eternally without an application of energy. For human beings, atrophy equals darkness. Put simply, unlike the Divine, human beings do not independently glow. Human beings become the vicegerents of God on earth only by exerting the required energy to bring the light of the Divine, the "light upon light," into their hearts, homes, relationships, communities, and mosques.

How do we know if the light of God is present? Is there a concrete way to identify whether our heart, in fact, responds to the "light upon light"? Or are we, as the Qur'an describes, like those lost in waves of darkness in a turbulent ocean (Q 24:40)?

Let me put it in the simplest way possible: light does not come from law. Nor does it not come from mere speech. It comes from a state of liberation, repose, and peace. In Islamic theology, light is a state of beauty and *ihsan* (equity and kindness). It is exactly contrary to the state of *qubh* (ugliness). Put simply, wherever you find anxiety, anger, or hate, light is absent. The very nature of God's light is repose and peace. Where there is love, there is light. Where there is happiness, there is light. Where there is suffering, depression, or anxiety, there is the absence of light. When human beings are in a position in which they are forced to lie, there is an absence of light. When human beings are angry instead of forgiving, there is an absence of light. When human beings are jealous or cause harm, there is an absence of light.

No amount of law or text can alter what a baby knows. When a baby is happy, it smiles and laughs. When a baby is unhappy, it cries. Human beings are asked to be as pure as a baby. If you seek to introduce God into that niche—whether your heart, home, or relationship—but the result is suffering, pain, anxiety, or restlessness, know that you have done something wrong. It cannot be. The very nature of "light upon light" is liberation and a sense of weightlessness, freedom, and empowerment. It is to exude a sense of happiness and beauty. I emphasize, again, that no amount of *hadith*, law, or text that you cite can change this basic and fundamental truth. If you go to a place that calls itself Islamic and you see that people are unhappy in the streets, know that it is not Islamic. If you go to a place and see suffering, pain, and hardship, then, regardless of the laws or the technicalities, know that there is no "light upon light." The very nature of our faith is to feel the liberating impact of God's light when it fills the "niche" of our hearts, homes, communities, and mosques.

In so many parts of the Muslim world, you go to a mosque and feel anxious about who you talk to. You are worried that the government has spies that may get you arrested if you talk to the wrong person or say the wrong thing. This is clearly, unequivocally, a blasphemy and a contradiction against Surah al-Nur and the Qur'an. Across the Muslim world, people are thrown into prison, tortured, molested, treated cruelly and unjustly, and yet people still speak of a "Muslim nation" and a "Muslim community." It is an absolute contradiction in terms. It is an impossibility. Any place in which people are rotting in prison unjustly, tortured and mistreated, is, by definition, not "light upon light." So many Muslim homes are plagued by authoritarianism, tension, anger, and jealousy. Regardless of how much the people in these homes may pray, fast, or listen to the Qur'an, the "light upon light" is missing. So many people claim to be religious. Yet, regardless of how much they pray or fast, if they are not in a relationship of peace, love, and beauty with creation around them, including other human beings, then the "light upon light" does not exist in that niche. It is a fraud. It is a lie.

Every week, I receive messages from young Muslims around the world who tell me things that make me feel ill. That make me supplicate to God, "God, have Your 'light upon light' fill this heart, and do not allow the darkness to invade it." One woman wrote to tell me that an *imam* (leader) at a recent wedding lectured those in attendance, directing his speech at women, that the Prophet said the majority of those in Hellfire are women. The misogyny, rancor, and insecurity of the male ego! It is clear that there is no "light upon light" in the heart of this *imam*. A speech like that at an event like that chases away the "light upon light." It is not "light upon light" to use God's religion to insult, degrade, or shame people. In any case, this is not an authentic *hadith*.[5]

This week, I received another message from a Muslim woman whose parents forced her to marry. Her husband then turned out to be abusive. Yet her parents repeatedly tell her that it is *haram* (forbidden) for her to divorce. Regardless of the abuse she suffers, they tell her that she must return to her husband. She wrote to me, explaining that if she leaves her husband, her parents will not take her back, and if her parents do not take her back, she will have no support. The *imam* in her community has also told her that it is a major sin to leave her husband and the community will not support her.

I wonder what happened to the niche of "light upon light." We do not need laws, lengthy discourses, or complex philosophy and theology to understand, quite simply, that the nature of God's light

---

5 See the discussion on this and similar *hadith* reports in Khaled Abou El Fadl, *Speaking in God's Name: Islamic Law, Authority, and Women* (Oxford: Oneworld, 2001), 225-232.

is to eschew and reject suffering, oppression, and injustice. If you want to know whether God's light exists, do not ask the person inflicting the suffering. Ask the person enduring the suffering. Ask the victim if they believe that God's light is present in a particular situation. Regardless of how many *hadiths* that husband and her parents cite, how many Qur'anic verses they hurl at their daughter, or how much theology and law they invoke, all I need is this single verse from Surah al-Nur. "Light upon light." I need only this to know what is right and wrong, what is Islam and what is not Islam.

Law, like philosophy, can have a corrupting impact. It can make people avoid dealing with the moral and ethical issue at hand. People often use law to escape ethical responsibility, as if citing the law gets them off the hook. Read Surah al-Nur. It starts with a discourse on law (Q 24:2-10), but it then suddenly reminds us that if law does not lead to "light upon light," it is pointless. That is the heart of Islam. That is the core of our faith.

Until Muslims remember that there can be no light where there is suffering, and that the very nature of suffering, anger, and hate is darkness, we will not return to the purity and power of our faith. This is why the Qur'an is an eternal and living revelation. It speaks to us with a moral and beautiful voice, but only if we are ready to listen.

18 December 2020

What Does Islam Offer?
On Taking God Seriously

Life never ceases to come up with its pleasures, distractions, delusions, and challenges. Each and every day, you are part of the theater of life. The theater of life is full of richness and meaning, but only if you can find the meaning. Life is like a dazzling show. It is full of surprises, distractions, glamour, and tragedy. But the meaning that lies at the heart of these events so often eludes us. It is the hardest thing to uncover, hold on to, and internalize in your heart, thought, and soul.

I daresay that what you internalize in your heart, mind, and soul is precisely the light of God. It is when you supplicate to God, "God, gift us with light. Gift us with light in our words, our thoughts, and our hearts. Gift us with light in our very being." Whether or not you know it or even like it, the extent to which God gifts you with light sticks to you as closely as a thumbprint. It is the very aura that you carry. It is the aura that you leave and enter your home with, go to bed with, wake up with. Yet, that aura is remarkably interconnected with the extent to which you manage to internalize, absorb, and remember the meaning that flows within and throughout life. It reflects the extent to which you make sense of what often appears as a chaotic set of events surrounding you, all the time.

People are born and die. People find and lose wealth. People marry and divorce. People find love and lose love. People rejoice and despair. These are all events. Without God, however, they have no meaning. They are just events. Without God, a job is just a job. A career is just a career. Life is just life. And death is just death. Only when you see the light of God flowing through everything is any of it gifted with meaning. God is light. If you see God in these events, then you see light. If you miss God in these events, then the absence of God is the absence of light, and the absence of light is darkness. Then, even if you rejoice at a career, wealth, or marriage, without God, its truth is darkness. When your heart is broken by death, divorce, betrayal, or the many things in life that sadden us, these things will truly become darkness unless you are able to see God in them, unless you see the light of the Divine speaking to you amid the heartache and tragedy, giving you meaning. And meaning consoles. Meaning soothes the soul. Meaning comforts and saves.

Be among those who long for meaning. Do not long for meaning only when you are sad. Long for meaning amid happiness and joy, and long for meaning amid tragedy and despair. Long for meaning when you find companionship and when you lose companionship. Long for meaning when you find success and when you confront failure.

Meaning, I underscore, is found only with God. There is no other meaning. Everything else is a delusion. Everything else is smoke and mirrors. The only reality and truth is the light of the Divine. If you perceive the light of the Divine—if you catch its perfume and if it touches you once in your life—then it becomes an addiction, a constant longing. It becomes a love that fills your being and makes you ache for its presence, companionship, and comfort. It carries you to a truth that we always overlook, namely, that we are divine because we are of the Divine. Every time you deal with your body, you are dealing with the property of the Divine. Every time you deal with your soul, you are dealing with the property of the Divine. Every time you deal with your intellect, you are, once again, dealing with the property of the Divine.

If your body, soul, and intellect belong to the Divine, what do they deserve from you? Reflect on this. In relation to the intellect, for example, if it belongs to the Divine, then how many books and how much learning would do the Divine justice? Can we put a number on it? At what point do we say, "I have served my intellect. I have served what belongs to the Divine"? The same applies to the soul and body. At what point do we think we have given the Divine its due?

There are those who think that their bodies, souls, intellects, lives, and careers are their own to do with as they please. Let me tell you: you are in darkness. The most glamorous and expensive lights in the world may surround you, but you are in darkness. On the other hand, there are those who are consistently mindful that their soul, body, and intellect have an Owner, and so have meaning and rights—the rights of the Divine. I often say to young people, "When you waste time, you are not wasting your own time. You are wasting God's time. When you hurt your body, you are not hurting your own body. You are hurting God's body. When you are ignorant, you do not insult yourself. You insult the intellect that belongs to God."

Many young people today ask what Islam has to offer. "What does Islam add to the picture?" The answer is: everything. It is exactly this perspective that lies at the heart of Islam. Islam is a reorientation in how we deal with the earth, trees, sun, moon, planets, stars, water, vegetation, animals, and the way we deal with our very being. Islam is the recognition of the truth of the light of God in existence. Islam is a response to every existentialist philosophy, sophistic leaning, and materialist orientation. Yet so few Muslims, sadly, understand Islam for what it is. Islam is not the laws. Islam is not the rituals. It is not the appearances. It is the heart and soul of the matter, the source of all meaning, the essence of being itself.

God did not leave us to our own devices to figure this out. God has spoken to you individually. God speaks to you every day, hour, and minute of your life. How? Through the Qur'an. The Qur'an is your personal revelation. "Don't they reflect upon the Qur'an, or are their hearts locked?" (Q 47:24) God speaks to us individually and eternally through the Qur'an. Muhammad al-Ghazali (d. 1416/1996) used to say that a house without the Qur'an is a tomb. He did not mean a house in which the Qur'an is not on prominent display for appearances. He meant that a house that does not hear the Qur'an every day is not blessed with the power of the Qur'an. It is a tomb. Regardless of how big or beautiful it is, in reality, it is a tomb.

And a human being who does not visit the Qur'an every day is a corpse. Can you pray five times a day and remain a corpse? Yes. Think of how we often memorize the short chapters so well that we can recite them in prayer while thinking about bills or other problems. We lose count of how many rak'ahs (prescribed units of prayer) we have prayed. That happens all the time. But, as Muhammad al-Ghazali would say, do not let your home become a tomb. Bring light and life into your home through the beauty and power of the Qur'an. Do not turn yourself into a corpse. If you do not make the Qur'an your close companion in existence, then do not be surprised when the light of the Divine, the light that tells you the truth of matters, eludes you and you struggle to find it and anchor it within you.

It is remarkable that we hear people in these odd times say that Islam is a tradition, not a religion. It is as if Islam can be an identity or just a garb that one wears. Islam is not just a face. Islam is Divine speech and Divine revelation. Your relationship to that Divine speech and Divine revelation is the beginning and end of it all.

The wise human being would be more than honored to live and die for the Qur'an, to have the Qur'an be the first thing they hear when they wake up, the last thing they hear when they go to sleep, and the very last thing they hear before leaving this earth. The wise person would want the Qur'an to be their companion. Every time they are happy, they go to the Qur'an to be reminded of how no happiness lasts. Every time they are sad, they go to the Qur'an to be reminded that no tragedy lasts. Every time they are reminded of death, they go to the Qur'an to remember the value of life. Every time they experience life, they go to the Qur'an to be reminded that it is all temporary.

The light of the Qur'an. What more could we want from our Lord? What more could God have given us? Do not blame God if the light of the Qur'an keeps eluding you because you are neglectful, arrogant, and ignorant. Humbly come to God and say, "God, I am tired. I surrender. I want the light. I want the Qur'an in my heart. I want the Qur'an in my intellect. I want the Qur'an before my eyes. I want the Qur'an in the moment of my death, in my grave, and in my resurrection, because this is Your speech and nothing honors me like Your speech."

God has given us so much to guide us to the light, but God constantly asks, "Don't you remember?" (Q 10:3; 11:24, 30; 16:17;

23:85; 37:155; 45:23). It means exactly that. So much guidance, but our egos constantly make us forget. We have moments of illumination and nearness, then we forget. We have moments of clarity, then we forget. We have instances of true perception, then we forget. God repeats the question because God knows the extent to which we are prone to forgetfulness. We remember what serves us or gives us pleasure. We conveniently forget what challenges us and what turns the eye of scrutiny upon us.

Look at Surah al-Furqan. This is among the most foundational and constitutional chapters of the Qur'an. God provides a step-by-step program in this chapter for those who want to find the light.

> *The servants of the Compassionate are those who*
> *walk humbly upon the earth, and when the ignorant*
> *address them, say, "Peace." (SQ 25:63)*

This verse refers to those who are humble to the core of their being. They are not arrogant or contentious. They do not go looking for an argument. They are not judgmental. From their humility and bashfulness, you would never know their degrees, wealth, or position. They do not flaunt their material achievements. That is not the point of their existence. They may have great achievements and accolades, but they carry themselves humbly. They know their place and they know that whatever goodness comes is from their Lord. They have nothing to be arrogant about.

How many Muslims who claim piety walk around like peacocks? In so many Islamic centers, you find wealthy medical doctors and lawyers walking with a swagger, even in the houses of God. They expect deference. They are in darkness. Without humility, you are in darkness.

> *and who pass the night before their Lord, prostrating*
> *and standing [in prayer] (SQ 25:64)*

This expression is so beautiful. They do not pray in public, but in the privacy of their homes. What do they do in the middle of the night when no one can see them but God? They supplicate and prostrate. They do not want others to see them. It is not about scoring points in the community. In fact, they prefer it that way. When all have gone to sleep, they get up, turn to God, and say, "God, have Your light touch us. We long for Your light."

> *. . . and slay not the soul that God has made inviolable,*
> *save by right . . . (SQ 25:68)*

They do not shed blood. The last thing in the world they want is to see bloodshed and the loss of life. They are not people of destruction or hurt. But it does not stop there.

> *. . . and who fornicate not . . . (SQ 25:68)*

They do not fornicate or commit adultery. They understand that the body is sacred, and that intimacy is sacred. They understand that you are intimate with someone either in the darkness of the demonic or in the light of God. There is no third alternative. If you are with someone, either the devil or God is your third, and they do not want sexual relations that involve the devil. So many Muslims today think that they can play legalities with God and do everything but intercourse. Are they insane? Penetration matters when talking about a criminal penalty, but it does not affect the moral status of the act. If you do everything but penetrate, you still fall under the category of *zina* (fornication/adultery).

What is even worse is that so many Muslims today "mosquito bite" this kind of intimacy as if it is nothing. "Yes, I fornicated in the past, but I do not anymore. God has forgiven me." Really? Do you know that? You have committed an infraction against creation itself. Approach God with humility, sadness, true regret, and say, "Please forgive me." Do not say, "God has forgiven me." Do not be like the fool who only begs for forgiveness in the Hereafter. It is no small infraction. It is not a coincidence that the Qur'an mentions *zina* immediately after killing. It is a huge thing. A sexual relationship without the light of God is darkness. It invites the demonic, and the demonic stains your aura. Every sinful sexual relation clings to your aura for decades to come if you do not sincerely repent.

Look at how Surah al-Furqan then teaches, humbles, and elevates us. After telling us to repent and do good if we err (Q 25:70-71), it reminds us of the seriousness of bearing false witness (Q 25:72). It then takes us to the heart and soul of meaning.

> *and who say, "Our Lord! Grant us comfort*
> *(qurrat 'ayn) in our spouses and our progeny,*
> *and make us imams for the reverent." (SQ 25:74)*

Qurrat 'ayn is a remarkable expression. It means: "Make our partners a source of true comfort, serenity, and peace." If you are married but have a wandering eye, that is not *qurrat 'ayn*. *Qurrat 'ayn* implies satisfaction, repose, and humility. It is to make our partners a source of true meaning, serenity, and tranquility. That only comes from a marriage in which God is the third partner. It is impossible to achieve that standard of *qurrat 'ayn* unless you invite God into the marriage and have God sign as the third partner in the marriage contract. Ask God for the light of the Divine to share your bed, your food, your space, your everything.

So many young Muslims today are on dating apps. They look at degrees, age, and ethnicity. But the most important thing is *qurrat 'ayn*, a partner who elevates you in your relationship with God, not someone who deprecates you and takes you to the path of Satan. Remember that we are either in the light of God or the darkness of Satan. Every marriage not anchored in God is anchored in something other than God, and everything other than God is Satan. The choice is yours. "Make us and our progeny an example unto believers" (Q 25:74). Reflect on that prayer. It is saying, "God, do not make our children the most impressive doctors, lawyers, and engineers. Do not make our children drive the fanciest cars or buy the most expensive properties. Honor and bless us, God, by giving us children who are an example unto others by way of You, Your light, and Your way."

The Qur'an is your constitution. It speaks to us all, every minute of every day. We just do not listen. But if you befriend the Qur'an and it befriends you, it will speak to you in every instant, challenge, and contingency that arises in your life. The voice of the Qur'an is often hard to hear because it is truthful and candid. It often makes us uncomfortable. It often makes us feel guilty. But it ultimately gives us that light. If we do not have the light, then we have darkness. And if we have darkness, then we have Satan. The choice is clear, if only we listen.

22 January 2021

3

The Qur'an as a Paradigm Shift

*This is the Book in which there is no doubt, a guidance
for the reverent, who believe in the Unseen and perform
the prayer and spend from that which We have provided
them, and who believe in what was sent down unto thee,
and what was sent down before thee, and who are certain
of the Hereafter. It is they who act upon guidance from
their Lord, and it is they who shall prosper. (SQ 2:2-5)*

How often does the Qur'an alert us to the fact that it is
intended to be a paradigm shift? The very opening of
Surah al-Baqarah directs our attention to the momentous reality
of revelation. This book, which prevails over all doubt, serves as a
guide to those who want to embrace and follow the path of guidance (Q 2:2). To follow this path, you must believe in the *ghayb*
(unseen realm) (Q 2:3). You must be among those who internalize
in your heart the non-material world. You must have sufficient

humility to say that there are things beyond what the senses rely on. You must be willing to see and hear with the heart, not just with the eyes and ears. You must be willing to recognize that God is ever-present, although God's presence does not translate within the realm of atoms and molecules. You must believe in God's will in the universe even if, on a daily basis, you see only the will of powerful human beings.

It often appears that only rich and powerful human beings act in this world. The rich and powerful determine our paycheck. The rich and powerful decide the laws of the land. They decide whether and to where we can travel. They decide so much in the material world. But the paradigm shift of the Qur'an is to say that over and above all of this is the reality and power of the Divine. It is not the case that everything begins and ends with the will of the rich and powerful. There is the prevailing, supreme will and power of God.

To follow this path, you must believe that the world of sensory experience, which is only a fraction of existence, is not the be-all and end-all. So much in the universe is unseen. This forces upon us a humility in existence. You must be willing to believe that this life is temporary and not the ultimate reality, because real life begins with the resurrection (Q 2:4). You must be anchored in the realization that death marks the beginning, not the end, and that death is not just a void of eternal silence.

The Qur'an is a paradigm shift. It tells us this on so many occasions, but there is a particular reason why it does so at the beginning of Surah al-Baqarah. This is because of the message of Surah al-Baqarah itself and what it teaches us about society, nations, history, and the very nature of life on earth. The chapter goes on, in fascinating Qur'anic style, to define two quintessential relationships: one with the nature of time, and the other with material possessions.

Regardless of how often you say, "I believe," what truly matters is that this belief impacts how you spend your time on this earth and that a good portion of your time is not spent pursuing material things—your ambitions, comforts, or temptations—but is instead reserved for God. This is the reference to prayer (Q 2:3). The five daily prayers are the minimum amount of time reserved for the Divine in your life. Upon waking up, you ought not to feel that the time in the day belongs to you, your career, whims, and desires. Rather, you should immediately know that a portion of the day must be reserved to invest in your relationship with the Divine. How much of the day depends upon your level of piety. We invest so much time in our careers and pleasures. But those who truly mean it when they say "I believe" invest in their relationship with God. Human beings also covet and are miserly with something else: their material possessions. Make sure, then, to consistently spend in the way of God (Q 2:3).

It is a remarkably coherent and powerful vision. The Qur'an can change your life. The Qur'an is a paradigm shift in existence, but only if you are willing to take your belief seriously in how you apportion your time and handle your material possessions.

In a series of famous *hadith*s, we read that what greatly concerned the Prophet is something that can be summed up in the word *taraf*.[6] The word *taraf* is fascinating on so many levels. It does not translate simply as luxury or pleasure. Rather, *taraf* expresses a dynamic in which you deal with life on earth with the expectation of fulfillment. *Taraf* is to ultimately become infected with the disease of hypocrisy. It is to say, "I believe," read the Qur'an, and even pray; but there is a huge difference between those who pray, and those who truly invest time in the Divine.

---

6 An allusion to the many *hadith* reports in which the Prophet expresses his fear that Muslims after him will succumb to materialism and worldly riches. See for example al-Bukhari (1344) and Muslim (2961).

We can pray and yet our minds are fully on this earth, thinking about worldly things. That is not the true meaning of "perform the prayer" (SQ 2:3). True prayer is an investment of time in the Divine.

The Prophet was describing a state in which Muslims, because of material temptations, engage in a process of intellectual and moral lethargy, a state in which Muslims interpret the Qur'an and even Islam itself in such a way that does not disturb their established comforts. We become so comfortable with certain things in life that they become our emotional supports, whether these are our jobs, our possessions, or our relationships with others. They can even be as small as our clothes, cars, or vacations. But they become our habitual comforts. If they exist, we are comfortable. If they do not exist, we are obsessed with making them exist. And our relationship to God is entirely contingent on their existence or lack thereof.

The Prophet was warning his *Ummah* (community of Muslims) against a situation in which those who read the Qur'an—which is, without doubt, "guidance" (Q 2:2)—say, "Yes, but my comforts must first be met. What makes me feel balanced, secure, and stable in this material world must first exist before I take it seriously that this is a book of guidance." If this is the case, then the place of this book has been lost. It is no longer an anchor or a guide. The book itself has become part of an apologist paradigm, affirming and legitimating your comforts in existence. But it does not challenge you. It does not drive you. It is, in fact, being driven by you.

We are one day away from starting *Project Illumine*, a journey with the Qur'an.[7] I confess that there have been many moments in which I have asked myself, "What is the point? What is there to teach people when God already told them that this book has 'no

___

7 Project Illumine officially commenced at The Usuli Institute in Columbus, Ohio, on 30 January 2021.

doubt' and is 'guidance' (Q 2:2)?" This, I am sure, is from Satan. This book clearly tells Muslims about the paradigm shift, about challenging the self, and not surrendering to our comforts and to the path of least resistance. This book explicitly tells Muslims to not think ill of each other, but we do. This book clearly tells Muslims to give their brothers and sisters the benefit of the doubt, but we do not. This book clearly says that Muslims, as brothers and sisters, should not treat each other with cruelty and harshness, but we *do* treat each other with a *lot* of cruelty and harshness. This book clearly tells us to not talk about others behind their backs, but we do. This book says so much about our relationship with time and material possessions. It is a total paradigm shift. We know what this book says, however, and yet we ignore it all the time. I ask myself, "If, God, You have already said this quite explicitly, what is the point?" This is most certainly the voice of Satan.

This is where your *iman* (belief) in the *ghayb* must come in (Q 2:3). For if you believe that God is ever-present, you must also believe that Satan is present. You must believe that Satan has access to you. "Give up," Satan tells you every day, every hour, and every minute. "Give up. There is no point. All is lost." But if you believe in God, you must believe that God is capable of achieving the good that you desire—but on God's time, not yours. God is capable of achieving the good, but God wants to see what you will contribute to that good. God does not need to wait to make goodness unfold upon the universe. God only waits to see what you will contribute.

A journey with the Qur'an cannot be just an intellectual journey. I have said it before and I will say it again: if your relationship with the Qur'an does not challenge, change, and improve you every day, then something is wrong. Go back to the basics. I tell my students that we have already completed eight chapters.[8] These eight chapters alone are sufficient to transform your existence on earth. If they have not done so, then you must reexamine your relationship to God and to your ego. Do you worship God or your ego? It is as simple as that.

The Prophet worried about *taraf* for his *Ummah*, but so much of *taraf* is not about material goods. It relates to our relationship with ideas and principles. It is when we gorge on words and ideas. It is when ideas come and go just like goods in the supermarket. We get some interesting ideas, and they go away. We consume some other ideas, and we flirt with yet even more ideas, but ideas lose their fundamental meaning in terms of their transformative capacity, in terms of how they define our relationship to values, time, principles, and material things.

This is what I worry about most. I worry that when I teach the Qur'an, people will listen and perhaps even be touched by what they hear. But a new sun will rise the next day, and the day after, and the day after, and nothing will have changed. The Qur'an will in no way have changed how they deal with time, material things, or the world of the *ghayb*. If so, pause and ask yourself, "What is wrong? Why am I not truly listening to the Qur'an?" If your thought processes, values, judgments, and relationships with others have not changed despite learning the Qur'an, pause and ask yourself, "What am I missing? Where have I gone wrong?" Take God seriously when God says that this Qur'an is a transformative book. This is the book that challenges the ego and tells you how to domesticate the ego, shrink its space, and replace the space left vacant with God.

---

8 At the time of this *khutbah*, the commentaries of the following chapters had been completed: Surahs al-Hadid (Q 57), al-Jathiya (Q 45), Ya Sin (Q 36), al-Sajdah (Q 32), al-Rahman (Q 55), al-'Ankabut (Q 29), al-Ahqaf (Q 46), and al-Hijr (Q 15). These were held throughout 2020 before Project Illumine formally launched in early 2021 after The Usuli Institute relocated to Columbus, Ohio.

Recently, a student asked me, "How can we tell what comes from God and what comes from the devil?" There is a roadmap. If something is dishonest, it is from the devil. If something leaves you with a sense of shame or anxiety, it is from the devil. If something makes you act cruelly and insensitively, without compassion or mercy, it is from the devil. If you hurt others and do not care, it is from the devil. If you transgress upon the rights of others, it is from the devil. But the path of God is clear. The path of God is transparent, honest, courageous, brave, kind, merciful, loving, and compassionate. Think of the people you know in your life. If you have hurt any of them, go back and mend the fences. Fix the breaches. Extend the face of the Divine on this earth before it is too late. Think of who may carry a grievance against you and fix it. Admit your fault. Extend a hand. Be the path to compassion and mercy so that people see the effects of the Divine and say, "We have seen a beautiful thing."

I once asked Muhammad al-Ghazali which of his fifty-eight books I should start with. His answer surprised me. Instead of his book on the *Sira* (biography of the Prophet) or the Qur'an, he said to start with his book on Islam and colonialism.[9] I have read and re-read that book several times in my life. In one chapter of the book, he writes that one of the most nefarious effects of colonialism was to convince Muslims that the Qur'an calls for an *ideal* situation that is, in reality, impractical, unrealistic, and unachievable, so Muslims are better served by focusing on the "real" empirical sciences and becoming medical doctors or engineers. What this means is that we deal with the Qur'an in our spare time as an extracurricular activity. It means the Qur'an is no longer our constitution for life.

---

9 Muhammad al-Ghazali, *Al-Isti'mar Ahqad wa Atma'* (Cairo: Nahdat Misr, 2005).

Remember that not so long ago, one became literate in the Muslim world by studying the Qur'an. Literacy was commingled with an education in the Qur'an. Before learning any sciences or mathematics, you learned the Qur'an. Your value system was shaped around the Qur'an before you were then molded into a doctor, engineer, or computer scientist. As al-Ghazali says, colonialism targeted this aspect and compartmentalized the Qur'an in our lives. The Qur'an became something to broadcast on radio stations or recite only upon a death in the family. As I attended al-Ghazali's lectures, I understood the extent to which his heart broke. On several occasions, he would be giving a lecture and choke up, as if he was about to break down crying. Back then, I was young and cocky, proud of my intelligence and memory. I wondered, "Why is he choking up?" Now I understand. It is because the Qur'an has become a stranger in the lands of Muslims. It is because our relationship to the Qur'an has become marginal. Because we can read "the Most Merciful, the Most Compassionate" in our prayers, but never ask if and how we fail to be merciful or compassionate to others, especially to our fellow Muslims.

This is not something for the intellect. It must be seen and felt by the heart. It is your heart that feels the suffering of others and makes you extend a hand to alleviate their pain. But what do you do when that heart is cold and unresponsive? What do you do when the heart feels nothing? What do you do when you have compartmentalized your life so that there is "prayer time" and "work time" and "relaxation time," but you do not truly feel accountable for your actions before the Day of Accountability? As a teacher of the Qur'an, how do you get the hearts of people to pulsate with the Qur'an? How do the words of the Qur'an become the blood that flows through your body? How does it become the spirit that animates your soul, intellect, and every fiber of your being?

You stand before God every night and say, "God, help me." As Moses supplicated to God, "I am truly poor, in need of Your aid" (Q 28:24). May God aid us as we begin this journey with the Qur'an so that, as the Prophet said, it may become the light of our being, the light of our minds, hearts, and eyes, and the very means by which we see, hear, and feel.[10]

You do not need to be here to accompany me on this journey. Hearts transcend distance. If your heart is in the right place, then you could be in the most distant place and still be present with us every minute of every day. You could be physically present here, but if your heart is cold and unresponsive, you may as well be in the most distant place imaginable. I invite all Muslims who truly have a passion for the Qur'an, who want to love the Qur'an, who want the Qur'an to be the light of their soul and intellect, to join us as we embark upon this journey of reflecting upon and discussing the revealed word of God.

29 January 2021

---

10 Al-Bukhari (6316) and Muslim (763).

4

The Challenge of the Qur'an

The Qur'an, God's revealed book, has set out for us a path that is an entire methodology of life. The point of the Qur'an is not to affirm, but, rather, to challenge what we are. The nature of God's revelation is such that if we find in it an affirmation of what we are, or an affirmation of our feelings and ideas, with nothing beyond this, then we have not given this book its due. We do not then have a relationship with the Qur'an.

The very idea of a revelation from God is to challenge, and inherent to the notion of a challenge is the demand for change. We do not read the Qur'an as a feel-good exercise. We do not read the Qur'an to affirm our presuppositions and natural inclinations. Rather, we read the Qur'an for guidance. To guide is to teach, and to teach must, necessarily, mean to challenge. Inherent in the very notion of a revelation from the Divine is the idea of a challenge. When God tells us that we have been created to compete in good deeds (Q 2:148; 67:2), embedded in this is the idea of a challenge.

The moral challenge for human beings is to go beyond what they know and are comfortable with. Otherwise, the notion of reward makes no sense. If the point of the Qur'an is to simply affirm our natural inclinations and biases—to rubber-stamp our material, psychological, and intellectual comforts—then what does God reward us for? Does God reward us for simply being what we are?

The idea of a challenge is inherent to the covenant that God offers human beings.[11] It is central to our role as God's vicegerents on earth (Q 2:30; 6:165; 10:14; 27:62; 35:39; 38:26). It is key to the idea of commanding the good and resisting the bad (Q 3:104; 3:110; 9:71; 9:112; 31:17). And challenge necessarily connotes progressive movement. If we are static, then we cannot say that there is a challenge posed and a challenge met. If we remain static while the world moves ahead, then we are simply in a regressive state.

Recently, someone showed me the curriculum of a new Muslim seminary in the U.S. The curriculum was good, but the problem is that it was identical to one that would have been taught in Damascus, Cairo, or Samarkand in the 12th century CE. A curriculum today cannot be identical to what was taught eight centuries ago, or even one century ago. Again, if you remain static while the rest of the world moves forward, then you are in a state of regression. You cannot then recognize or meet a challenge.

The idea of our being vicegerents of God necessitates a dynamic of progression. If human beings were created like zombies, unchanging and unmoving, then we would not need to read the Qur'an as

---

11 The most common Qur'anic terms for the covenant between God and human beings are ʿahd (Q 2:100; 9:75; 16:91; 33:15; 48:10) and mithaq (Q 2:63; 4:154; 5:14; 33:7). Other verses widely seen as central to the Qur'anic concept of covenant are Q 7:172; 30:30; 33:72. On the nature, implications, and significance of the covenant between God and human beings in the Qur'an, see The Usuli Institute, *Surah 2: Al-Baqarah Original English Commentary* (Project Illumine *Halaqas*, October-November, 2021).

posing a challenge and demanding progress. The same applies if time did not move forward in a linear fashion—if one could wake up on one day living a year ago, the next day living ten years ago, and the third day living ten years from now. Yet, the way God created time on earth is that it moves forward. Creation itself is in constant change (Q 55:29), and human beings are constantly changing. While we maintain the same outward physical appearance, what is inside our heads drastically changes from one day to the next, from one year to the next. How we understand such basic concepts as love, family relations, mercy, loyalty, compassion, and justice is constantly changing. Why? Because the systems of neurological synaptic devices that God placed in our brains are constantly rewiring themselves.

We have the same two eyes throughout our lives, but perception varies from one time to another. Perception varies from one place to another. Had God willed, none of this would be the case. Had God willed, consciousness and understanding would be uniform and redundant. But this is not what God wills. God created for us the logic of challenge and progression. What many call "evolution" is the process by which every created being on this earth confronts a challenge, adapts to that challenge, and progresses. Scientists overzealously call this process "evolution," but what they describe is, fundamentally, the process by which God teaches us through the created world. All living beings confront, deal with, and adapt to challenges. In so doing, they supplicate and worship the Divine.

Think of any job. A healthy institution will reward workers who are disciplined, creative, and innovative. We reward workers who confront problems and come up with solutions. We do not reward, nor are we supposed to reward, workers who ignore or fail to see problems. When it comes to our Islamic tradition, however, we forget this. When it comes to the Islamic sciences, we forget this. When it comes to the *Shari'a*, we forget this. Instead, we celebrate those who fail to see problems or who fail to come up with innovative solutions to problems. Even better, we celebrate those who do not want to hear about problems. We only want people who can memorize al-Nawawi's (d. 676/1277) *Riyad al-Salihin* ("The Gardens of the Righteous") or who can repeat the systems of *hadith* classification that were invented by al-Bukhari (d. 256/870), al-Nasa'i (d. 303/915), or Muslim (d. 261/875) centuries ago. While we understand the logic of creativity and innovation in our work, we want none of this in our religion. As a result, we fall behind, and this beautiful and remarkably rich tradition that flourished for centuries before colonialism remains the playground of hobbyists and the least creative, least intelligent people. It does not attract problem-solvers. It does not attract people who are restless and who desire progress. Instead, it attracts those who are ethically and morally dull. It attracts those too lazy to even notice a moral challenge, let alone rise to meet it.

Listen to the words of your Lord:

> So be steadfast, as thou hast been commanded—and those
> who turn in repentance along with you—and be not
> rebellious. Truly He sees whatsoever you do. And incline not
> toward the wrongdoers, lest the Fire should touch you—
> and you will have no protector apart from God. Thereafter
> you will not be helped. And perform the prayer at the two
> ends of the day and in the early hours of the night. Truly
> good deeds remove those that are evil. This is a reminder
> for those who remember. And be thou patient. Truly God
> neglects not the reward of the virtuous. So why were there

not among the generations before you those possessing merit,
who would forbid corruption upon the earth, other than a
few of those whom We saved among them? Those who did
wrong pursued the luxuries they had been given, and they
were guilty. And thy Lord would never destroy the towns
unjustly, while their people were reforming (SQ 11:112-117).

This is from Surah Hud. God demands that we follow the path of diligence and conscientiousness, but about what? God tells us to not surrender or be submissive and subservient to the unjust (Q 11:113). God tells us that many past nations were destroyed because the majority failed to resist *fasad* (corruption) (Q 11:116). God then tells us the natural law of things: if you are unjust, you will be destroyed by your injustice; but if you are just, God will stand with you (Q 11:117).

In every nuance of this discourse is a challenge to rise to the occasion. To refuse to surrender and submit to the unjust requires that we first meet the challenge of understanding justice. And we cannot understand justice unless we understand that the balance of rights, wants, and duties changes from one age to another. After this comes another challenge: organizing life in such a way that does not grant hegemony to the unjust, to those who are corrupt, tyrannical, despotic, and who think of themselves as demigods. We must then organize life to resist corruption. To understand corruption, we must understand the epistemologies of our age. Centuries ago, for example, we did not pollute the oceans or kill whales. Today, this is part of what it means to corrupt the earth. If we talk about justice and injustice in the way that Abu Hamid al-Ghazali (d. 505/1111) spoke about it in his time, it is not going to work. Centuries ago, there was no pornography. Sexual abuse behind closed doors was not a huge social problem. In our day and age, it is. People watch pornography and the devil enters their hearts. Centuries ago, there was no World Bank. Today, studying the World Bank, what it does and does not do, is essential to understanding justice at an international level.

We cannot fight corruption if we fail to realize that faith is about confronting a challenge, and if we fail to understand that God demands us to be fully aware of the historical moment in which we live. This is the nature of life on earth. Perhaps in the Hereafter there will be no challenges and we can live in comfort and happiness. On this earth and in this life, however, faith can never be a ticket to lethargy, laziness, or ignorance. Faith can never be an excuse for the pretenses of piety without the substance of justice. Yes, it is wonderful that there are those who want to study the chains of transmission of al-Bukhari and Muslim. Yes, it is wonderful to know the differences between the authentication of al-Bukhari and Muslim, what "*hadith hasan sahih*" means in al-Tirmidhi (d. 279/892), or the differences between al-Nasa'i and al-Tirmidhi. It is all very nice. But it is hardly enough. Living in the past is not meeting a challenge. Living in the past is escapism, indolence, and intellectual laziness. Islam can never be used as an excuse for this kind of immorality.

There is no question that one of the things we have lost as Muslims is our sense of the obvious. It is obvious, for example, that progress is the nature of human sociology—"progress" in the sense of moving forward, though not always for the better. It is obvious that human life is constantly challenged, and those who move ahead are those who meet the challenges of their time. It is obvious that to succeed in a field, one must attract the best minds to that field. This is all obvious but, again, part of what we have lost, as Muslims, is our sense of the obvious. Furthermore, our Islamic tradition has become plagued by affectation. Affectation is about optics, not meaning. Affectation is to sound like a person of the *Sunna* or look like a person of the *Salaf* (predecessors). Substantive issues, however, like the nature of justice or corruption, cease to have meaning. As a result, we, as Muslims, have stopped making sense.

Consider some recent events. After the war on Gaza, Jewish communities around the world mobilized to defend the criminality of Israel.[12] Everyone knows that the West Bank is occupied territory according to international law. The West Bank was conquered in 1967, as was the Gaza Strip. Under the Geneva Conventions, you cannot annex occupied territory; you cannot expel people from their homes; you cannot deny people living under occupation the right to self-defense. Nevertheless, the U.S. moved its embassy from Tel Aviv to Jerusalem—which is occupied territory—and the Biden administration has let the decision of the Trump administration stand. Israelis often talk about Jerusalem, the West Bank, and Gaza as if they have no special status under international law. After the recent war on Gaza, Israeli settlers insisted on organizing something called the "March of the Flags," in which they raised Israeli flags and, once again, violated the sanctity of the al-Aqsa Mosque. During the march, participants chanted "Death to Arabs" and cursed the Prophet Muhammad. This is a regular practice among Israeli settlers, many of whom are American.

Imagine if this was a demonstration in which Arabs chanted "Death to Jews" and cursed Moses. The whole world resonates with condemnations of anti-Semitism but, yet again, when the very essence of this obscenity is perpetuated against Muslims, the world is silent. There are no condemnations. There is no talk about Jewish

---

12 Between 10 May 2021 and 21 May 2021, Israel launched a military assault on the Gaza Strip which, by the time the ceasefire was signed, resulted in the death of 261 Palestinians, 13 Israelis, and an estimated $380 million in physical damage in Gaza.

fanaticism. There is no talk about extremism in Israel or "political Judaism." There is no talk about the inherent problem of aggressive Israeli expansion. There is none of that. For Israel is not cursed with rulers like Mohammed bin Salman or Abdel Fattah el-Sisi, who are themselves Islamophobes. Israel is not cursed with being ruled by self-hating Jews in the way that Muslim countries are cursed by self-hating Muslim rulers.

Is this not injustice? Is this not corruption on earth? Our Prophet is cursed in the al-Aqsa Mosque, and the entire Muslim world, once again, is silent and oblivious. How many *khutbah*s (sermons) have talked about this? How many Muslims did anything about it? We Muslims sit and talk about Islamic issues and the vast majority of what we talk about is unimportant and irrelevant. It makes no difference to the world. You can take ninety-five percent of Muslim conversations, throw them in the garbage, and the world would not change one iota.

A Muslim family in Ontario was recently run down and killed by an Islamophobe, someone weaned on the ideas of Robert Spencer, Daniel Pipes, and the like.[13] In 2017, another Islamophobe gunned down six people in a Quebec mosque.[14] If Muslims had a correct sense of priorities, the whole world would understand that Islamophobia is racism and that the likes of Robert Spencer and Daniel Pipes solicit murder. Everyone would understand that when you support people like that, either in buying their books or listening to their lectures, you participate in an ugliness equal to Nazism or fascism.

---

13 A reference to the murder of the Afzaal family, which took place on 6 June 2021 in the town of London, Ontario, in Canada, after a driver intentionally struck the family, killing four people, a mother, father, daughter, and grandmother, and injuring a nine-year-old boy.

14 A reference to the incident known as the "Quebec Mosque shooting," which took place on 29 January 2017 in Quebec City, Canada, after a gunman killed six people at the Islamic Cultural Centre of Quebec City as Muslims gathered for prayers.

But Muslims do not have a clear and correct sense of priorities. And because they do not see their religion as demanding progress—as demanding that they recognize and overcome challenges—they turn their religion into a drug, akin to a tranquilizer or morphine, with which they make themselves numb. That is the problem.

Recognize that there is a huge difference between those who see Islam as truly taking people from darkness to light (Q 2:257; 5:16; 14:1, 5; 33:43; 57:9; 65:11), and those who do not even understand what darkness and light are, who are focused on stroking their egos while using the Qur'an, God's revealed book, to affirm all their weaknesses, rather than as a fuel to recognize, confront, and meet the challenges of their age.

18 June 2021

5

The Butterfly Effect: Choosing the Divine or the Demonic

One year ago, I started my commentary on the Qur'an in which I focus on the role and core message of each Qur'anic chapter, particularly the ways in which each chapter was understood by the original recipients of the Qur'an. The last chapter that we dealt with was Surah al-A'raf, which is one of the longest chapters of the Qur'an.[15] I typically spend five to six hours on each chapter, sometimes more. What always strikes me is how much more could be said and how much must be left unsaid due to the constraints of time and the necessity of moving forward. We talked about al-A'raf for several hours. As with every chapter of the Qur'an, however, what you touch upon is just the surface. Within the Qur'an are folds of meaning, all tucked within one another. You peel away one layer

---

15 The Usuli Institute, *Surah 7: Al-A'raf, Original English Commentary* (Project Illumine *Halaqa*, July 2021).

to reveal a deeper layer. You peel away the deeper layer to reveal an even deeper layer in an endless array of meanings and enlightenment.

Like all books, however, the Qur'an interacts with its audience. The message of the Qur'an depends upon the ability of the reader to receive the message. For all books, regardless of how brilliant the message or how eloquent the language, the quality of the audience is an essential component in the chemical reaction that takes place to produce meaning. If the reader is seriously flawed, inattentive, or negligent, for example, then the equation to produce meaning is deeply affected and becomes reactive to the vulnerabilities and shortcomings of the reader. The same applies if the reader imposes their own epistemological framework upon the text.

The Qur'an is a book of virtually limitless meaning. It can lend the most enlightening insights into the human condition, origin, and fate. It can illuminate the past, present, and future. But it needs readers of high intellectual caliber and pure heart and intention. Like everything else that is worthwhile, the Qur'an needs deliberation, insistence, and persistence. The Qur'an is a text that, by its nature, does not function like fast food. By its nature, it is a rich meal that can only be truly appreciated and valued by those who have done the hard work of developing their sense of taste and comprehension.

While we have devoted several hours to al-A'raf, I return in this *khutbah* to certain verses in the chapter to elaborate upon certain points and to illustrate the critical role of the reader and what he or she brings to the dynamics of the text itself. In al-A'raf, God addresses all human beings with a message that deserves pause and reflection:

O Children of Adam! We have indeed sent down upon you
garments to cover your nakedness, and rich adornment.

But the garment of taqwa, that is better. This is among the
signs of God, that haply they may remember. (Q 7:26)

One of the blessings of God is not only the raw material but also the "know-how" to do something that we do all the time without much thought: cover our bodies. God gifted us material that can be processed and manufactured. God gifted us the ability to process this material to wear clothes. But as soon as God says this, God adds, ". . . But the garment of *taqwa*, that is better" (Q 7:26). We must always remember that the *taqwa* we wear is far more important than the material covering our bodies.

Taqwa is not simply "fear of God" or "reverence." In this context, it means moral probity. It means being keenly aware of the difference between optics and reality. It is to know that there is an external shell and an inner reality. God addresses us fully aware of our tendency as human beings to think that if something is covered up, then the problem is solved. God knows our tendency to deal with reality as if what cannot be seen or heard does not exist.

It is a remarkable way of alerting us to something of a paradox. Yes, the material that we process and use to cover our bodies is a gift. God could not have put it clearer in one simple sentence: we must not forget that even something as simple as the raw materials that we manufacture to cover our bodies would not be possible, but for God. But physical appearance can often obscure reality. We must be keenly aware of the fact that regardless of what we wear externally, what is inside is far more important. In one simple verse, God alerts us to a point of order and a principle that we should reflect upon. If the optics matter more than the substance, there is a problem. If we tend to define moral worth according to external appearance, there is a problem. If, as individuals, we are obsessed with how we present ourselves to the world—in other words, obsessed with what people think of us rather than the true core of our spirit—there is a problem.

God then takes us to another point. God tells us to reflect upon how we arrived at the dichotomy between optics and reality in the first place.

> *O Children of Adam! Let not Satan tempt you,*
> *as he caused your parents to go forth from the Garden,*
> *stripping them of their garment to show them their nakedness.*
> *Surely he sees you—he and his tribe—whence you see*
> *them not. We have indeed made the satans the*
> *friends of those who do not believe. (Q 7:27)*

In the story of creation, Satan got Adam and Eve to exercise a choice. God created Adam and Eve with the ability to make moral choices. Upon creation, however, there was no occasion to exercise this ability. Adam and Eve only knew that with which every baby finds itself, namely, an innate and intuitive sense of well-being and goodness. As pure as the smile of a baby. No choices had yet been exercised. Human beings had been created in light and remained in light. Then came the point in which Adam and Eve, for the very first time, exercised a moral choice. Satan got them to reflect upon eating from a tree. This is like the first time an infant, at some point in its development, makes a choice for itself. For the very first time, that choice may take the infant away from God or closer to God.

We could of course say that the infant is not accountable, but that is not the point. The point is the nature of the choice made. The point, to put it simply, is that we were created with the ability to choose good and bad. We were created in a state of goodness, and we remain in a state of goodness and purity until we exercise a choice that pleases demons.

Your choices as a human being will please either God or demons. Very few things in existence are neutral. All choices function like a butterfly effect, either resonating toward the Divine or the demonic. If we had impeccable wisdom, we would be able to see each choice for what it is. As human beings, however, our perception is limited, and we see only a small part of our choices. As soon as Adam and Eve made a choice, they engaged the dynamics of good and evil, darkness and light.

Notice, in the same verse (Q 7:27), that Satan caused Adam and Eve to exercise a choice that took them out of heaven and stripped them of their "garment," exposing their "nakedness." But at this point we must pause: Adam and Eve were created naked. They were already naked in heaven. In fact, the Qur'an tells us that only after exercising the wrong choice did they become aware of their nakedness. It was at that point that they covered their bodies. How, then, could the Qur'an say that God stripped them of their clothes? For they were already naked.

Read the Qur'an too fast and you fail to notice things like this. But when God speaks, God speaks specifically, intentionally, and purposefully. God is not simply talking about clothing. If we read the verse this way, it will not make sense. It is at this point that we realize that the true cover for a believer is their *taqwa*, and that *taqwa* is far more important than optics. What Satan did, then, is get Adam and Eve to engage the possibility of the obscene by relinquishing the choice of goodness. We now see clearly how the Qur'an cares far more about the state of the soul than physical appearance. We now understand that while God created Adam and Eve in purity, their exercising of choice engaged the possibility of the impure and corrupt.

In the same verse, God goes so far as to warn us that Satan and the demonic see us from where we do not see them (Q 7:27). This could mean that demons observe us, but we should reflect on it further. Like the entire unseen realm of *jinn* and angels, Satan and the demonic see the truth of who we are. They are not fooled by optics. The fact you can dress like a *Shaykh* does not convince Satan that you are a *Shaykh*. The fact you can dress like a king does not mean Satan respects you. Learn to see the truth of things. For even Satan, not just God, can see the truth of things.

What does God say next? ". . . We have indeed made the satans the friends of those who do not believe." (Q 7:27). Know that God has created a law in the universe: light attracts light, and darkness attracts darkness. If your internal truth is one of darkness, then your satanic energy will attract "satans" or demons that will become your "friends" and allies. Any Muslim who reflects upon this will never care to spend more than a few seconds worrying about their external appearance. They will become fully engaged with the imperative of internal reality. Note, too, that nothing attracts the demonic like hypocrisy. If you tend to wear the best garments to communicate status or belief, whether explicitly or subtly, then you should be on high alert. For if the external expression is inconsistent with the internal truth, you have created a state of hypocrisy. And hypocrisy is a natural playing field for the demonic.

There is a further point. God immediately warns us of those who commit obscenities. We see this in the next verse:

> *When they commit an obscenity, they say, "We found our fathers practicing it, and God has commanded us thus." Say, "Truly God commands not indecency. Do you say of God that which you know not?" (SQ 7:28)*

46

"We found our fathers practicing it" means, in practical terms, "Well, everyone does it." This verse requires that Muslims first understand that "obscenities" (*fawahish,* sing. *fahisha*) are known by nature. This means that there is a natural law and that obscenities are encoded in natural law itself. It means that, from an Islamic perspective, what are considered "obscenities" ought to be discoverable by intuition and reason. It means that Muslims should be at the forefront of articulating what those are. But the verse shows that we often lose sight of this intuitive knowledge due to social pressure and flawed cultural constructions. Culture makes us ignore and normalize all types of wrongs that take us toward the demonic, not the Divine. We tell ourselves that these acts are habitual. But habitual is not moral. Simply because something is cultural and custom does not make it moral.

God forces us to reflect upon the difference between the superficial and external, on the one hand, and true reality, on the other. God tells us that reflecting upon this difference determines nothing less than whether we are on the side of the Divine or the demonic. God then says that social pressure, habit, and custom do not excuse immorality. God puts the onus on us to understand what is moral and to reflect upon, articulate, and teach morality. Isn't this the Straight Path (Q 1:6)? Isn't this an entire way of life? A way of life does not comprise laws that were written in medieval handbooks one thousand years ago. These handbooks can be consulted to study history, human interpretation, and examples of human effort. But we are never off the hook. We must strive to understand in every moment in which we live the difference between the superficial and the real, morality and immorality, the ethical and the unethical, and what brings us closer to God and what takes us closer to the demonic.

I know what I say is unpopular, but there are no quick fixes. No beard, *hijab*, prayer bead, or prayer rug—in short, nothing that is optical—will lead us to comprehend the difference between a *fahisha* and a *hasana* (morally beautiful act). We cannot understand the difference between a *fahisha* and a *hasana* without moral probity and ethical consciousness. And moral probity and ethical consciousness come from education, cleansing, discipline, hard work, perseverance, and intelligence. There are no shortcuts.

We Muslims went astray when we stopped understanding the Qur'an. We read the Qur'an, but it is as if we no longer have ears with which to hear, eyes with which to see, or hearts with which to feel. We read the Qur'an, but it does not penetrate. We Muslims lost our way when we started thinking there are shortcuts to realizing the Godly and avoiding the demonic. Every single choice we make on every single issue—who to speak to, what to eat, drink, or wear, where to walk, and where to sit—by its very nature either implicates the Divine or engages the demonic.

A wise person would understand that we need to understand the Qur'an, but we also need to read history with moral probity, moral consciousness, and an exacting and demanding ethical awareness. I therefore want to mention a small snippet from the life of the Prophet that would allow us to be in harmony with the Qur'an, if only we could understand. We all know of the Companion of the Prophet, Salman al-Farsi. Salman came from a noble family in Persia. Since his childhood, however, Salman was troubled. He saw the privileges that his family enjoyed, the fancy clothes, the comfortable furniture, and the luxuries. But he also noticed, once he stepped outside his home, the misery and injustice on the streets. When he started to question and discuss this with his family, they referred him to the clergy of the temple. He went to the clergy and found that they defended these injustices and inequities as natural, telling him that he is from a superior class that is, by the nature of things, entitled to superior things. Salman lost his faith in the religion of his family and embarked on a plan to travel in search of the truth. Salman first studied and briefly embraced Christianity, but he soon noticed that the priestly class was corrupt, collecting charity from the poor only to enjoy the pleasures of life at their expense. He left Christianity and continued to travel, only to eventually be captured by highway robbers who sold him into slavery. At this point, Salman could have become clinically depressed. He could have said, "Look at how I ended up. I used to be a noble man from Persia. God, I searched for You, and this is what You do to me? You turned me into a lonely slave working in the fields?" Salman could have looked for a psychiatrist to prescribe Prozac or give him tranquilizers. He could have taken drugs to relieve the stresses and pressures of life. But he did not. Salman continued, even as a slave, to search for the truth. He went on to study Judaism because his owner was Jewish.

Ultimately, Salman did not approve of the idea of Jews as the chosen people. He saw in this an unwarranted and immoral ethnic bias and privilege. This continued until God brought the Prophet to Salman. Salman said that when he met the Prophet, he realized that he had met the ethical paradigm and example that he had been searching for all his life. He fell in love with the Prophet and the message of Islam, which, unlike so many modern Muslims, Salman knew to be exactly the opposite of the message of the priestly classes in Persia and Christianity and the privileged rabbinic class in Judaism. When the Prophet migrated to Medina, Salman converted to Islam as a slave. He knew this would make his Jewish owner unhappy. He knew his Jewish owner would make his life miserable. But this was the nature of the man. Salman announced that he was now Muslim, whatever the consequences.

When the Prophet arrived in Medina, he told Salman to talk to his owner about purchasing his freedom. Salman's owner promised to grant him his freedom if Salman planted three hundred palm trees, stipulating that they must be healthy and productive palm trees. The owner added that Salman must also pay him a large sum. The Prophet learned of the demands of the owner. Did the Prophet say, "It is a shame, but we have bigger problems. We have just migrated to Medina and lost all our money and possessions"? Did the Prophet say, "I have relatives who are far more important"? Did the Prophet say, "He is a Persian"? No. What were the ethics of these Muslims? The Prophet drew on the community to pay Salman's ransom. Muslims donated whatever palm trees they could. Some donated one palm tree, others donated two, others three, and yet another would donate ten. They donated baby palm trees in sacks. But they did not stop there. Muslims would donate the palm tree and plant it on the land of the Jewish owner, ensuring that it was healthy and productive. The Muslim community as a whole paid Salman's ransom of three hundred healthy palm trees. The Prophet then gave Salman the money for the Jewish owner. This is how Salman became a free man.[16]

From the moment Salman was freed until the time of his death, he says, he never heard a single Muslim say, "We paid for your freedom." The Prophet never made Salman feel as if he owed the Prophet a dime. Not only this, but when the Prophet heard that an Arab had an argument with Salman and chided or shamed him for

---

16 For an overview of the story of Salman al-Farsi that includes the details mentioned in this *khutbah*, see Martin Lings, *Muhammad: His Life Based on the Earliest Sources* (Rochester, Vermont: Inner Traditions, 2006), 124-125 and 215–216.

being Persian, the Prophet became upset, his face became red, and he said, "People, your God is one and your father is one. Whoever speaks Arabic is an Arab. Indeed, Salman is to be considered from among us, the family of the Prophet."[17] A greater vindication of ethnic equality is not possible.

I submit to you that the Prophet and his followers knew this not because of any law book, but because of an innate understanding of what a *fahisha* is. An innate understanding that racism is a *fahisha*. Ethnocentrism is a *fahisha*. Injustice is a *fahisha*. Slavery is a *fahisha*. Leaving a Muslim brother in a condition of slavery is a *fahisha*. It was this innate understanding of morality, ethics, goodness, purity, and light. It was an innate understanding of what takes you toward God and what throws you toward the demonic. It was, in short, an innate understanding of the Qur'an.

May we someday attain this level of innate ethical understanding.

9 July 2021

---

17 See Lings, *Muhammad*, 224. See also the *Musnad* (22961) of Ahmad ibn Hanbal (d. 241/855).

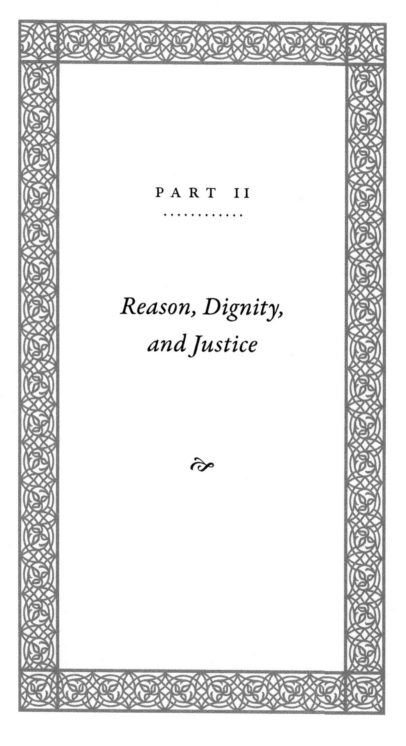

PART II

· · · · · · · · · · · ·

*Reason, Dignity,
and Justice*

℘

6

The Prophet's *Hadith*
on the Intellect

Of all the religions of the world, only one has truly sanctified the role of the intellect. There is so much in our Islamic tradition that honors, praises, and elevates the role of the intellect in human affairs. The true nature of piety is not ignorance or obliviousness. The true nature of piety is a fully engaged intellect that is disciplined in the path of God. It is easy for the ignorant to claim piety. If you lower the bar and remove all challenges, however, then your claim to competence is empty. It is worthless. The true nature of piety is a fully engaged intellect that wrestles with all the challenges that logic and thinking pose to human beings. It is to employ the gifts of the intellect in a relationship with God. Again, it is easy to be ignorant and pious. That is not much of a challenge. You can keep yourself ignorant and then claim to be the most pious person in the world, but your *iman* is, in fact, empty. Your piety is empty because it is based on absolutely nothing.

The intellect is the gift that God gave to Adam. The intellect is the very reason for God commanding the angels to bow before human beings in the story of creation (Q 2:34; 7:11; 17:61). It is the intellect that makes human beings the vicegerents of God, worthy of carrying the covenant and trust as God's representatives on earth.

I am interested in the extent to which Muslims are unaware of their own tradition, and how much the Islam that is made available to Muslims is stripped of its spirit and soul, the soul that, at one time in history, inspired Muslims to create a civilization unlike any other. I want to share a rather long report by the Prophet about the intellect. It is a report that I have never heard cited or discussed in over thirty years in the United States. When I would go to Islamic centers and attempt to even discuss this *hadith*, I would be met with very strange resistance, often by the same people who claimed fidelity and loyalty to the *hadith* tradition. In fact, I still remember, thirty years ago, that someone who has since become a rather well-known Muslim responded to this report by saying, "There is no intellect in Islam." This report is considered *sahih* (authentic) by the standards of traditional *hadith* transmission. It is reported from Ibn 'Abbas and can easily be found in a number of books of *hadith* and in non-*hadith* works, including Abu Hamid al-Ghazali's *Ihya' 'Ulum al-Din* ("The Revival of the Religious Sciences"), where it is discussed at great length.

The Prophet is reported to have told Ibn 'Abbas, one of the most honored Companions:

> *To everything, there is a central motor that allows it*
> *to work and allows it to be, and the true motor of the*
> *believer is the intellect. To everything, there is a base and*
> *a foundation, and the base and foundation of the believer*

is the intellect. To everything, there is a pillar upon which it stands, and the pillar of faith is the intellect. To every person, there ought to be an objective, and the objective of the true believer is the intellect. To every merchant, there is a commodity, and the commodity of diligent, striving Muslims is the intellect. To every home, there are people who are responsible and accountable, and in the homes of the truly faithful, it is the intellect that holds everyone to account and to which responsibility is owed. To every people, there is a lineage and genealogy, and the true lineage and true genealogy of the believer is the intellect. For every journey, there is a purpose, and the true purpose of the journey of the believer is the intellect.[18]

In another report, the Prophet is asked, "Who is the most knowledgeable of people?" He answers, "The most rational," meaning the person with the greatest intellectual capacity. "And who is the best worshipper?" The Prophet says, again, "The most rational." "And who is the best of people?" Yet again, the Prophet says, "The most rational." The Prophet then ties the intellect to ethical character: "For it is the truly rational human being who is capable of the greatest amount of goodness." [19]

Go back and assess these traditions. The Prophet affirms the intellect as the pillar of Islam upon which the entire faith stands; without the intellect, religion cannot be. But what type of intellect is the Prophet talking about? It is the type that can do mathematical equations or study the empirical sciences? Is that the kind of intellect

---

18 Al-Ghazali, *Ihya'*, 109.
19 Al-Harith bin Abi Usama, *Bughyat al-Bahith 'an Zawa'id Musnad al-Harith* (Medina: Markaz Khidmat al-Sunna wa al-Sira al-Nabawiyya, 1413/1992), 2/809.

upon which religion and piety are based? Partly, yes, to the extent that a truly rational and logical human being cannot stand ignorance. In other words, if your field is medicine or chemistry, you cannot be the "most rational" if you are ignorant of medicine or chemistry. But beyond that, as is pointed out by Abu Hamid al-Ghazali and many others, the Prophet is referring to the type of intellect that is not satisfied by habit, culture, and social mores. It is the type of intellect that understands ethical principles and virtue, and is able to reason what ethical principles and virtue entail in the life of a believer.

Shaykh Muhammad al-Ghazali used to say that the idea of a Muslim who does not value the intellect as the foundation upon which their entire faith stands is a contradiction in terms; the idea of a believer who is ignorant is a contradiction in terms, because a true believer would never shut down the role of the intellect.

The role of the intellect, however, is severely under-utilized when all it does is memorize. The ability to memorize is largely genetic. We play no role in how much we can memorize. Memorizing a great deal of knowledge, including even the Qur'an or *hadith*s, is, still, a severely underused intellect. A computer can do that. You can teach a monkey to memorize and parrot something. The intellect (*al-'aql*) does not mean memorization. It means analysis, development, and the ability to take the data that you have acquired and utilize it in a rational and logical fashion. The idea of an Islam that is unreasonable or irrational according to the epistemology of the age—"epistemology" meaning the systems of knowledge of the age, how we think what we think—is a contradiction in terms.

Let me put it bluntly. It is a severe defect in *'aql* for someone whose field is medicine to be ignorant of medical sciences. For a doctor, a true *'aql* mandates that that doctor learns their field. The same is true for an engineer. If an engineer is ignorant of the latest developments in engineering, then they lack *'aql* because they cannot think in a way that is fitting for their time and place. We then come to the Islamic sciences. The same is true for a *faqih* (jurist). Someone who claims to study God's law but is ignorant of developments in legal sciences, legal history, legal philosophy, legal sociology, and the epistemologies of their day and age is, by definition, disqualified. Claiming to be a *faqih* while being ignorant of all this is to lack true *'aql*. It is a disqualifier. You may have memorized the Qur'an, *hadith*s, and books of *fiqh* (jurisprudence) that were written centuries ago, but if you are not competent in the sciences and systems of knowledge of your day and age, you are disqualified. For you do not have true *'aql*.

Muslims fell behind when they bought into the idea that their religion rejects reason, is uncomfortable with reason, or that, somehow, reason opens the door to Satan. Muslims fell behind when they came to believe that Islam does not demand the rigorous, consistent, and systematic application of reason. If you want to see the material consequences of this, go to any Islamic center. The minute you enter an Islamic center, you enter a bubble of irrationality. The same person who in the real world could be a successful doctor or engineer—the most rational human being in their profession—suddenly, upon stepping into an Islamic center, starts thinking in a bizarre and twisted fashion. It is as if reasonableness, logic, and making sense are not required once you enter an Islamic space. It is as if, once we enter an Islamic space, we are ruled by the dictates of "The Prophet said such-and-such . . ." regardless of whether or not our understanding of that *hadith* leads to logical and reasonable consequences.

The Prophet told us that *iman* is defective without the proper application of reason. Your claim to be a Muslim who submits to God is defective. It is not genuine, for you have lowered the standards so that you can master them. What type of standard is that? You will not succeed by doing what dictators in the Middle East do, that is, eliminating all competition and declaring yourself the winner. That is not piety. That is egoism masking as piety. A true Muslim is educated, rational, and reasonable—within the epistemology of their age. A true Muslim is not scared of learning, knowledge, and education. A true Muslim understands the relationship between piety, reason, and virtue.

We do not teach this to our children. That is why, after thirty years, I have never heard this *hadith* taught in any Islamic center. Many years ago, in an Islamic youth camp, someone—an engineer—heard me lecture on this *hadith*. His immediate response was to say that the *hadith* "cannot be authentic." I tried to tell him all the books where we can find this *hadith*, but he continued to refuse to accept its authenticity.

Islam has become a religion that turns people off because of its unreasonableness. Either what we demand of people is truly unreasonable, or we fail to explain the reasonableness of what, we claim, the religion demands. Either way, it is our failure. Do not blame people when they turn away because those who speak for this religion are those whose true field is medicine or engineering, or those who claim that there is no role for *'aql* in Islam. Meanwhile, we live in society through the virtues of *'aql*. We know from experience that we need *'aql* to get through school or college, to make a living, and to raise our children. We need *'aql*, quite simply, just to live in good standing in society. Yet, suddenly, when it comes to Islam, we are told that there is no role for *'aql*. What do you think will happen? What quality of people will stick around after they are told something like that?

I mean every single word I am saying. I mean it when I say that Islam is the only religion that humanity has ever known that sanctified and praised the intellect to the extent of declaring it as the foundation of being. It is incoherent to find Muslims in their current state, that is, as a people who are *not* ignited by their faith to demonstrate the wonders of the intellect by engaging the fields of philosophy, sociology, and anthropology in the name of God. People who do not say, "I am a distinguished philosopher *because* I am a Muslim." That is what we truly lack.

The revolution must start with you. Do not expect your leadership to change. The doctors who have grown accustomed to sitting on the boards of Islamic centers because of their donations are not going to change. The engineers who like to play the role of *imam* and stand at the podium, blabbering on about this *hadith* or that verse—neither of which they are qualified to talk about—are not going to change. The *imam*s who took a shortcut to knowledge by flying to al-Azhar or Saudi Arabia, learning some Arabic, memorizing some *hadith*s, and declaring themselves jurists are not going to change. What will change things is for you to demand standards. For you to say, "If you put yourself in a position of authority, then you must address my reason. You must make sense. If you are not making sense, get out of the way. You are not qualified to stand where you are." The Prophet taught us that as we are, so our leaders will be. If we are losers, our leaders will be losers. But if we are accomplished human beings who honor Islam and give Islam its due as the religion that liberated the intellect from the Dark Ages, then God will give us the leaders we deserve. "As you are, so you will be led."[20]

---

20 For a discussion on this *hadith*, see 'Abdul Rahman al-Kawakibi, *Taba'i al-Istibdad wa Masari' al-Isti'bad* (Aleppo: Matba' al-'Asriyya, n.d), 22. In a similar vein, Ibn Qayyim al-Jawziyya (d. 751/1350) writes, "Ponder upon the wisdom of God by which God has made peoples' kings, leaders, and those in authority over them of the same kind as their own deeds. It is as if peoples' deeds appear in the form of their kings and leaders." See Ibn Qayyim al-Jawziyya, *Miftah Dar al-Sa'ada wa Manshur Wilayat al-'Ilm wa al-Irada*, ed. 'Abd al-Rahman bin Hasan bin Qa'id (Mecca: Dar al-Fawa'id, 1432 H), 2/721.

Islam is the religion of reason. The religion of dignity. The religion that demands that a Muslim be an example of a civilized human being in every day and age. The Prophet taught us that Muslims are like a single body; if you hurt the arm, the entire body is in pain.[21] So I must ask you: where is the logic and rationality when we see a country like Israel systematically killing and imprisoning our Muslim brethren, occupying the al-Aqsa Mosque, and yet receiving a warm welcome from the UAE, Bahrain, and elsewhere? Where is the rationality when fellow Muslims help Israel impose an illegal boycott of Gaza that has turned Gaza into a huge concentration camp? Where is the rationality when Israel and its supporters are the biggest advocates of Islamophobia around the world, yet Muslim nations embrace Israel as a friend? Where is the rationality? Where is the logic?

Look at the conflict in Nagorno-Karabakh between Azerbaijan and Armenia. Do the UAE, Saudi Arabia, and Egypt support Muslims in this conflict? No. They support Armenia. How many of us know that in the late '90s, thirty percent of the population in this region was Muslim? The Christians of the region exterminated Muslims and turned mosques into pigsties. This genocide occurred without a single Muslim country saying anything, except Turkey. Today, Saudi Arabia, the UAE, and Egypt stand with the aggressor against Muslims suffering the aggression—just to anger the Turks. Where is the rationality? I do not need expertise in *fiqh* to tell me something is wrong. Muslims were ethnically cleansed from the region, but no one cared when the mosques were turned into churches and pigsties. No one cared about the thousands of Muslims who were exterminated.

What is happening? So long as we get to perform the *hajj* (pilgrimage to Mecca), we are fine? What has gone wrong with the

---

21 Al-Bukhari (6011) and Muslim (2586)

Muslim intellect? The corruption of the intellect is the kernel of the corruption of ethics. An irrational human being lacks mental capacity, and a person who lacks mental capacity is often incapable of ethical choice. Mental capacity is a prerequisite for accountability and responsibility.

Several *jumu'as* (Friday congregational prayers) ago, I made an angry comment about those who would object to a woman giving the *adhan* (call to prayer). I said that I would discuss whether a woman's voice is *'awra* (private parts that must be covered) once we take care of our priorities, such as liberating the al-Aqsa Mosque.[22] But I have a greater point to make. Is it not irrational, when your *Ummah* is falling apart all around you, to even notice and be preoccupied with an issue like the *'awra* of a woman's voice?

In my view, part of what makes an irrational person is the inability to prioritize. Part of what makes a rational human being is the ability to prioritize. Before I go out, I must get dressed. If I do not get dressed, I cannot go out. That is prioritizing. That is what rational people do. If you reverse the process—go out naked and then get dressed—you lack mental capacity. Quite possibly, you are insane. Before I can eat, I need to work to earn a salary to have the money to buy food. These are logical priorities. If you are incapable of prioritizing, you lack either intelligence or mental capacity. A huge part of intelligence is knowing what comes first, what comes second, and what comes third. In fact, when I grade a paper, half the grade is based on how the student has presented their information. Someone may have the greatest ideas in the world, but if they do not know how to prioritize and present, they lack competence.

---

22 See The Usuli Institute, *Women Giving the Adhan & Misplaced Priorities of Modern Muslims* (Excerpt, 24 September 2020).

I was disturbed by the number of people who disliked my comments. It disappointed me in the *Ummah*. I was even more disturbed by one of the comments that said, "First get her to stop doing *adhan* and then we will liberate al-Aqsa." My response? You lack a sense of priorities. You lack mental capacity. You are insane.

But there is a more fundamental issue. Many Muslims do not know that we have a long tradition of women reciting the Qur'an, performing the *adhan*, and even heading Sufi *tariqa*s (orders) that dates back centuries. Leave the Arabian Peninsula and understand that Islam is not limited to Arabia. Islam is an entire *Ummah*. Here are just some of the names of female Qur'an reciters today: Maghfirah Hussein, Puja Syarma, Farhatul Fairuzah, Hajar Nasser Al Sayed, Iman Talbi, Asma Barour, Zahraa Helmy, Halima Baturic, Wafiq Azizah, Atiiqah Suhaimi, and Sharifah Khasif, who is a truly amazing Malaysian reciter. There is Leila Hassan, Nawal El Rifa'i, Farah Amchishu, and Khadija Azdad. From Morocco, there is Hajar Boussaq. There is the famous Jennifer Grout, of course, whom many know. Long before this, many people do not realize that Umm Kulthum—*the* Umm Kulthum— started as a reciter of the Qur'an. She left the field of Qur'anic recitation to sing romantic songs. I will comment on this shortly. But long before Umm Kulthum, there was Sakina Hassan, *Shaykha* Mabrukah, and *Shaykha* Munira 'Abduh, among many, many others.

The sad thing is that the same Wahhabi Islam that vilifies the idea of women reciting the Qur'an and performing the *adhan* is now opening bars in the Hijaz.[23] Instead of inviting female Qur'an

23 An allusion to the spread of so-called "*halal* bars" in Saudi Arabia in recent years under the auspices of the Crown Prince, Mohammed bin Salman. For more, see Khaled Abou El Fadl, *The Prophet's Pulpit: Commentaries on the State of Islam—Volume I*, ed. Josef Linnhoff (Dublin, Oh: Usuli Press, 2022), 52, n. 23. On Wahhabi jurists condemning certain forms of Qur'an recitation while allowing for mixed-gender music concerts, see Abou El Fadl, *The Prophet's Pulpit—Vol. 1*, 93-94.

reciters, they invite Nicki Minaj and Mariah Carey to perform.[24] The Islam that has convinced you that a woman's voice is *'awra* is the Islam that has betrayed you, but you remain ignorant. The opinion that a woman's voice is *'awra* is based on a single *hadith* that is inauthentic in every way; the Prophet is said to have heard a woman singing from behind a window and told her to stop. Alongside this, however, we have many reports of female Companions teaching and speaking, and a long tradition of women reciting the Qur'an and performing the *adhan*.

My problem is that when women recite the Qur'an and give the *adhan*, they do not end up on radio stations. Only male reciters are broadcast. Most recording companies do not want to record women or sell their recordings. So what happens to women with the gift? Many do what Umm Kulthum did. Eventually, they give up reciting the Qur'an and sing romantic songs instead. Imagine if Umm Kulthum had remained a Qur'an reciter. Imagine if that amazing voice had remained in the service of the Qur'an. There is an Egyptian woman with a voice of the same quality as Umm Kulthum. Her name is Somaya Eddeb. When she recited the Qur'an, your heart trembled. But she then married one of those men who says that a woman's voice is *'awra*. She started wearing the *niqab* and now no longer recites the Qur'an in front of men. She has even pleaded with people on Facebook to take down all her recordings, claiming that it is *haram* (forbidden). That woman with a golden voice, who could make hearts tremble out of love for God through her recitation, now hides her gift.

Is that rational? Is that *'aql*? Is it rational to talk about a religion that wants to silence half its population? How much *'aql* do we need

---

24 On Mariah Carey performing in Saudi Arabia, see Abou El Fadl, *The Prophet's Pulpit—Vol. 1*, 93, n. 39.

to understand that it is patriarchy, not the Prophet, that silences women? It is insecure and authoritarian men whose egos are so easily threatened by women who can look at them and say, "I am your equal." These men and their fragile egos are the problem. That is the truth. They should say *"Astaghfirullah"* (May God forgive me) and listen to the recitations of these women. A reciter like Hajar Boussaq has an angelic voice. See how she will move your heart when you listen to the Qur'an from the perspective of a female voice. We do not want another Umm Kulthum who turns to love songs because no one will record her reciting the Qur'an. We do not want another Somaya Eddeb who now says that her voice is *'awra*. We want the rational position that states that women have piety too, women have a relationship with God too, and God has given some women a beautiful voice that they can place in the service of God. Who are you to say that it is *haram* based on nothing other than a *fatwa* (non-binding legal opinion) from the same people who are now building bars in the Hijaz?

The religion of the intellect is surrounded by ignorance and irrationality. This is not right. The solution starts with you. Stop being a male chauvinist. Stop being small-minded and ignorant. Make a commitment that your piety must shine upon humanity with reasonableness and virtue.

2 October 2020

7

A Living Islam
or A Dead Islam?

We always begin in the name of God, the Most Merciful, the Most Compassionate, who gave us the most sacred trust. The trust is that we inherit the earth and discharge our obligation to take care of what belongs to God, in God's name, to achieve God's purposes. This is the basic relationship between human beings and their Lord. It is a covenantal relationship. Our Lord is the Creator of the laws of nature and all the basic elements, from the smallest to the biggest, that make our world. All this was entrusted to us. It was given as a sacred trust. It is a very simple and straightforward formula: we either act on this earth in God's name, in which case we have discharged our obligation and covenant toward God, or we do not act in God's name, in which case we are transgressors.

If we act in God's name, then we must act within the objectives and purposes set by God. If you own something and entrust it to a trustee, you have the right to tell the entrusted party what is expected of them. This is the basic reality of a believer. A believer is aware that they exist in this world as a trustee, because nothing in the material world—not our bodies, nature, the skies, earth, oceans, or rivers—are, in fact, ours. They have an Owner, the One and Only. Because they have an Owner, a believer is a trustee. A wise trustee would read the terms of the trust. A trustee who does not honor the trust is a transgressor.

We all, at some level, know this, but we often forget it. God repeats in the Qur'an the same basic message that is found in the Torah and the New Testament. God says: "O believers, establish justice and bear witness for God" (Q 4:135). The sacred trust is that we establish justice on earth. God is sanctified and beautified when we establish justice, but the opposite is also true; every injustice is a blasphemy against God. The Qur'an tells us in the most simple and straightforward terms that God does not love the unjust (Q 3:57, 140). God condemns injustice, iniquity, and corruption on earth (Q 5:33; 7:56; 26:151; 47:22). The Qur'an tells us that God will hold each of us accountable for the times in our lives when we upheld justice, goodness, and beauty, and for all the times that we failed to do so.

Let me say something that is critically important but often overlooked. In Surah al-Nisa', God tells us to "establish justice and bear witness for God" (Q 4:135). In the very next chapter, Surah al-Ma'idah, God says: "O you who believe! Be steadfast for God, bearing witness to justice" (SQ 5:8). So God changes the formula slightly. In Surah al-Nisa', God tells us to first establish justice and then bear witness for God. In Surah al-Ma'idah, God tells us to first uphold Divinity and then bear witness for justice. What is the implication here? What is the message? It is the interchangeability between Divinity and justice. It is clear that without justice, you cannot have Divinity, and without Divinity, you cannot really have justice. This is what should be settled in the heart of every Muslim. The idea of a Muslim who lives in injustice is antithetical to the very notion of Divinity. Injustice negates Divinity.

God establishes the intimate link between Divinity and justice. There is simply no way to discharge the covenant unless we affirm both Divinity and justice. We cannot discharge the covenant if we do not recognize the Owner, the One who created the trust and gave us our charge. Nor can we discharge the covenant unless we recognize that this Owner wants justice. It is incumbent upon us, then, as human beings entrusted with creation, to always concern ourselves with the nature of justice.

While justice is an objective concept, its application is contextual and circumstantial. What counts as justice in one time and place may not count as justice in a different time and place. But God gave us parameters for justice because God speaks to us as rational human beings. If we were cattle without reason, God would speak to us differently. As rational beings, however, when God tells us to not cause corruption on earth (Q 5:33; 7:56; 47:22), implicit in this is that we understand what "corruption on earth" means. God gave us guidelines. God made it very clear, for example, that failing to care for the poor and orphans is corruption on earth (Q 2:215; 76:8). Can any Muslim deny that this has been made clear? God made it clear that if we do not take care of and have good relations with our neighbors, it is corruption on earth (Q 4:36). God made it clear that if we do not honor and respect our parents, it is corruption on earth (Q 17:23-24; 29:8). God made it very clear that adultery or fornication is corruption (Q 25:68). God gave us many guidelines—moral and ethical guidelines—to help us recognize and think through the obligation of establishing Divinity and bearing witness for justice, and establishing justice and bearing witness for Divinity.

God made something else very clear. "Whosoever slays a believer willfully, his recompense is Hell, abiding therein. God is wroth with him, and curses him, and prepares for him a mighty punishment" (SQ 4:93). The consequence for intentionally killing a believer is Hellfire, the wrath of God, and God's curse. Three consequences, each worse than the other. How could God have made it clearer that murder and killing is inexcusable? The consequences are so grave in the Qur'an that not even *kufr* (unbelief/ingratitude) has these three cumulative consequences.

How is it, then, that everywhere we turn, we see Muslims killing Muslims? God tells us that killing takes us out of God's mercy. If Muslims understood this, the possibility of a Muslim even thinking of killing another Muslim would cease. It is the very definition of corruption on earth. Graver still is when the powerful kill the powerless and oppressed (*al-mustad'afun*), those unable to even defend themselves. That is the worst situation of all. It is *taghut*. For the powerful to kill the powerless with impunity is a breach of God's covenant so fundamental, so thorough, as to be absolute corruption on earth.

A Muslim must understand this. A Muslim must understand that when God tells us to establish justice and bear witness (Q 4:135; 5:8), we have no choice but to stand up, resist, and speak out on behalf of the disempowered and oppressed. If you fail to do so—especially when there is no imminent threat to you personally, meaning no one will hurt or kill you for doing so—then nothing is left of your Islam. You are only technically Muslim. You are a Muslim by label or performance, but not by truth and substance, nor by beauty and justice.

I say this because we are living in a very serious moment with very serious problems. Muslims are being murdered all around the world, in China, Myanmar, and all over the Middle East, at a rate never seen in history. After the so-called Arab Spring, a movement in which Muslims demanded the right to self-determination, true despots in the Muslim world launched campaigns of repression and persecution that are unprecedented in history. Muslims have been put to death in Yemen, Libya, Syria, and Egypt. I work in the field of human rights, and I was working on the case of someone who was executed in Egypt. His name was Ahmed Hindawi. He was a professional boxer who had won championships. He had nothing to do with the crime for which he was accused. He was, in fact, in police custody at the time. But it did not matter because he had certain religious and political ideas, so the government tortured him, sentenced him to death, and executed him. Yet the regime of Abdel Fattah el-Sisi has faced no consequences. Look at how Sisi is received in the U.S., Europe, and at the U.N. If that does not keep you up at night, then there is something wrong with your Islam. You do not understand God's message about the oppressed, murder, and injustice.

Recently, in Saudi Arabia, thirty-seven people, mostly Shi'a Muslims, were executed. A Muslim cannot live with that. If you do not care, perhaps because most of the victims were Shi'a, then you are not a Muslim. The biggest calamity is the recent news that Saudi Arabia plans to execute three very important Muslim scholars after Ramadan: Salman Alodeh (b. 1376/1956), Awad al-Qarni (b. 1376/1957), and 'Ali al-Omari (b. 1393/1973).[25] Whether or not you agree with these scholars is not the point. The point is that there is a development in our Muslim world of great importance. It is something we must all be aware of.

---

25 As of January 2023, each of these figures remain imprisoned in Saudi Arabia. Each was arrested in September 2017.

Islam is being split into two groups. It is not about terrorism versus non-terrorism. It is not about Muslim Brotherhood versus non-Muslim Brotherhood. It is not about secular versus religious. What, then, is it about? It is about those Muslims who are willing to tolerate injustice, who say that our duty is to do our prayers, fast, and do nothing else, on the one hand, and those Muslims who are *not* willing to tolerate injustice, on the other.

What "crime" have these scholars committed? Why does Saudi Arabia plan to execute them? Quite simply, it is because they dared to disagree with the rulers. They dared to disagree with Saudi policy toward Iran, Qatar, the Arab Spring, and what the rulers call "political Islam." They dared to say that we do not have an obligation to obey the ruler if the ruler commands us to commit a sin.[26] They dared to affirm the *hadith* of the Prophet: "There is no obedience to a created being if it means disobedience to the Creator."[27]

This is a historic moment of great consequence. It is as if the powers of corruption on earth are telling Muslims, "Forget all this stuff about a covenant, bearing witness, and establishing justice. Your role is to do your *salah* (prayer), fast in Ramadan, and not concern yourself with issues of justice, social policy, equity, fairness, or democracy. Islam does not involve itself with any of that. Keep it to yourself. Or, if you must talk about it, do not bring God into it."

The issue, brothers and sisters, is not political Islam versus non-political Islam. The issue is a living Islam versus a dead Islam. There are rulers, like the rulers of Egypt, Saudi Arabia, and the UAE, who want an odorless, tasteless, and silent Islam. An Islam that is not about a covenant, justice, or establishing ethics in the public sphere. An Islam

---

26 For more on the question of political quietism and obedience to unjust rulers, see Abou El Fadl, *The Prophet's Pulpit—Vol. 1*, 28-31, 141-152, 157-158, 165-169, 189-190.
27 Al-Bukhari (7144) and Muslim (1840).

that you keep to yourself while you let despotism thrive, unhampered and unchallenged. That is why Saudi Arabia and the UAE have even spent money trying to get Muslims in the U.S. Congress unelected.[28] They see the prospect of an American Islam that is politically engaged and that cares about social justice as dangerous to them. They want a dead Islam. They want an Islam that cares about whether or not you use a *miswak* (teeth-cleaning twig), but does not care about who is in prison, who gets tortured, and who gets executed.

That is the significance of this moment. Again, whether I agree with Salman Alodeh, Awad al-Qarni, or 'Ali al-Omari is not the point. I would love to debate and disagree with them after they are released from prison and free from oppression. But when their lives are threatened, I stand by them because I am an ethical Muslim. So should you.

Why am I talking about this? It confounds me that those loudest in condemning the news of their likely execution are non-Muslims. Muslims, in their *jumu'a*s and *khutbah*s, say not a word. Not only this, but many American and European Muslims follow *imam*s who are close to Saudi Arabia, the UAE, and Egypt. A famous American *imam* has even said, "It is my honor to have a close relationship with the Emirates." This, after the UAE and Saudi Arabia have sold out Jerusalem, sold out the Palestinians, opposed democracy, and thrown everyone who represents ethics, morality, and justice from an Islamic perspective into prison! Yet so many American Muslims still follow this *imam* and regard him highly.

That is not Islam. If that is Islam, who wants to be Muslim? Islam is about justice and ethics, and God is about justice and ethics. It is not about *hijab*, *salah*, and *sawm* (fasting). These are but means to

---

28 See Hamid Dabashi, "Why Saudi Arabia hates Muslim women in the US Congress." *Al Jazeera* (27 January 2019).

an end. Your *salah* should make you a warrior for justice. If it does not, then you do not understand what *salah* is about.

God promises damnation to those who kill prophets and to those who kill people pursuing justice (Q 3:21). So let me put it very simply. If Salman Alodeh, Awad al-Qarni, and 'Ali al-Omari are put to death, then the legitimacy of Saudi Arabia as the "Guardian of the Two Holy Sites" is null and void. Then they have no right over the Holy Sites. Muslims must then demand that the guardianship of the Holy Sites is handed over to a confederacy of Muslim states or even to a U.N. body that is not marred in bloodshed and injustice. If Saudi Arabia murders these scholars, then I urge Muslims around the world to boycott *hajj* and 'umrah (lesser pilgrimage).[29] They already discriminate against Palestinians, Turks, and Iranians. They have already committed a genocide in Yemen. They have already worked with oppressors in Sudan against the people of Sudan. They are working with oppressors in Tunisia against the people of Tunisia. The leadership of Saudi Arabia has clearly become a force of corruption on earth. I condemn all corrupt governments, but this is like when the Qaramita occupied Mecca. The record of Al Saud is as bad as the Qaramita. If they kill people of that stature, then they have lost all moral claims over the Holy Sites.

I know that people follow and love the *imam*s who talk about *wudu'* (ablution), *salah*, and the *hijab*. I know that I am one of only a handful of Muslims around the world who testifies at *jumu'a* for justice, on behalf of God, by condemning this ugliness and corruption for what it is. I established an entire career pointing the finger at Saudi Arabia. I am willing to sacrifice my life to protect these

---

29 For more on the question of spending money on *hajj* and 'umrah while both are under the control of the Saudi regime, see The Usuli Institute, *The Myth of the Decent Person and the Sin of* Hajj (*Khutbah*, 24 June 2022) and *The Sin of* Hajj *Explained* (Excerpt, 4 July 2022).

scholars because I am a Muslim who understands my obligations toward God. But what kills me is that I am a minority. What kills me is that not too many Muslims are willing to stake their position and make clear what Islam is about. Islam cannot be about oppression and injustice. The same *imam* who is close to the UAE has also said, "In Islam, you cannot rebel against a ruler." Read my book on rebellion in Islamic law.[30] Get an education. Islam is not about quietism and the abandonment of ethics in the public sphere. Islam is exactly about ethics in the public sphere. It is not about a theocracy in which a government takes power and rules in the name of God. I would oppose that as injustice and corruption on earth. But it *is* the right of a Muslim to speak for and pursue justice. How can someone say that this is not part of Islam? These people are killing our religion! They are murdering our faith. They are selling our soul.

If Muslims in the West, who enjoy the freedom and protection to speak out and not end up in prison, do not speak out, then who will? I can nearly forgive an *imam* in Egypt who does not speak out because he knows that as soon as he says anything, he will be arrested, tortured, and murdered. But Muslims who live in safety in the West—what is their excuse? Pray with me that God guides whoever has the powers of rationality, justice, equity, and morality. Enough blood has been spilled. They have already murdered thirty-seven Shi'a Muslims. There are so many executions all over the Muslim world.

Enough.

Pray with me that God protects the lives of these scholars, as well as the lives of so many others.

24 May 2019

---

30 Khaled Abou El Fadl, *Rebellion and Violence in Islamic Law* (Cambridge: Cambridge University Press, 2001).

8

The Mystification of Power

The Prophet Muhammad, in so many of the lessons that he imparted to his *Ummah*, taught a path of personal integrity, self-respect, dignity, and honor. He taught a way of existing in society that is aspirational in nature. Many of his lessons set as a moral objective a certain type of character and ethic that the individual must, as a Muslim, be endowed with and seek to fulfill. We find one such lesson in a well-known *hadith* that is reported by Abu Saʿid al-Khudri, who heard the Prophet say, "Let no person, because of the fear of people, fail to speak the truth."[31] The *hadith* clearly says that if you believe you know the truth, then you have an obligation to speak it, elaborate upon it, expound it, and defend your perspective, whatever that perspective is.

There are two core prongs in this moral lesson about integrity and dignity. The first is the ability to search for, discover, and investigate the truth. This *hadith* would make no sense if a Muslim was denied

---

31 Ibn Majah (4007).

the ability to search for and investigate the truth. The second prong is that once you become convinced that something is indeed the truth, then, as the Prophet says, you must not let the fear of others render you silent. The first prong is the obligation to search, and the second is the obligation to speak.

I keep returning to the idea of following the *Sunna* of the Prophet because so many pontificators in the modern age pretend to be people of the *Sunna*. When you scrutinize what they mean by "*Sunna*," however, it is only the most superficial things. They ignore the heart and soul of what the true *Sunna* of the Prophet is about. In fact, they butcher it. They adhere only to the most superficial things about hygiene, appearances, or other affectations, ignoring what truly matters. The true *Sunna* of the Prophet is to have the ability to search for and speak the truth. If you do that, then you follow the *Sunna* of the Prophet. If you do not do that, then you do not follow the *Sunna* of the Prophet.

Reflect on this for a second. What is required—socially, culturally, and politically—to create a social order that enables people to search for, scrutinize, and study the truth? If you want to follow the *Sunna* of the Prophet but find that searching for the truth is too expensive, for example, then that is an impediment to what the Prophet taught. If searching for the truth means that your family will starve because you do not earn enough to feed them, that is a violation of the *Sunna* of the Prophet. If searching for the truth is unavailable because you are illiterate, or because the means to education are unavailable, that is a violation of the *Sunna* of the Prophet. If searching for the truth is unavailable because you live under a despotic system in which you are told that the truth is the province of those who rule, and that you should concern yourself with your personal affairs, then that, too, is a clear violation of the *Sunna* of the Prophet.

The Prophet says that if you are convinced that something is the truth, then you have an obligation to speak it, and the failure to do so is a major problem. We must therefore think of what conditions are conducive to the fulfillment of that moral command. We cannot tell people to be interested in the truth if they are too poor, too hungry, or too sick, for example, or if searching for the truth means they could be arrested, tortured, or killed. If we want to follow the *Sunna* of the Prophet, we cannot have a tyrannical society. We cannot have a society in which the aristocracy, rich, or powerful tell us, "Obey, and do not ask any questions." By definition, that violates the *Sunna* of the Prophet, because that is not what the Prophet did with his people.

He was the Prophet of God and yet not once in the recorded *Sunna* did he ever tell his followers, "You have no right to question my political decisions." Rather, he did the opposite. Time and again, his economic policies were questioned. His fiscal policies were questioned. His military policies were questioned. His political policies were questioned. And he tolerated it all. Not once do we find in the huge corpus of the *Sunna* any occasion in which the Prophet became angry when people questioned him. He did say, "If the Qur'an tells you something, do it. But if I tell you something about money, politics, commerce, or social policies and you question me, I will not pull rank over you."[32]

The Prophet was the antithesis of something that existed in the medieval world and that still exists in the Muslim world. I speak here of the mystification of power. It used to be that rulers would tell those over whom they ruled, "You are too uneducated, too simple-minded, and too uninspired to question our decisions. Power

---

32 A likely gloss on the famous *hadith* in which the Prophet is cited as telling the Companions, "You are the most knowledgeable of your worldly affairs." See Muslim (2363).

is a mysterious thing. We, as rulers, have been invited to share in the mystery of power that you, the laity, are not privy to, so do not interfere." A hallmark of the Islamic revolution—which long preceded the French and English revolutions—was the de-mystification of power. When a woman challenged 'Umar ibn al-Khattab in the mosque over his policy on the payment of dowries, when rebels challenged Uthman ibn 'Affan, or when so many challenged the rule of Abu Bakr, not once did these Caliphs respond by saying, "Do not interfere in matters of politics. You are not equipped to do so." They refused to mystify power. Instead, they said, "We think that we are right and that you are wrong."[33] But there is a world of difference between saying this, on the one hand, and claiming that power is a mysterious God-given right, on the other.

This is a critical lesson. The first prong requires a social and political order that allows for the investigation of truth and individual persuasion. The second prong requires these conditions even more so. I cannot tell people that they have an obligation to speak the truth and to not let the fear of others silence them if the cost of speaking the truth is imprisonment, persecution, torture, or death. I cannot urge people to follow that lesson from the *Sunna* if I do not create the conditions that allow for its fulfillment.

So many of those who are still under the influence of colonialism love to speak about so-called "Oriental despotism" and "Islamic tyranny." They have the minds of their colonizers. They may have the skin color of the colonized, but their intellects, souls, and consciences are one and the same with their colonial masters. Reflect but a little and you will see that the true *Sunna* of the Prophet is not about

---

33 The then-Caliph 'Umar ibn al-Khattab, it should be noted, famously accepted the rebuttal of the woman and immediately acknowledged his mistake—an even clearer demonstration of the de-mystification of power.

growing a beard, wearing a *jalabiyya* (one-piece garment), drinking water in three gulps, cleaning your teeth with a *miswak*, or separating men and women in public gatherings. The *Sunna* of the Prophet is an investment in the individual. Investing in the individual means dignity, which comes with the freedom to investigate and speak the truth. It is entirely meaningless to tell people to follow the *Sunna* of the Prophet if they do not have the conditions that are conducive to the fulfillment of that truth. If ignorance, poverty, or oppression reign, there is simply no way of fulfilling the teachings of the Prophet.

Taking our tradition seriously means realizing that, since its inception, this is a tradition that invests in the individual and elevates them to the heights of dignity. It means realizing that the mystification of power is fundamentally inconsistent with the ethical legacy of the Prophet.

The tyrants of the modern Muslim world tell us that politics is the business of the rulers and that we should leave it to them; they know what we do not. If the UAE builds the "House of Abraham," for example, which threatens to change the very nature of Islam by creating a single mesh of Islam, Judaism, and Christianity, calling it "tolerance," the tyrants of modern Islam tell us that we cannot have an opinion about it; it is entirely up to the rulers; they know best.[34] If the Saudi King buys yet another yacht, painting, or chateau in France, we are told that it is none of our business. If the traitorous ruler of Egypt, Abdel Fattah el-Sisi, wastes billions building a fancy new city for Egypt's elite, we are told, "This is the business of the ruler. Do not talk about it."[35] Even here, in the United States, the

---

34 The House of Abraham will be a museum "dedicated to interfaith harmony" in the UAE. It has been widely celebrated by the UAE and other media outlets for its "tolerance."
35 A reference to the so-called "Capital Cairo Project" which aims to construct a new capital city to alleviate overcrowding in Cairo. This move is widely seen as a political statement by Sisi.

attitude of the students of 'Abdullah Bin Bayyah, Hamza Yusuf, and Zaytuna College is to not question policies like the Muslim ban.[36] It is entirely the same dynamic. "This is God's will. You do not understand power. Do not talk about it. Just take care of your family." The medieval paradigm that Islam came as a revolution against has returned! The aristocracy of Mecca are back in power. This time, however, they are in charge of our very religion. It is as if we have not progressed one iota.

There is a new trend in Saudi Arabia. Aisha al-Muhajiri, an elderly woman in Mecca who does nothing but teach and preach the Qur'an from her home, has been arrested and disappeared. Not only that, but the organization *Prisoners of Conscience* has reported that Saudi intelligence will arrest anyone who inquires as to her whereabouts or the reason for her arrest. Al-Muhajiri is not the first Qur'an teacher to be arrested in Saudi Arabia. This is a new trend in the land of the Two Holy Sites. People who do nothing but teach the Qur'an at home are picked up and arrested. Consider this alongside the case of Ahmed Sabi' in Egypt, about whom I have spoken several times, and who is still in prison for daring to criticize the Pope.[37] Add to this all the reform-minded Muslim scholars in countries like Saudi Arabia, the UAE, and Egypt who are rotting in prison, like Salman Alodeh, Awad al-Qarni, Safar al-Hawali, and so many others.

Where do we find the mystification of power? We find it when you try to talk about these people but are told that these are "political matters," that the rulers "have their reasons," and that you "cannot ask." We find it when you are not allowed to seek the truth because

---

36 For more on the Muslim ban, see Abou El Fadl, *The Prophet's Pulpit—Vol. 1*, 127 and 151.

37 For more on Ahmed Sabi', see Abou El Fadl, *The Prophet's Pulpit—Vol. 1*, 160-162, 172, 182-183. Note that Ahmad Sabi' was eventually released from his Egyptian prison, without explanation, in September 2022, after this *khutbah* was delivered.

you do not even know the charges or the alleged evidence. We find it when you are told to stay quiet, keep out of it, and simply focus on raising your children. Even if you are made aware of the truth, you are then told, "Keep it to yourself. Stay quiet." Therein lies the mystification of power.

Alongside the arrests of Qur'an teachers, Saudi Arabia has announced that it will build the first church in Arabia. The UAE is building the "House of Abraham," which will dilute the Islamic faith. Egypt has announced that all Qur'an and *hadith* references will be removed from educational curricula from next year, except for religion classes. If you dare to ask, "Why are you imprisoning Muslim scholars but building a church in Arabia? Why are you removing all Qur'anic references from the curriculum? Why have you torn down hundreds of mosques in Egypt?"—you are told it is none of your business.

What is happening to the *Ummah*? The mystification of power is nothing but a legitimation of tyranny and despotism. It is degradation and humiliation. It is a complete eradication of the Prophet's *Sunna*.

It is very simple. Regimes like those in Egypt, the UAE, or Saudi Arabia know that they have no legitimacy. So why does Saudi Arabia arrest an elderly Qur'an teacher while building a church? It is because Mohammed bin Salman (MBS) wants the new Biden administration to overlook his despotism and gross human rights violations. "Yes, I am a despot. But look, I am willing to build churches for you. I know you fear Islam, so I am willing to fight Muslims for you." It is the same in the UAE with Mohamed bin Zayed, who is willing to be friends with Israel, build the "House of Abraham," and say that Islam, Christianity, and Judaism are one, all so that the U.S. will overlook that he is a tyrant murdering people in Yemen and imprisoning his own people in droves. It is the same with Sisi in

Egypt. "I know that you know I am a tyrant who maims, tortures, and kills. But I am willing to take Islam out of the hearts of people."

In this, our politics in the West remains deeply hypocritical. We announced to the world long ago that we are a secular society. We built Western society on the profound assumption that we are doing not the will of God, but the will "of the people, by the people, for the people." The separation of church and state was a core principle of the French Revolution. It carried over to the American Revolution. Yet, there is one area that has remained deeply hypocritical. Throughout the colonial period, we tolerated the most tyrannical governors so long as they allowed evangelism, missionary work, and the building of churches. While our domestic politics is the byproduct of the French Revolution and the English Reformation, our foreign politics remains thoroughly archaic.

Are we willing to tolerate a tyrant like MBS because he built a church in Arabia? Of course. People in the U.S. State Department who may have never entered a church in their lives have an innate sense of victory when they see this kind of missionary work taking place. We have done the same with Israel. We are willing to tolerate the worst of tyrants, the most disgusting human rights abusers on earth, so long as they are friends with Israel. Sisi's regime carried out the worst civil massacre in the modern age at Rabaa.[38] But we tolerate and forgive anything he does so long as he allows Christians to build as many churches as they want, and so long as he supports Israel. It is thoroughly hypocritical. It is straight out of the Crusades. It is as if, domestically, our intellects have joined the twenty-first

---

38 Egyptian security forces operating under the command of Abdel Fattah el-Sisi killed over nine hundred protestors participating in a sit-in in Rabaa al-'Adawiyya and al-Nahda squares in Cairo, on 14 August 2013. *Human Rights Watch* has described the incident as a crime against humanity and as "one of the world's largest killings of demonstrators in a single day in recent history."

century, but externally, vis-à-vis the Muslim world in particular, our intellects remain locked in the medieval age, the age of Crusades and religious wars. The arrests of Qur'an teachers and the building of the first church in Arabia are but displays to please the West. Muslims, meanwhile, get nothing but the mystification of power. They have no right to either seek or speak the truth.

Why should we care? I will say it again and again. So long as the likes of MBS rule over Mecca and Medina, God will never bless us as a people. So long as al-Azhar is in a country ruled by the likes of Sisi, God will never bless us as a people. So long as Muslim institutions in the West continue to live oblivious to the dignity of their fellow Muslims around the world, God will never bless us as a people. So long as we, Muslims in the West, continue to care more about whether the hair of a woman is fully covered than whether Salman Alodeh is perishing in prison, God will never bless us as a people. So long as we, Muslims in the West, continue to care more about whether men and women are properly separated in prayer than about the dignity of Muslims around the world, including the genocides in China and Myanmar, God will never bless us as a people.

The *Sunna* of the Prophet is there for all who want to follow it. But it is not about clothes. It is not about hygiene. It is not about looks, smell, or taste. The *Sunna* of the Prophet is about ethics, dignity, and virtue. The *Sunna* of the Prophet is to live in a society where you can investigate the truth and, once convinced, be free to speak the truth without fear of punishment. *That* is the *Sunna* of the Prophet. Until we realize this, God will never bless us.

19 February 2021

9

The Unshackling of
Human Beings

The Qur'an is like a living prophet. It speaks to us. But it cannot have an impact in this world unless an audience is willing to listen to its words and implement them into an actual way of life. The Prophet died and left us with the eternal word of God, but where are those ready to receive the word of God and take on the obligation of inheriting the earth and fulfilling the covenant with God? Jews often speak of their covenant with the Lord. Christians speak of a different covenant. Both feel bonded to the Lord in some sort of an agreement or contract. The Qur'an repeatedly emphasizes the covenant binding Muslims to God and tells us that this covenant means that we must bear witness for God.[39] It is remarkable to see Muslims in the condition that they are in today. If only the Qur'an could speak. I wonder what it would say about modern Muslims.

---

39 On the idea of covenant in the Qur'an, see footnote 11.

I spoke yesterday to a delegation from Indonesia. I was asked a question that I often hear when speaking to Muslims from outside the Arab world. The questioner said that, as a Muslim, he looks at the affairs of the Arab world. He sees the oppression, suffering, and hardship. It makes him wonder: why did God put Islam in this spot of the world?

This is the most uncomfortable reality. Anyone who studies and reflects upon the Qur'an will experience a dizzying sense of cognitive dissonance. For the simplest example, look at verse 157 of Surah al-A'raf:

> *Those who follow the Messenger, the unlettered Prophet,*
> *whom they find inscribed in the Torah and the Gospel*
> *that is with them, who enjoins upon them what is right,*
> *and forbids them what is wrong, and makes good things*
> *lawful for them, and forbids them bad things, and*
> *relieves them of their burden and the shackles that were*
> *upon them. Thus those who believe in him, honor him,*
> *help him, and follow the light that has been sent down*
> *with him; it is they who shall prosper. (SQ 7:157)*

In this verse, God calls upon non-Muslims, particularly Jews and Christians, to follow the Prophet. God reminds them that Muhammad is mentioned in the Old and New Testaments. But this verse has an even greater significance. It alerts them to the fact that the perennial truth of Muhammad represents the truth of Judaism and Christianity. Let us remember that the Torah, without corruption, would have played no ethnic favorites. It would have no racial group as a chosen people. We Muslims believe in the one and only God who is Just, Merciful, and Compassionate, a God that does not favor one group over another. The New Testament calls for the worship of the one and only God. It calls for the worship of God who is Father of all. Jesus never said that he was God. Nowhere in the New Testament, even as it exists today, does Jesus claim to be God. The message of Muhammad is the original monotheism that, in their hearts, they know to be true.

Jews and Christians are then reminded in this verse of the most remarkable and basic fact: this message is fundamentally about morality, virtue, and ethics. It is about enjoining the good and forbidding the bad (Q 3:104, 110; 7:157; 9:71, 112; 31:17). "Enjoining the good" means living a virtuous life. It is a life that requires reflection upon the nature of goodness, beauty, and ugliness.

Then comes the most remarkable statement by God. This message is about liberating human beings from the "burdens" that crush them and the "shackles" around their necks.

The verse then takes us back to the most fundamental theme in the Qur'an: the path of the Prophet Muhammad is the path of light (Q 2:257; 5:16; 14:1, 5; 33:43; 57:9; 65:11). It so often boils down to a simple question: do you embody the light of the Divine, or do you embody the darkness of the absence of the Divine?

Since its inception, Islam has stood for the removal of the "burdens" that crush the human soul and spirit. It has stood for the removal of the "shackles" of oppression and subjugation. We see this when Ja'far ibn Abi Talib went to Abyssinia and the Meccans sent a delegation to try to bring him back. Ja'far defended himself before the Abyssinian King. His words were simple and straightforward. He informed the Abyssinian King: "We were a people without morality. We would steal from each other. We would assault and oppress each other. God then sent to us a Prophet who taught us basic, straightforward morality. Now we are kind to our guests. We honor our parents, family, and neighbors. We do not allow the strong to oppress the weak."[40] It was a beautiful, simple, and straightforward representation of the Islamic message.

Of course, literalist commentators read this verse (Q 7:157) and claim that Islam came to abrogate the oppressive legal commands of Judaism and Christianity. But this is without substance. For we do not truly know what these oppressive commands in Judaism and Christianity were, nor what Islam came to abrogate. If anything, Islam came with laws and restrictions that did not exist in Judaism and Christianity, such as the prohibition of alcohol. Rather, the Qur'an is clearly referring to a concept that hearkens back to the covenant between God and Muslims. It is a concept that is inherent in the very idea of worship, namely, that we worship only God and that we are a people who embrace our dignity and freedom—our freedom to choose, reflect, and pursue the rights that we are entitled to. The idea of oppressed, subjugated, and powerless Muslims does not cohere with the Qur'an.

My Indonesian friend has a point. The Islamic message was once so clearly identified with the idea of liberation from oppression, whether of caste systems, class structures, or slavish obedience to landed noblemen. It was a universal message of justice and dignity. How could the region in which this message originated now be plagued by such corruption and oppression?

Dignity allows human beings to flourish. Dignity allows human beings to create civilizations. No civilization in human history was founded by people who did not have a sense of their own dignity. People without a sense of dignity are defeated. They are unable to

---

40 On this famous episode from the *Sira*, see Ibn Qayyim al-Jawziyya, *Zad al-Ma'ad fi hadyi khayr al-'ibad* (Beirut: Dar Ibn Hazm), 374-378. For a brief overview, see Lings, *Muhammad*, 84-86.

think creatively. They do not flower into something meaningful. They become a redundancy. Eventually, they die with very little effect upon this world.

If Islam did not liberate the souls of its followers, it would have never flowered into the civilization that we have seen in history. The Qur'an liberated the human soul long before the Founding Fathers of the United States told people, "Cast off your shackles." The rallying cry of the American Revolution was one of liberation against the shackles of oppression. Yet, hundreds of years before this came the Islamic revolution with the very same cry, "Cast off your shackles!"

My answer to my Indonesian friend is to remember that Judaism was born in Palestine and initially emerged among a Semitic people who, at the time, did not even have the Hebrew language. The Hebrew language itself was the language of the inhabitants of Palestine who, at the time, were not Jews. As the followers of Moses settled in Palestine, they borrowed the Hebrew language from the inhabitants of Palestine. Moses and his followers did not speak Hebrew. Remember that while Judaism started in Palestine, the complex narrative of the religion did not unfold in Palestine. And while Christianity was also born in Palestine, the complex narrative of the Christian faith did not unfold in Palestine. The nature of religions—if they are real religions—is that they are messages of liberation that do not remain wedded to their historical and geographic circumstances.

We live in an age in which it seems "Arab" and "Muslim" are nearly indistinguishable from one another. But this is not inevitable. Nor is it necessary. The history of Islam, were it limited to Arabia, would have never become the history of Islam. The history of Islam is a history of Persians. It is a history of Turks, Africans, and South Asians. It is a fallacy to simply look at where Islam originated, see the amount of oppression, and say, "Islam is in deep trouble." We must transcend ourselves. We must understand that true Islam is wherever the message of the Qur'an is received, regardless of ethnicity or geography. True Islam is wherever human beings throw off the shackles that oppress them and reclaim their basic sense of human dignity upon which everything else is built.

The Qur'an reminds us that a Muslim cannot be Muslim if they do not call for the removal of the shackles of oppression, nor if they fail to even notice the shackles of oppression. I must, therefore, keep referring to something that should weigh heavily on the conscience of every single Muslim: the abysmal human rights record wherever Muslims dwell. The oppressed of the earth are inordinately Muslim. And, sadly, the oppressors are often Muslim. This is not the case in Myanmar and China where the oppressors are clearly not Muslim, but those who tolerate the oppression of the Rohingya and Uyghur Muslims *are* Muslim. There are those who think that tolerating oppression, living in despotism, and accepting dictatorship and injustice can somehow be made consistent with Islam. Particularly Islam! Read the Qur'an and you will find that God repeatedly tells us to remove the burdens of oppression and break the shackles of bondage. We live in a day and age, however, in which Muslims are the most oppressed people on the face of the earth.

We got into this situation neither by accident nor overnight. We got into this situation after generations of Muslims, who *could* have made a difference, observed and experienced injustice and chose to tolerate it. They chose safety over truth. Every Muslim, born or convert, must deal with the sins of our forefathers who tolerated the shackles of oppression and did not rebel. We are all forced to wrestle with the same historical questions. How could it be that this religion that came to liberate human beings from oppression is now marred in the ugliness with which it is marred today?

To the very extent of the sins of our forefathers is our obligation to correct the path. This is why the generation that must correct the course of Islamic history bears a responsibility that is far greater than any previous generation. We cannot correct the path or bring the Islamic message back to its pristine clarity and luminosity without major corrective action. Major corrective action requires enormous investment. It requires great sacrifice by the best kinds of people. The best of Muslims must be willing to sacrifice their entire lives to correct the course, intellectually and educationally, and break the yokes of bondage. We are not going to do this by working as medical doctors during the week and focusing on Islam on the weekends. We are not going to do this by teaching Islam in our free time. That is the past. It is only possible if a sufficient number of the brightest Muslim minds are willing to sacrifice their entire lives to educate fellow Muslims, correct the path of history, challenge the burdens of despotism, and point the finger at what is wrong by saying, "This is wrong and we cannot tolerate it."

Before the *khutbah* today, I received a message from the grand-daughter of Yusuf al-Qaradawi (d. 1444/2022), thanking me for mentioning her parents in an earlier *khutbah*.[41] The mother and father of this poor woman—the daughter and son-in-law of Yusuf al-Qaradawi—have been imprisoned in Egypt for a number of years. They are held in solitary confinement in abysmal conditions that rise to the level of torture under any human rights standard. There are reports that they are being subjugated to a slow and torturous death. Their only crime is that they are the daughter and son-in-law of Yusuf al-Qaradawi.

---

41 See The Usuli Institute, *What Does Your Iman Amount To?* (*Khutbah*, 5 March 2021). Note that Yusuf al-Qaradawi was alive at the time this *khutbah* was delivered. He has since died, aged 96, in September 2022, several months before this book went to press.

I remember when Yusuf al-Qaradawi was a superstar among Egyptian Muslims. I remember when Yusuf al-Qaradawi attended a conference in Qatar and a huge crowd formed around him, trying to shake his hand. I remember the long list of *Shaykhs*, including the former *mufti* of Egypt, Ali Gomaa, waiting humbly and patiently to have just five minutes with him. In that visit to Qatar, I was not even allowed two minutes with him. I was not important enough. He was a superstar. I watched the long line of *Shaykhs* clamoring to greet al-Qaradawi, sit with him, and maybe even take a picture with him—for that was a sign of great prestige. It was so prestigious that one could return to the U.S. and use the picture to be elected as the *imam* of a mosque or the chairman of its board.

This was back in the '90s. I remember saying to myself, "I wonder if a day will come in which the Qatari government becomes angry at Yusuf al-Qaradawi and expels him. Will all these people stick around, or will they disappear?" I corrected myself. "Do not think badly of people. Shame on you." But what happened? Yusuf al-Qaradawi became a persona non grata in Egypt. Saudi Arabia and the UAE turned on him as well. He can only live in safety in Qatar. Were he to set foot in Egypt, he would be promptly arrested and likely killed. And, lo and behold, all those who once flocked around him have disappeared. Al-Qaradawi was once such a superstar that everyone claimed to be his student or friend, even if they had only briefly met him once. Suddenly, however, after Saudi Arabia, the UAE, and Egypt turned on him and made him a persona non grata, it is as if all these so-called former students and friends had never heard of Yusuf al-Qaradawi. They had never met him. They never knew him. This includes 'Abdullah Bin Bayyah, who I once saw in Egypt fawning over al-Qaradawi, calling him "the great scholar." Today, Bin Bayyah will not lift a finger to help him. Al-Qaradawi's daughter and son-in-law have been tortured to the point that she appeared in court and begged the judge to sentence her to death because she cannot stand living anymore. She has been tortured so much that she told the judge, "Please, kill me." Meanwhile, all the *imams* here in the U.S., who once upon a time claimed the honor of meeting, knowing, and studying with al-Qaradawi, utter not a single word.

If the Sisi regime in Egypt did nothing else but oppress the daughter of Yusuf al-Qaradawi—if they did everything else perfectly and this was their only sin—it would *still* be enough to condemn them in this world and in the Hereafter. Similarly, if the Saudi regime did nothing but imprison and oppress someone like Salman Alodeh—if this was its only sin—it would *still* be enough to condemn them in this world and in the Hereafter.

You can measure the health of the *Ummah* by how it treats these figures. Salman Alodeh is a scholar larger than life. He is an *Ummah* in and of himself. And as much as I disagreed with Yusuf al-Qaradawi at so many points in my career, I have the sense and humility to know that he is an *Ummah* in and of himself. He has guided thousands upon thousands of Muslim youths. He has written countless books on Islam. He has lectured for thousands upon thousands of hours. For a scholar like that to sit in isolation in Qatar, unable to leave for fear of what may happen to him, and for his heart to break over the fate of his daughter and son-in-law, speaks volumes about this *Ummah*.

You can expand the *Haram* (holy site) as much as you want. However, if you oppress someone like Salman Alodeh or Yusuf al-Qaradawi, no amount of service to the *Haram* will make up for those sins. You can measure the health of an *Ummah* by looking at its shackles and studying upon whose necks these shackles are tied.

All nations have shackles. Power is oppressive, arrogant, and ugly. But if you study the shackles and upon whose necks these shackles are tied, it will tell you if this *Ummah* has a chance.

The shackles of the Muslim *Ummah* are tied around the necks of Salman Alodeh and Yusuf al-Qaradawi. Yet most Muslims are silent. It is disgusting. We Muslims need to reclaim our representation in the world. We Muslims need a representative to speak on behalf of Muslim interests, dignity, and freedom. We must demand moral and authentic representation. And it is due time that we Muslims search all the means to recreate the institution of the Caliphate once again.[42] Not as an imperial power, but as a moral force speaking on behalf of Muslim dignity and Muslim rights. As an institution chartered upon the principle of speaking truth to power, defying oppression, and removing the shackles that bind human beings. In the world today, there are over one billion Muslims, but we have no Muslim representation, and no Muslim voice.

12 March 2021

---

42 For more on the need for modern Muslims to imagine and strategize for the rebirth of a symbolic Caliphate, see Abou El Fadl, *The Prophet's Pulpit—Vol. 1*, 129-138.

10

The Unspoken Truth about Sexual Abuse and the Rights of Victims

This *khutbah* deals with a difficult and sensitive subject that must be addressed with honesty and candor. Part of this *khutbah* will be technical, but it is not technical for the sake of technicality. We must sometimes address technicalities to make a moral point. When technicalities obstruct morals and ethics, it is the job of the moral scholar and jurist to address those technicalities in order to make space for morality and decency.

Recently, a well-known Muslim figure passed away. This figure was rather controversial. Although he was a popular *imam* with young people to whom he may have provided guidance and inspiration, there were allegations of sexual misconduct. This has become rather common in our community. And it has become quite common for sexual misconduct to be dressed up in legalities, in other words, for it to occur under the pretense of a marital relationship. Straightforward sexual abuse of girls—or, in some situations, boys—is rarer. What is more common in our community, sadly, is for an *imam* to use his position to convince women, often converts, to marry him even though he is already married. The marriage is secret and pursuant to a secret contract. The marriage is consummated through some form of sexual relationship. Eventually, the woman discovers that she lacks any of the rights or recognition of a wife. She discovers that she has simply been used sexually. And she is then, quite often, discarded.

In the case of this *imam* who recently passed away, there have been allegations by female victims who were misled or influenced to enter into marital relations with him. The issue is that after this man died, everyone wanted to remember the good he had done and ignore the rights of the victims of sexual abuse. This is rather typical of our community. Unsurprisingly, these women felt re-violated and re-traumatized. What they had gone through did not seem to matter to the Muslim community. Following what has become the norm in our Muslim communities, the victims were told that the Prophet taught us to only speak about the good that the deceased have done, and to abstain from talking about their misdeeds. For years now, I have seen victims, primarily women, suffer sexual abuse only to be told by the community that exposing their abuser is "un-Islamic." If their abuser passes away, they are told to only speak of the good that their abuser did.

The immorality of this is rather obvious. For we are making choices as to whose rights we uphold and whose rights we disregard. Do not blame God: it is your decision. God presents us with choices in life, and these choices often involve a tension between the competing rights of human beings. Whose rights do you honor, and whose rights do you de-emphasize and ignore? That is a choice. It is a moral choice. Do you focus on the rights of a man who may have served God in certain regards, or do you focus on the rights of victims who have been used and discarded after performing a certain function in a man's life?

Let us examine the famous *hadith* that tells us to only speak well of the dead. This *hadith* is recorded by Abu Dawud (d. 275/889) and al-Tirmidhi (d. 279/892).[43] It is also found in *al-Mustadrak* by al-Hakim al-Nishapuri (d. 405/1014) and in the *Sunan* of al-Bayhaqi (d. 458/1066).[44] But al-Timirdhi, al-Bayhaqi, and al-Tabari (d. 310/923) themselves comment that this *hadith* is problematic because of its chain of transmission. It is narrated by a man named Ata', who claims to have heard it from 'Abdullah ibn 'Umar, who heard it from the Prophet. But the narration goes back to a man named 'Imran ibn Anas al-Makki, who was an unreliable narrator of *hadith*. There is disagreement as to whether 'Imran invented *hadith*s or if he was used as a placeholder by inventors of *hadith*. In any case, as has been recognized by *hadith* scholars for a long time, this *hadith* is weak. Even the modern scholar of *hadith*, Nasir al-Din al-Albani (d. 1420/1999), categorized it as a weak *hadith*.

So much injustice and immorality has been justified on the basis of a *hadith* that, through the technicalities of the science of *hadith*, has long been recognized as unreliable. Many Muslims will at this point respond by citing other *hadith*s that tell us to speak well of the dead, such as "Do not curse the dead for their affairs are now with God,"[45] "If your companion dies, do not speak ill of them,"[46] "Only mention good things about the dead,"[47] and "Do not speak ill of

---

43 Al-Tirmidhi (1019).

44 The full name of the work is *al-Mustadrak 'ala al-Sahihayn*, a five-volume *hadith* collection. The *Sunan al-Kubra* or *Sunan al-Kabir* is a major *hadith* compilation containing almost twenty-two thousand *hadith* reports.

45 Al-Bukhari (1393).

46 Abu Dawud (4899).

47 Al-Nasa'i (1935).

the dead so that you do not hurt their loved ones."[48] Each of these *hadiths*, while less famous, are more reliable. As jurists recognized centuries ago, these *hadiths* teach a general moral rule: once a person dies, we must forget our petty disputes and personal grievances and, as a general matter, learn to honor and not disrespect the dead. However, this must be understood in light of what God teaches us in the Qur'an. This is the other side of the coin. God does not forbid and, in fact, even encourages those who have suffered an injustice to speak up. "God loves not that evil should be spoken of openly, save by one who has been wronged" (SQ 4:148).

Refrain from ill-talk, then, but do not refrain from speaking up if you have suffered an injustice.

Moreover, in another authentic *hadith*, it is reported that the Prophet heard people speaking well of a dead person, and responded, "May God accept." On another occasion, the Prophet passed by a group of people speaking ill of a person who had just died, and said, again, "May God accept."[49] In the *hadith*, the Prophet explains that our role is to witness the deeds of a person; if their deeds were good, then we may speak about these deeds, and if their deeds were bad, then we also have an obligation to testify about these deeds. Notice in the *hadith* that the Prophet heard people speaking ill of a dead person but did not tell them to stop. If this man left behind a bad reputation, so be it. The Prophet did not tell people to stop criticizing or exposing what he had done.

As scholars recognized centuries ago, it all goes back to a juristic principle about the rights of people (*huquq al-'ibad*) and the rights of God (*huquq Allah*). As to the rights of people, the presumptive

---

48 Al-Nasa'i (4775).

49 Ahmad bin Hanbal, *Musnad Imam Ahmad bin Hanbal*, ed. Shu'aib al-Arnout and 'Adil Murshid (Mu'assasat al-Risalah, 1421/2001), 20/268.

demand upon us is that the entire community must fulfill the rights of people. As to the rights of God, the presumptive demand upon us is forgiveness. Put differently, God will vindicate God's own rights in the Hereafter, so we, as a community, are obligated before all else to address the rights of those whose rights have been violated in the here and now.[50]

Apply this to our situation. We cannot disregard the testimonies of victims just because they are women. We cannot blame them for the violations against them. We cannot ignore their rights just because we like to venerate *imams* at the expense of less illustrious, less connected, and less celebrated women. The whole community has an obligation to fulfill the rights of those whose rights have been violated.

It is time for real scholars to speak up when a man dies and the whole community rushes to cite a *hadith*—a *hadith* they have not studied, the context of which they do not understand, and without understanding the jurisprudence surrounding it—to idolize a male figure at the expense of female victims. It is then time for real scholars to say, "That is unethical. That is immoral. It is not right. This is not Islam. This is not *Shari'a*." Men who use their charisma, knowledge of the Qur'an and *Sunna*, and purported closeness to God to obtain license to the bodies of women do not act in a righteous manner. When the community covers up for these men, it becomes complicit in their crimes. These women are then not only violated by their abuser. They are re-violated by the entire community.

Do you really think that God will bless and support a community that uses and abuses the *Sira* of the Prophet to ignore the rights of

---

50 For more on the juristic principle between the rights of people vis-à-vis the rights of God, and the notion that the rights of people precede the rights of God, see Khaled Abou El Fadl, *Reasoning with God: Reclaiming Shari'ah in the Modern Age* (Lanham, Md: Rowman & Littlefield, 2014), l-lii and 320.

abused, exploited, and misled women? Do you think that God will look at this and be perfectly fine with it? If you do, then you are deluded. If you do, then you do not understand what Islam, the Qur'an, the *Sira*, and the *Sunna* are all about. If you do, then you are a continuation of the misogyny, exploitation, and abuse.

When will Muslims learn that God gave us an overriding principle that trumps all else? It is summed up in one word: *haqq*, which means truth, morality, justice, and righteousness. When will we learn that those who remain silent before *haqq*, meaning those who are silent when rights are violated, are "silent devils"?[51] Again, the juristic principle is that the rights of people precede the rights of God. What, then, of the community that dismisses the rights of people? What of the community that looks *haqq* in the face and says, "We have other priorities"? What do you think God will do with a community like that? What does one say about a religion that supposedly tells women to swallow their pride, live in humiliation and indignity, and suffer in silence?

We keep hearing of scandals in so many Muslim communities. Some have escalated to the point that the police were involved. Some *imam*s have been arrested, convicted, and even sentenced to prison. For every *imam* who is arrested, however, there are ten others who are never exposed, never arrested, and never sent to prison. Only in extreme cases or when a parent in the community is willing to break ranks and go to the police are the *imam*s exposed and arrested.

---

51 A reference to the famous statement, "The person who refrains from speaking the truth is a mute devil" (*al-sakit 'an al-haqq shaytan akhras*). Both al-Qushayri (d. 465/1072-73) and al-Nawawi (d. 676/1277) attribute this to the early scholar and Sufi Abu 'Ali al-Daqqaq (d. 405/1015). Islamic sources typically discuss this in relation to the Qur'anic command to enjoin the good and forbid the bad (Q 3:104; 9:71) and the famous *hadith* of the Prophet: "Whosoever of you sees an evil, let him change it with his hand; and if he is not able to do so, then (let him change it) with his tongue; and if he is not able to do so, then (let him condemn it) with his heart," which is found in both Muslim (49) and al-Nawawi's collection of forty *hadith*s (34).

These cases are truly alarming because they often involve underage girls who were entrusted to an *imam* after the parents wanted her to learn the Qur'an, the *Sunna*, or the *Sira* of the Prophet, only for the *imam* to violate this trust and abuse the minor. In some cases, the victims are of age. In all cases, however, there is an enormous amount of pressure upon our children and women to keep their mouths shut and not expose these *imams*.

The problem is that we do not vet our *imams*. The problem is that we live in a world of pietistic affectation. If someone has a good memory and can rattle off Qur'anic verses and *hadith*s, regardless of their moral character or whether they are properly vetted, the community falls for that person so easily. The problem is that there are many computer scientists, engineers, or businessmen who are so eager to teach minors and we do not ask ourselves why. Just because they speak piously to the parents does not mean that they are trustworthy, ethical, or reliable.

What is far more important than religious garb and symbolism is that we teach our children to have dignity and pride. Children must be taught, very clearly, that if they think they are being touched inappropriately, then it is necessary to talk to their parents and for the parents to provide them with a safe space. It is equally important that parents are, in turn, provided a safe space to discuss the concerns of their children with figures of authority in the community. It is imperative that we do *not* say, "But he recites the Qur'an beautifully. He talks about the *Sunna* of the Prophet. He made girls wear the *hijab*, so it cannot be true." If there is an allegation, then it is morally and Islamically incumbent upon the community to act promptly, to investigate, and to protect.

The effect of an abusive *imam* upon a community destroys an entire generation. I know many children who were sexually abused by *imam*s and who grew up resenting Islam and resenting the Muslim community. That, sadly, is the reality. We cannot put our heads in the sand and say that God said there must be four witnesses to the act (Q 24:4-5). If only people bothered to be educated! The requirement for four witnesses is in the context of a formal prosecution by the state in which the state demands the criminal penalty for adultery or fornication. Aside from that formal procedure, four witnesses are not needed. When the issue is whether to protect a minor, you do not need four witnesses. When the issue is whether to terminate someone's employment, you do not need four witnesses. When the issue is whether to stay married to someone, you do not need four witnesses.

Stop acting like lawyers who think they know what they are doing. Have the humility to admit that you know nothing about law if you are not trained as a lawyer. Rely on morality, not law, because you *are* qualified to speak for ethics, but you are *not* qualified to pretend to be a jurist. It is a crime for which you will be responsible in the Hereafter if you do not encourage the abused to speak up and provide a safe space. Not just a safe space, in fact, but a comforting shoulder, support, and understanding. It is better to have someone who cannot recite the Qur'an lead prayer than someone who recites beautifully but is otherwise an abuser and an immoral, degenerate human being.

This is the voice of *haqq*. This is what *haqq* sounds like. The voice of *haqq* is pure, clean, sensible, and straightforward. The voice of *haqq* is not convoluted. It does not perform cartwheels. The voice of *haqq* is as clear and pure as *al-Sirat al-Mustaqim* (the Straight Path) (Q 1:6). The *haqq* is that there have been too many abuses by religious figures. The *haqq* is that we must do more to protect children and women from abuse. The *haqq* is that victims grow up to be a problem for themselves and for others. And the *haqq*, finally, is that it is our fault.

24 September 2021

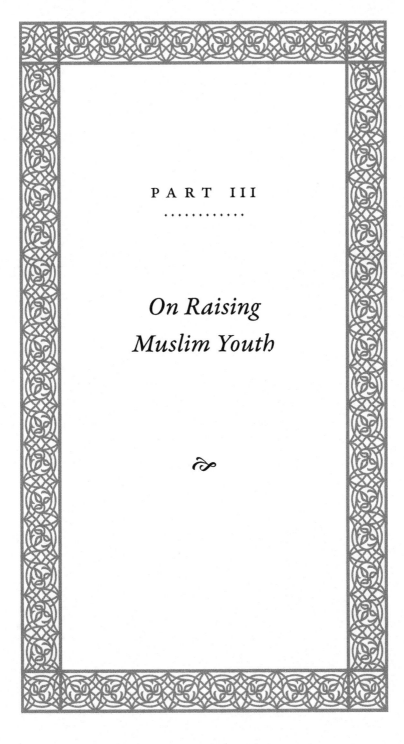

PART III

· · · · · · · · · · · ·

*On Raising
Muslim Youth*

৵

11

Why Our Youth Leave Islam:
When Moses Will Not Confront
the Pharaoh

A Muslim must affirm that God is not marginal to their life. God is not a mere footnote. God is not a complementary item, like a spice added to food. A Muslim does not use God to simply boost the ego. Rather, God is the direction and the goal. God is the objective and the anchor. God is the beginning and the end. God is the difference between light and darkness, beauty and ugliness, justice and injustice. This has always been the message of Islam. You soon realize, upon even a cursory reading, that the main theme in the Qur'an is the contrast between those who live their lives without acknowledging or embracing Divinity, on the one hand, and those who understand that Divinity is the core of their very being, on the other. The latter do this not because they have a political agenda, but because they understand that we are simply an extension of the Divine.

The nature of *kufr* is to fail to acknowledge that you are an extension of Divinity. *Kufr*, literally, means ingratitude. It is ungrateful to deny the truth of the blessings of the Divine. It is ungrateful to respond to what you receive by denying either the thing received, or the Giver of the thing received. *Kufr* can, of course, mean the denial of the very possibility of Divinity, but this is not the type of *kufr* to which the Qur'an refers. In the Qur'an, *kufr* refers to those who refuse to acknowledge that they are, in fact, a natural extension of the Divine. It refers to those who see themselves as "stand-alone" human beings, with a relationship to the Divine that is ambiguous and unclear. They may not say outright, "We do not believe in God," but they do not invest any serious thought, attention, energy, or moral deliberation into what it means to be an extension of the Divine, or what it means to exist in full view of the Divine, rather than in full view of the self, family, tribe, nation, job, or hobbies. This is *kufr*. We have all been in situations in which what matters most to us is the opinion of our family, friends, or community. When we do this, we acknowledge that we are an extension of these categories. So often, however, we do not acknowledge that we are an extension of the Divine.

We are from the Divine, by the Divine, and to the Divine. This is not just theoretical talk. We use the word "theology" to describe a system of belief, but the word is often abstract. Theology, however, describes a pulsating and living reality. How do we think and talk about the relationship between human beings and their Maker?

We commit large and small acts of *kufr*. Narcissists live their entire lives engaged in a huge act of *kufr* because their existence begins and ends with them. They do not think beyond the self. Small acts of *kufr* occur every time we lose sight of our umbilical connection to the Divine. Every time we confront life without thinking of the role of the Divine in it, it is a small act of *kufr*. Every time we are anxious or worried about something without being fully cognizant that everything in life is from God and for God, it is a small act of *kufr*. Hopefully, it is a momentary lapse. Every time we think about right and wrong without thinking about what God wants from us, it is a small act of *kufr*. Every time we indulge a whim or desire and do not think about whether the Divine approves or disapproves—whether it affirms or deprecates our Divinity—it is a small act of *kufr*.

The theology of *iman* and *kufr* is the core of what it means to be Muslim. It did not start with the Prophet Muhammad. All the prophets came with the same basic message: "Make a decision. You either acknowledge that you live in the light of God, from God, and to God, or you do not. God is either part of how you decide to manage yourself, your family, career, and existence in every way, or not." If not, then that is precisely what *kufr* is all about. *Kufr* is not simply atheism. *Kufr* is not simply about violating the technicalities of law. You could be the most diligent practitioner in the world, but if your prayer and fasting do not increase your awareness of your umbilical relationship with your Creator, then your practice does not increase your *iman*. If it does not increase your *iman*, and you always slip into these mini states of *kufr*, then the technical laws are not achieving their objective.

This is critical to remember. Today, everywhere we turn, Islam is being emptied of its substantive meanings. It is as if Islam is being intentionally eroded so that it no longer has any coherence as a system of belief. Those who imagine that Islam is simply a bunch of ritualistic practices without a vigorous theology commit a great crime against Islam. No religion can survive on habitual practice alone without a system of thought that supports, explains, and legitimizes that practice. Think about it. If you have a religious practice but no vibrant theology to go with it, then the practice itself eventually loses all meaning. You then get precisely the mess that we are in today, with Muslims all over the world suffering crises of faith. "I do not know why I pray or fast. I do not know why I do this or that." That is precisely because of the state we are in.

The point of a *khutbah* is not to simply exchange religious jargon and dogma and then set people on their way. The *khutbah* was designed so that those with the most theological knowledge—of course, we have a problem with our so-called "religious experts" today—address the Muslim congregation and bring theology into real life. Today, people fall asleep in *khutbah*s all over the Muslim world, complaining that they get nothing from the *khutbah*. This is because *khutbah*s every-where repeat the same theological dogma but do not bother to relate that dogma to real, unfolding events in the life of the community. In doing so, the *khatib* (speaker) betrays their trust. It is precisely because of this dynamic that so many Muslim communities do not even bother insisting that the *khatib* be a theological expert or the most knowledgeable. They see no value in that because they know that he is not going to say anything that actually relates to the life of the community. This is a disaster. It is a disaster because, for centuries, *jumu'a* has been a barometer of the health of the *Ummah*.

Let me cut to the chase. Why did theology become so divorced from reality all over the Muslim world? Why can we attend *jumu'a* after *jumu'a* anywhere in the Muslim world and find that they all, more or less, sound the same? They all cite the Qur'an and *Sunna*, but they are all marginal and irrelevant to the real-life affairs of human beings. I can sum it up in one word: *taghut*, which means oppression and injustice. The biggest demon haunting the Muslim world is the demon of *taghut* and our silence before *taghut*. *Taghut* is the demon of oppressive injustice. It is the demon of our cowering and kneeling before oppression and injustice.

If you acknowledge that you are an extension of God, then you affirm, by definition, that anything that oppresses God's creatures and spreads injustice and suffering is an offense against the Divine. "As an extension of the Divine, I cannot accept it. I cannot abide by it." I have said before that Islam, like all the Abrahamic religions, praises the poor and the oppressed. It praises those who suffer on earth. Not once does it praise the powerful, mighty, and wealthy. You will find God among the weakest and most oppressed on earth, not the most powerful. That is why Islamic theology condemns the evil of blind, oppressive, and suffocating power. You cannot align yourself with God and, at the same time, align yourself with oppression. If you fail to understand that Islam is an unabating call for justice, liberty, and dignity—that Islam supports the weak and oppressed, saying, "Claim your dignity. Raise your head for you are an extension of the Divine"—then you have not understood Islam at all.

I always pause at a narrative in the Qur'an that makes me tremble every time I recite it. It is when God tells Moses to confront the Pharaoh because the Pharoah is a man of *taghut* (Q 20:24, 43). The Pharoah is an oppressor, a despot, a tyrant. Moses is initially told to approach the Pharoah with kindness and advise him in the hope that he will change his ways (Q 20:44). Moses' response tugs at the hearts of so many Muslims of conscience. It reflects the plight of so many Muslims in our day and age. Moses and his brother, Aaron, say to God: "Our Lord! Truly we fear that he will deal hastily with us, or that he will transgress" (SQ 20:45). Yes, they will confront the Pharoah, but this is a tyrant, a horrible human being. Moses and Aaron are scared. They are scared because they know what tyrants do. They know that tyrants imprison, torture, and kill.

But then comes God's response: "Fear not, I am with you. I hear and I see" (Q 20:46). This gives me shivers. I get shivers because Moses and Aaron were prophets, but not all prophets were promised by God that they will be protected from harm. We know the story of Moses and Aaron—the parting of the Red Sea, the drowning of the Pharoah's army—but we should not forget that some of the followers of Moses did not make it. Some were tortured to death. Others were imprisoned. Do not forget that while God guaranteed victory to Moses and Aaron, we modern Muslims, who confront the ugliness of tyranny and despotism, have no such guarantee. If we are lucky, our fate will be exclusion and marginalization. If we are unlucky, it will be far worse.

What does it mean to confront the Pharaoh? It is to speak the word of truth and Divinity before the tyrants of the earth.

This, my brothers and sisters, is why so many young people suffer crises of faith. It is why so many people are turning away from Islam. Even if young people are too fearful to join you in confronting tyrants, they will at least respect you. They will look up to you. They will honor your sacrifice. In turn, they will honor the system of belief that you embody. If, however, they see that those who are meant to be role models fail to confront the Pharaoh of their age, and instead cower in fear and engage in hypocrisy and double-speak, then they will say, "Well, if these people do not stand up for the paradigm of *iman*, maybe it has no meaning."

We live in odd times. There is a famous and fairly promiscuous Egyptian actress called Somaya El Khashab who is known for her belly dancing and eroticism. This woman was recently given the seal of the Prophet in Saudi Arabia. This is the ring that the Prophet used to wear on his finger with which he would stamp his correspondence. The image was turned into a symbol that is given to dignitaries in

Saudi Arabia. The seal of the Prophet was not given to a great scholar or to someone who stands against tyrants and defends human rights. Rather, it was given to a woman who embodies sexual promiscuity. Saudi Arabia, of course, denies the claims, but I investigated it carefully. The facts indicate that, indeed, she was given a medallion with the image of the seal of the Prophet.

If this was a stand-alone event, I would not have bothered to mention it. Alas, it is not. Recently, I heard the strangest *fatwa* from the former *imam* of the *Masjid al-Haram* (Great Mosque of Mecca), 'Adil al-Kalbani. I once saw a video of this *imam* playing cards in a new entertainment center, smiling broadly. This is after spending thirty years telling us that cards, chess, backgammon, and music were *haram*. Al-Kalbani was asked, "When I attend a music concert"—perhaps the questioner meant a Mariah Carey concert—"should I clap or dance?"[52] Can you imagine the Prophet being asked this question? Al-Kalbani, the "great religious scholar" from the land of the so-called "Guardian of the Two Holy Sites," replied, "It depends. Are you better at clapping or dancing? If you are good at clapping, clap. If you are good at dancing, dance. If you are good at singing, sing."

The head of the Muslim World League, Muhammad bin 'Abdul Karim al-Issa, recently met with Jewish representatives at the Holocaust memorial. In a well-publicized event, he gave a long speech about how Muslims must acknowledge and fully condemn the evils of the Holocaust, which I fully agree with. At the time he said this, however, Israel was once again bombing Gaza. He did not say a single word. He went out of his way to lament the Holocaust, but he did not say a single word about the ongoing genocide in

---

52 See footnote 24.

China against Muslims. Why? It is because his boss, Mohammed bin Salman (MBS), has not said a word. Nor did al-Issa say anything about the genocide against the Rohingya. Again, this is because his boss, MBS, does not want him to. Nor did al-Issa say anything about the continuing slaughter of Palestinians since 1948, leave alone the other massacres taking place in Iraq and Afghanistan or the millions of Muslims who have perished in the past twenty years.

It is good to testify to the truth by condemning the evils of the Holocaust. When you present only part of the truth, however, you are lying. It is fraud and deception. The truth cannot be segmented. It is beyond the pale to kill six million Jews, but it is equally so that an even higher number of Muslims have died in wars that the U.S. and Israel are often involved in over the last twenty years.

Consider another recent episode. 'Aid al-Qarni became very popular among Muslims in the U.S. and Britain. His book, *La Tahzan* ("Don't Be Sad"), was sold everywhere and translated into countless languages. 'Aid al-Qarni once declared that music is from Satan and that no Muslim can ever question that music is *haram*. Recently, however, he sang a song for MBS—apparently, that is not *haram*. But he has gone even further than this. In a recent interview, al-Qarni apologized on behalf of the so-called "Islamic Awakening" movement to which he belonged during the '80s and '90s. He said the movement made many "mistakes," spread "militancy" and "extremism," and that, on behalf of this movement, he "apologizes to the Saudi people." Of course, he does not explain precisely what he is apologizing for. Is it for teaching women that they are simply a form of *fitna*? Is it for teaching that Muslims should be suspicious of, if not openly hostile to, non-Muslims? Is it for teaching that Islam is about nothing more than beards, *hijabs*, and other minutiae? What, precisely, is he apologizing for? Al-Qarni is influential. He has traveled to over 40 countries. Yet, in the interview, he explains just two things: that "bad Islam" is "political Islam" and the Islam of the Muslim Brotherhood; and that "good Islam" is the Islam of the Saudi Crown Prince, MBS. To add to this farce, *Dar al-Ifta' al-Misriyya* in Egypt issued a *fatwa* immediately after the interview to state their full support of al-Qarni and endorse his apology, but to add that "bad Islam" is also the Islam of Turkey and Qatar.[53] "Good Islam," of course, is also the Islam of Abdel Fattah el-Sisi.

Put the picture together. The seal of the Prophet is given to a representative of promiscuity. The former *imam* of Mecca gives a truly nonsensical *fatwa*. We are told that "bad Islam" is "political Islam" and that "good Islam" is the Islam of MBS and Sisi. So, the Islam that has murdered six thousand people in Egyptian prisons in recent years is "good Islam." The Islam that murdered thousands at Rabaa is "good Islam."[54] The Islam that continues to disappear and torture people in the most savage way in Egypt is "good Islam." The Islam that inflicts genocide upon Yemenis by the UAE and Saudi Arabia is "good Islam." The Islam that supports the armies of Khalifa Haftar in Libya so that it can bomb and kill civilians in their homes is "good Islam." The Islam that does not protest the continued bombing of Palestinians in Gaza is "good Islam." I listen to Israeli media. They openly boast that they are living in a golden age. "We are killing Palestinians and the only countries that have protested so far are Jordan and Turkey. We love it." That is "good Islam"?

This is why I stand with Moses, recalling his feelings when God told him to speak the truth to the Pharoah because the Pharoah

---

53 *Dar al-Ifta' al-Misriyya* is an Egyptian Islamic advisory, judiciary, and governmental body established as a center for Islam and Islamic legal research in Egypt. It purports to offer Muslims religious guidance and advice through the issuing of fatwas on contemporary issues.

54 On the Rabaa massacre in Egypt, see footnote 38.

had become an oppressor. Under oppression, you cannot worship God. You are too terrified. Hypocrisy rots your heart. Your true "god" becomes whoever has the power to hurt you, not God. 'Aid al-Qarni's true god is MBS. The god of the former *imam* of Mecca is the King and Crown Prince of Saudi Arabia. The god of the *mufti* of Egypt is Sisi, not God.

I then come back to us. We no longer know what Islam stands for. We used to have a sense that Islam is anchored in a universe of ethics and morality. But look at what is happening in the Muslim world. Look at all the examples. Role models keep falling before our eyes, left and right. This resonates with our children when they are not proud to be Muslim because they simply do not know what to take pride in as Muslims. Let us teach our children that the very essence of Islam is the call that Moses receives to confront the oppressor, the tyrant, because the tyrant is unjust (Q 20:24, 43). That is Islam. When that tyrant grabs you, imprisons you, tortures you, deports you, de-naturalizes you, marginalizes you, and ostracizes you, God says, "Fear not, I am with you. I hear and I see" (Q 20:46). That is Islam.

Let us teach this to our children. Let us pray that God has mercy on those of us who heed this call and who embody the truth of the extension of Divinity by standing up to tyrants. May they not suffer like so many brave heroes have suffered, those who have stood up to tyrants in our day and age.

10 May 2019

12

On Preserving Women and Female Reciters of the Qur'an

I receive a considerable amount of correspondence. Every week, Muslims with a range of different issues write to me. I try my best to respond, but I am usually not successful because of the sheer amount of correspondence. What is most difficult is the correspondence that I receive from women with a problem that I truly wish, in our day and age, was no longer a problem. It is hard to believe that it is still a problem. These are women who find themselves trapped in abusive marriages or in marriages that they did not desire in the first place and were forced, often by their parents, to enter into. It is quite remarkable that many of these women are in the United States. For these women, the issue is often the lack of communal support. A consistent theme is that they approach local *imams* in their communities and do not find a sympathetic party that is willing to help them. The women complain that the *imam*

and community counsel patience, effectively condoning the abuse that they are subjected to by their husbands.

In this *khutbah*, however, I want to focus on another kind of abuse. It is the abuse of Muslim women who are pressured into entering marriages that they do not desire.[55] It is quite remarkable, again, that in the U.S. today we still have many women who come from traditional families that emigrated to the U.S. and that try to solve the anxiety they feel as immigrants by forcing their daughters into undesirable marriages. The position of the parents is easy to understand. These parents are typically worried that their daughters will fall in love with the wrong type of man. They fear that their daughter may even want to marry a non-Muslim. Often, however, this is not the only source of anxiety. Many families want their daughters to marry someone of the same ethnicity and cultural background. If they are Indian, for instance, they not only want their daughter to marry someone who is Indian, but someone from the same area in India, and so of the same ethnicity, language, and culture. The family exerts a tremendous amount of pressure to get their daughters to marry these men.

Quite often, these relationships soon run into problems. Culture plays a huge role in shaping and forming human psychology. If you are raised with the expectation that your parents will choose your marital partner, then, psychologically, in your consciousness, you may prepare yourself throughout life to enter a relationship that is chosen for you by your parents. You may not see this as coercion. You may even find this arrangement desirable. You may be excited and happy when your parents pick someone for you. And once you

---

55 For a further discussion on the issue of women being pressured by their families to marry and the selective use of *hadith* reports to sanction this, see Abou El Fadl, *Speaking in God's Name*, 192-197.

enter a marital relationship, the entire culture in which you live helps you preserve the marriage, for better or worse. It is highly unjust, however, for Muslims who are immigrants to the U.S. to try to force that way of seeing and doing things onto their daughters who have been raised in a very different cultural setting and who grew up under very different circumstances.

I am not saying that all arranged marriages are unfair and unjust. Not at all. Often, in certain cultures, arranged marriages are not coercive. I have seen in my own family in Egypt how female relatives handle an arranged marriage. The idea of coercion never crosses their mind. They are happy with the person their parents pick because they know that it is not only a marriage of man to woman, but of family to family. The daughter knows that her family is part of the marriage to the other family. She knows the culture is set up to help her negotiate her relationship with her husband. The culture is such that relatives and neighbors are involved in the marriage. Every person in the village is involved in the marriage to some degree. There is a long-established practice of handling marriages this way, so the psychological makeup of people is such that an arranged marriage does not produce trauma. It does not produce harm.

But it is very different when there is, in fact, trauma and harm. It is very different in the case of a woman whose expectations in life are different because of her different cultural experiences. This woman may rebel against her culture and believe in her autonomy and right to choose her partner. In these cases, entering a marriage under pressure and coercion produces deep injury to the psychology of the coerced person. This is the serious problem.

I receive so many messages from young Muslim women of various cultural backgrounds who complain that, since reaching their 20s, their parents have pressured them into marriages with men who are simply of the same ethnicity or background. They complain that these relationships are loveless. Often, the threat is that if they do not agree to marry this person, the parents will terminate their education. They will no longer be allowed to go to college. They will be cut off and considered a rebel. In extreme cases, there are even threats of physical violence. Once in these marriages, the daughter is told that it is her duty to remain married even if she does not love her spouse. Even if she cannot stand her spouse. If she attempts to leave her husband, she will be disowned. In this scenario, it has become common for the poor woman to seek out *imams*, only to find that the *imams* are unsympathetic, uncaring, and often side with the parents. The woman is told that honoring parents is a religious obligation. In other words, she is told that it is an obligation to remain in a coerced and loveless marriage.

Let me put it very bluntly. I am baffled by parents who expect their daughters to surrender their bodies to men whom they do not love. God has not willed that I have a daughter. If I did, however, the idea that I would expect my daughter to give herself sexually to a man whom she does not love shakes me to the core. Strip away all the niceties. Is this not, essentially, what we are doing to these women? "Whether or not you love or even like the man, live as a wife and perform as a wife. If you do not, you will be ostracized by the community. You will be disowned by your family." These parents are without honor.

Let me send this message loud and clear. If, as a parent, you expect your daughter to lay in the bed of a man she does not love, then you are a parent without honor. Because of your own insecurities, egoism, and misogyny, you expect your daughter to submit her body without love, feeling, and passion. And you then claim to love your daughter! You then claim to be a parent of honor, religion, and faith. That is not Islam. No matter how hard you try to dress it up as Islam, it is not Islam. God tells us that God created partners so that we may find peace and repose (Q 30:21). God tells us that God wants relationships of love (*mawadda*) and mercy (*rahma*) (Q 30:21). How, then, can parents force their daughter into a relationship in which she does not feel any love? Are the parents submitting their bodies to this man every night? You cannot force your daughter into this position and then stroke your ego, thinking yourself to be a wonderful Muslim.

Ibn 'Abbas reports that a woman came to the Prophet and said, "My father forced me into a marriage that I did not want." The Prophet did not respond by asking how she was forced. Rather, the Prophet simply said, "You have a choice. Return his dowry and you are free, or stay in the marriage."[56] In a famous report, a man coerced his daughter to marry her cousin. The woman complained to the Prophet, adding that her father did it to elevate his own social and economic status. The Prophet immediately brought the father and husband, and said, "She has a choice. If she wants, she can return the dowry and she will be free. Or she can keep the dowry and stay in the marriage." At this point, the woman utters a statement that resonates throughout the centuries. The woman says, "I actually *do* want to stay in this marriage, but I did what I did to affirm a principle. I wanted women to know that it is up to us, not our fathers."[57] So, this woman ultimately stayed in the marriage, but she sought to make the point that it is up to women, not their fathers, to decide to whom they surrender their bodies.

Patriarchy had a huge problem with these reports in which the Prophet clearly and unequivocally believes the woman. No

---

56 Abu Dawud (2096).
57 Ibn Majah (1874) and al-Nasa'i (3269).

investigation. No interrogation. The Prophet did not ask, "Were you really coerced? How so?" Yet, many Muslim jurists—who, of course, were men—still claimed that there has to be proof that the coercion is compelling. This is a product of patriarchy. The will of God is very clear: God does not like coercion (Q 2:256). The *Sunna* of the Prophet is very clear: your body is yours; you decide who to surrender it to. It is obscene that there are still Muslims today who expect women to give their bodies to men, even if unwillingly, and claim that the angels will curse them otherwise.[58]

Let me share a recent incident. I informed one woman about the famous story of the Companion, Thabit ibn Qays. Thabit was married to a woman who told the Prophet that she wanted to leave him. The wife was very blunt: "I find no fault in him, neither in his personality nor religion, but I just cannot stand him." The Prophet said the same thing: "He gave you a garden as a dowry. Return the garden, and you are free." The woman in question then went to an *imam* and, as usual, the *imam* told her that she has to stay with her husband. "But I cannot stand him," the woman responded, "and how about the story of Thabit ibn Qays?" This *imam* said to her, "Thabit ibn Qays was a very ugly man and that is why the Prophet gave his wife the right to divorce him." Look at the bigotry! There are versions of this report in which the wife of Thabit tells the Prophet that her dislike of Thabit was such that, but for the fear of God, she would spit at him every time she saw him. Interpreters—who, again, were men—asked, "Why would she spit in his face? It must be that Thabit was ugly." So they inserted this reasoning as justification for

---

58 For an extensive discussion on the *hadith*, attributed to Abu Hurayrah, that cites the Prophet as allegedly saying, "If a man calls a woman to bed and she refuses to come, the angels will continue to curse her until the morning," and similar *hadith* reports that denigrate the moral status of women, see Abou El Fadl, *Speaking in God's Name*, 210-18.

the narration. They inferred that Thabit ibn Qays was an ugly man. Research the story of Thabit, however, and you find that this is the only time he is described as an ugly man. The far more common and authentic version of the narration cites the woman as saying, "I do not fault his moral character or piety, but I fear that if I stay married to him, it will test my faith. It will make me less pious as a Muslim."[59]

This is not because Thabit was an impious man. It is because a life without love can test your faith. A life without love can make you do what many women do today—blame Islam for their predicament. A life without love can lead many women to start losing their relationship with God. They no longer feel anything when they pray or read the Qur'an. After all, they live a life of sexual captivity. They feel forced to surrender their bodies to men whom they do not love to appease their parents. Yes, it tests your faith. If there are children, then we must talk about the rights of the children. If there are no children, however, then the priority must be a relationship that draws you closer to God. If you exist in a loveless marriage, you will often not know how to love God. But what often happens with these poor women is that their parents push them into these marriages and then pressure them to get pregnant. Once they are pregnant, they are stuck. For we must always think of the rights of the children.

Muslims need to grow up. God taught us the principle of non-coercion (Q 2:256), and our Prophet repeatedly taught that women have a right to autonomy and freedom in marriage. Reflect on this. Every jurist will accept that it is *haram* to force a woman to eat or drink when she does not want to eat or drink. If you force a woman

---

59 Al-Bukhari (5273) and al-Nasa'i (3463).

to exercise when she does not want to exercise, it is *haram*. If you force a woman to do anything, it is *haram*. But then, lo and behold, somehow, when it comes to having sex with husbands whom they do not love, some jurists say that refusing sex could cause the angels to curse them all night! How could it be that coercion is condemned in all affairs except for a woman's bodily and sexual integrity? Men must learn that the sanctity of a human body, at a minimum, starts with the principle of non-coercion. You cannot torture a human being. You cannot rape a human being. You cannot make another human being suffer. So if you make your own daughter suffer in the most degrading way, do you really think you are a Muslim? Do you really think your prayers and fasts are accepted? Do you think that anything about you as a Muslim is accepted? You are a parent with no honor.

Why don't all those who like to call themselves "feminists" do something for the sake of these women? Why not raise funds so that when a Muslim woman wants to leave her husband, she can hire legal representation? Many of these women are trapped in these relationships because they have no means. They cannot hire a lawyer. They cannot get a job. They live in fear of social exclusion, stigma, and even of their parents doing them harm. To all so-called feminists: let us do something real. Let us work together to raise money so that if these women want lawyers, we get them lawyers. If they want shelter, we get them shelter. If they want jobs, we get them jobs. If they want protection from their parents, we get them protection. This is the feminism that I understand, but it is also the Islam that I understand. This is what my Islam teaches me. I do not get this from Western values. I get it from the heart of my *iman*.

Yes, misogyny crept into the Islamic tradition and sullied the waters. There is a *hadith* reported by Abu Hurayrah that says, "If a woman asks her husband for a divorce without just cause, she is cursed by the angels until the Final Day." Jurists, however, said that this *hadith* is too weak to have any legal import. Yet Muslims today make this isolated *hadith* equal to the many reports that affirm the right of a woman to choose her partner in marriage. What I mean when I tell Muslims to grow up is that it is time to recognize that our tradition—like all religious traditions—has been sullied by misogyny and patriarchy. It is time to have the bravery to say that what is misogynistic cannot come from our Prophet because it contradicts the Qur'an. The Qur'an honored women and told them that their relationships with their husbands must be built on love and mercy (Q 30:21). The Qur'an did not tell women to shut their mouths and surrender their bodies to men whom they do not love. It just cannot be. If you do not see that, then there is a serious problem in the way that you understand Islam.

Some will hear this and say, "Khaled Abou El Fadl is a liberal." So defending the integrity and honor of a woman is "liberal"? It is not Islam, but "liberal"? Shame on you. Or they will say, "Khaled Abou El Fadl is Westernized." Since when did honor, integrity, and justice become "Westernized"? If this is not Islam, why are you Muslim? The justice, ethics, and virtue that I learned are from the Qur'an and the *Sunna* of the Prophet. My sense of virtue does not come from liberalism or anything else. It comes from Islam. So should yours.

Last week, I talked about female reciters of the Qur'an.[60] I started to count the number of female reciters from the past century whose recitations I could find online. To date, I have found around seventy, and I am still counting. But I want to comment on some misunderstandings that I found in the scholarship on the tradition of female reciters.

---

60 See Chapter 6: *The Prophet's* Hadith *on the Intellect* in this volume.

At the end of the nineteenth and beginning of the twentieth century, the Qur'anic radio station in Egypt started broadcasting famous female reciters like Sakina Hassan, Munira 'Abduh, Karimal Adliya, Munira Ahmadul Khudari, and Adliyat Ibrahim. This tradition continued until the end of the 1930s, when Egypt suddenly stopped broadcasting female reciters. That rule continues until today. I read in the literature two things upon which I must comment. The first is the claim that the tradition of female reciters of the Qur'an started around one hundred years ago and derives from the practice of female wailers at funerals, where women would be hired to scream and cry. The second thing is that, according to the literature, radio stations stopped broadcasting female reciters because of a *fatwa* by al-Azhar in the 1930s that stated that the voice of a woman is part of her *'awra*.

Both of these points are wrong. The tradition of female reciters of the Qur'an did not emerge from the tradition of female wailers. The profession of female wailers is well-known. It is an established profession in countries like Egypt that dates back centuries and has nothing to do with the guilds of Qur'an reciters that include women and have chains of transmission going all the way back to the Prophet. These female reciters were taught by their female teachers, who were taught by their female teachers, and so on. The tradition of female reciters of the Qur'an, then, goes back centuries, not just one hundred years. Many people do not know that these female reciters taught men who became famous reciters themselves. Until today, there are famous female reciters in Morocco, Egypt, Algeria, Indonesia, and Malaysia. The second point to note is that female reciters disappeared from the airwaves not because of a *fatwa* by al-Azhar. There is no such *fatwa*. Female reciters disappeared because of the influence of Wahhabi and puritanical Islam from the 1940s. Especially after the *Nakba* in Palestine, Muslim culture became increasingly conservative.[61] As always happens, Muslim men responded to political and military defeat by taking it out on women. Misogyny, sadly, always reaches its height in periods of military, political, and cultural defeat.

I close with an important point that I would be remiss not to mention regarding the ongoing war between Azerbaijan and Armenia over a region called Nagorno-Karabakh. This region is historically part of Azerbaijan, but it has a majority population who are ethnic Armenians. Nagorno-Karabakh declared itself an independent state in an act that was recognized by no country except Armenia. Armenia sent military forces to "protect" the enclave. Many do not know that ethnic Armenians in Nagorno-Karabakh evicted the Azeris from the region. They killed around thirty thousand Muslim Azeris and ejected approximately one million. The cause of the war is that Azerbaijan wants Nagorno-Karabakh back, considering it land that belongs to Azerbaijan that has been occupied by Armenia. That is also the position of the United Nations and international law. The ethnic cleansing that took place in Nagorno-Karabakh against Muslims is a genocide.

Here is what is extraordinary. The city of Los Angeles has made an official declaration supporting the Armenians. The declaration refers to Nagorno-Karabakh by its Armenian name, Artsakh. Armenian Americans stood next to lawmakers from Los Angeles, the Mayor of Los Angeles, and other officials to support Artsakh, even though it is not recognized by any other country in the world. They stated that Artsakh has the right to be a free country and any war by

---

61 Lit. "the disaster" or "catastrophe," the term refers to the destruction of Palestinian society and homeland in 1948 and the permanent displacement of a majority of Palestinians upon the formal creation of the state of Israel.

Azerbaijan to evict the Armenian army is illegal. They claimed that Turkey and Azerbaijan are sending "terrorists" and "jihadis" from Syria and Libya to fight Christian Armenians. There is no evidence of this, of course, but we all know why they said it. They said it to invoke the Muslim terror card.

Why did the city of Los Angeles do this? Because of the political influence of Armenian Americans. This is the problem with Muslims. So many Muslims live in Los Angeles, and yet they are powerless. They are not involved in politics. They have no political clout, because while Armenian Americans donate huge amounts to buy political influence, rich Muslims spend their money on expensive cars and fancy homes. With all the Muslim millionaires living in Westwood, Beverly Hills, and Malibu, the city of Los Angeles has completely ignored the ethnic cleansing of Muslims. According to the Mayor of Los Angeles, the Armenians of Nagorno-Karabakh are blameless, faultless, and innocent. They did not commit ethnic cleansing. They did not slaughter Muslims. They did not close mosques and turn them into barns for animals. The politicians did not even mention Muslim victims at all. They spoke only of how "jihadis" are flocking to fight their Christian brethren. The city of Los Angeles now demands that the federal government stands against Turkey and Azerbaijan and supports the independence of the Christians of Artsakh.

Where is the Muslim Public Affairs Council? Is it not an LA-based organization? Where is the political clout that they have worked to develop over thirty years? Where are all the rich Muslims, and where are their donations?

9 October 2020

13

Addressing the
Generational Divide

We are approaching the month of Ramadan, the crux of the entire year. Ramadan is our marker. We count our lives by how many Ramadans we have lived through. Ramadan is not just a month of fasting and charity. The fasting, prayers, and charity are all part of a dynamic in which we look inwardly, think of the year that has passed, and reflect upon the years to come, if God wills that we have years to come. It is a month in which we seek to discipline the body, control our urges, reflect upon the past, and make resolutions.

Ramadan is our review board. It is the month in which we review what we have done and think about the trajectory of our lives. A Muslim must undertake an internal review of their own beliefs, convictions, and conduct. There is also an external review in which a Muslim looks at the state of the Islamic world, the *Ummah*, more generally. We start, of course, with our most immediate community and extend this outward until we reach a point of reflection about the entire Muslim *Ummah*. We start locally and extend globally. But we should also reflect beyond the Muslim *Ummah* and think of the state of the world itself.

This Ramadan arrives under rather exceptional circumstances.[62] The entire world is confronting a global pandemic. This Ramadan, those who are afraid of themselves will find no escape from themselves. Those who are easily distracted may find it much harder to be distracted. It is a Ramadan that, I think, none of us imagined we would ever confront in our lifetimes. No public gatherings, no collective *iftar* (evening meal), and no prayers in the mosque. It is a challenge, but it is also an opportunity. It is an opportunity to turn inward and worship God away from public scrutiny and the gossip of our communities. It is an opportunity to truly reflect within and contemplate your place, my place, and our place in the world in which we live.

There is a very practical aspect to each Ramadan. No Muslim can ignore the fact that so many Muslims around the world will confront this Ramadan in severe hardship. I refer to those Muslims who have been imprisoned unjustly. The coronavirus cannot cause us to forget the Uyghur Muslims who confront this Ramadan in concentration camps. This Ramadan, so many Uyghurs face illness, death, and suffering. We know next to nothing about them, except what has been leaked. We cannot forget them in our prayers. Nor can we forget the thousands of Muslims, including scholars like Salman Alodeh, who, yet again, will fast under impossible circumstances in political prison. Ramadan is a barometer of the health of the *Ummah*. Another Ramadan arrives and Muslims are still suffering so much injustice, corruption, and inequity. This is a measure of

---

62 This *khutbah* was delivered in April 2020 at the height of lockdown measures as a result of the global COVID-19 outbreak.

our well-being. Ramadan is not a time to be selfish. It is not about simply feeling better about oneself as a Muslim. It is about how we can improve as Muslims while scrutinizing what we can each contribute to the *Ummah* and the world around us. That is the Islamic ethic. That is what Islam is all about.

There will be other opportunities, however, to talk about Ramadan. In this *khutbah*, I want to focus on a sad reality. This Ramadan arrives amid a virtual flood of young Muslims who are confused, if not skeptical, about their faith. So many young Muslims are unsure about their place in the world. They are not sure what they are supposed to do with their lives. Worse, they feel ambivalent about their identity as Muslims.

There is a clear generational gap to this dynamic. Many young Muslims are skeptical, if not outright disappointed, about the generation that raised them. Many young Muslims look at the generation that raised them and wonder whether that generation did a horrible job with the lives they were given. This is because they look around and see the state of the Muslim world. This younger generation was raised in an age of Islamophobia, social media, and mass communication. We cannot ignore how they were raised in an environment that has been colonized by Islamophobic discourses. If they were raised in a Muslim country, they were raised under despotism, injustice, and a great deal of hypocrisy. If raised in a non-Muslim country, they were raised with discontent and double standards, a world in which action is very different from speech, platitudes, and dogma. For young Muslims, the generational gap has bred confusion and disappointment.

Few of them, however, openly confront their parents' generation with their disappointments. "Why have you given us a world in which there is so much inequity and bloodshed?" Indeed, very few of the older generation are satisfied with the world they are handing over to their children. It is not as if the parents think they have done a wonderful job. But there is no adequate language by which the parent can tell their child why the world has become the way it is. In other words, if parent and child spoke honestly and openly, they could share their collective confusions and disappointments about the state of the Muslim world. They would find, in fact, that the feelings of alienation are something that they can bond over.

I want to focus on one aspect of this. I want to reflect upon how we got here and how the Qur'an speaks to us, giving us solace and direction in times like these. The Qur'an is a living prophet. It came to speak to every day and age. God, in God's wisdom, revealed the Qur'an to the Prophet in Mecca and Medina as events unfolded. Yet the way the Qur'an was revealed and what it said to the Prophet were intended as a demonstrative living example to address every age to come.

The opening verses of Surah al-Baqarah address the early Muslim community in Medina, which faced an environment as hostile to Islam as the world we live in today. In Mecca, Muslims faced open and sworn enemies. Like today, the Meccans were hostile to Islam and openly oppressed Muslims. Yet this, in many ways, was the easy part. In Medina, Muslims faced a far greater challenge. The Jewish tribes in Medina had a complicated and ambivalent relationship with the Prophet. On the one hand, there was a formal alliance between the early Muslims and the Jewish tribes, the so-called "Constitution of Medina." Yet the Jewish tribes of Medina were well established and had grown accustomed to dealing with the Arab tribes of Medina from a position of superiority. They controlled much of the financial market of Medina. The Jewish tribes were also literate and educated, unlike most of the Arabs of Medina. Beyond the formal alliance, then, the rhetorical and propaganda war never truly ended. Islam was the new religion on the block, so to speak, and Muslims faced criticism, skepticism, and doubt from more-established Jewish tribes. Add to this the problem of the so-called "hypocrites" among the natives of Medina, who nominally converted to Islam but remained sworn enemies of the Prophet. The hypocrites only pretended to convert. They uttered the *Shahadah* (testimony of faith), but mocked, jeered, and sought to subvert the new religion of the Prophet from within.

Reflect on the position of the early Muslims in Medina. They arrived in Medina having fled the sworn enemies of Islam—the Meccan Quraysh, the external enemy—but soon faced the Jewish tribes and the hypocrites. Imagine being among these early Muslim pioneers. Imagine facing external and internal enemies. Now think of this in relation to our time. How does Surah al-Baqarah address us and speak to our present circumstances?

This is the Book, there is no doubt in it. It is a guide
for those who are mindful of God. (Q 2:2)

It is as if God is saying that God knows we are going through the hardest time. God knows the road ahead is difficult. God is saying, "I know you exist as an island in a sea of hostility, but if you want to walk this journey, the starting point is that this Qur'an is the truth. There is no doubt in it." We must always ask ourselves a fundamental question that the Qur'an, incidentally, posits numerous times: is God's word sufficient for us, or not? No one can convince you that this is a book from God unless you are willing to accept the testimony of God. If you are not sure that God is testifying, then you do not actually know if you are a Muslim. If you do not truly believe that this is God's testimony, then there is a problem from the get-go. God is assuring you. Take God's word that this is the Book in which there is no doubt, and that it is a guide for those who live in reverence of God, those for whom God is an important part of their existence.

> *Who are steadfast in prayer and spend from the wealth*
> *that We provided them. Those who believe in the revelation*
> *sent down to you (Muhammad), and in what was sent*
> *before you, and firmly believe in the life to come in the*
> *Hereafter. They are the people who are rightly following*
> *their Lord and it is they who shall be successful. (Q 2:3-5)*

There are those who believe, pray, and are generous with God's money, knowing that it is not really their money. Having told us this truth that should anchor our lives, Surah al-Baqarah then addresses the sources of confusion, ambivalence, and alienation in the psyche of the early Muslims and in our psyche today.

> *As for those who are bent on denying the truth, it makes*
> *no difference to them whether you warn them or not.*
> *They will not believe. God has sealed their hearts and*
> *their ears, and over their eyes there is a covering, and*
> *they will receive terrible punishment. (Q 2:6-7)*

If your relationship to the truth is affected by the beliefs of others—if you are the type to look around and say, "But I know so many who never respond to the call" or "There are so many whom I respect and it confuses me that they are not Muslim," which was very much like the early Muslims—then God is intervening to tell you, explicitly, "Here is the truth. This is the truth." Know that God is speaking to you. Know that if your psychology is dependent upon who converts to Islam and who does not, then you have a very hard road ahead of you. Your belief in God cannot be contingent on your relationship to other human beings. That is a fool's errand.

There are believers, deniers, and then the most serious and dangerous category of all.

> *There are some who say, "We believe in God and the last day," and yet they are not really believers. They seek to deceive God and the believers but they only deceive themselves, though they do not realize it. In their hearts is a disease which God has increased . . . (Q 2:8-10)*

This is because if you seek beauty and goodness in your life, God will help you achieve it. If you seek hypocrisy and ugliness in your life, God will help you achieve it. God enables you to do what *you* want to do.

> *. . . They will have a painful punishment because they have been lying. When they are told, "Do not cause corruption in the land," they say, "We are only promoters of peace," but it is they who are really causing corruption, though they do not realize it. And when they are told, "Believe as other people had believed," they say, "Are we to believe just as fools have believed?" Surely they are the fools, even though they do not realize it. (Q 2:10-13)*

The third category are those who are nominally Muslim. They say the *Shahadah* and call themselves Muslim, but they philosophize a great deal about their state. "We are good people. Does it really matter if we do not pray or fast in Ramadan?" Even if they do pray, they do so artificially. Even if they do fast in Ramadan or wear the *hijab*, they do not care about injustice. They do not really care about Muslims suffering around the world. They are nominal Muslims in terms of their ethics and morality.

These poor examples of godliness are the greatest test for our children and the new generation, for they break Muslims from the inside. Officially, they are Muslim, but their conduct betrays a great deal of ugliness that cannot be reconciled with Islam. The Qur'an insists on calling these people "hypocrites" and, in so doing, the Qur'an teaches us a very valuable lesson: hypocrites are to be identified by their conduct, not by the declarations they make about themselves. Talk is cheap. Look at the effects of their conduct. Do they benefit or corrupt the Muslim community?

This Ramadan finds Muslims in a state that is directly addressed by Surah al-Baqarah. The Qur'an reminds us that our anchoring point is to know that this is God's Book and God's revelation (Q 2:2). God did not create this world so that everyone would become Muslim. There will always be those who are skeptical about God and Islam. There will always be those who reject the message and who do not, and will not, believe (Q 2:6-7). Yet I want to further discuss the third category, those who are officially Muslim but who, substantively, have very little to do with Islam.

Recently, I read two books that left me reflecting on Surah al-Baqarah and the state of modern Muslims. I urge everyone to read these books. The first is titled, *MBS: The Rise to Power of Mohammed bin Salman*.[63] It portrays the life and rise to power of the Saudi Crown Prince. Reading the book, you are struck by how this young prince, the effective custodian of Mecca and Medina

---

63 Ben Hubbard, *MBS: The Rise to Power of Mohammed bin Salman* (New York: Crown, 2021).

and leader of perhaps the most important Muslim country, is so thoroughly alienated from Islam. MBS throws lavish parties that cost millions of dollars. He buys a yacht for half a billion dollars. He buys a painting for hundreds of millions of dollars. He has parties in which he serves foreign diplomats the most expensive alcohol. Everything he says to Europe and the U.S. is to appease non-Muslims and convince them that Saudis are worthy of their respect. At the same time, MBS shows zero regard for the opinions, autonomy, or sovereignty of Saudis themselves.

The second book is titled, *Into the Hands of the Soldiers*.[64] It examines the Egyptian revolution, how it failed, and the coup that followed. The book shows how key figures in the Obama administration, such as Chuck Hagel, Rand Paul, James Mattis, and Michael Flynn, had strong feelings about Islam. Read Michael Flynn's book, *The Field of Fight*.[65] He is very open and honest about his views. Flynn is a Christian evangelical who thinks Islam is evil. The attitude of these figures who worked in the Obama administration, and later in the Trump administration, is one of clear hostility toward Islam. These are rabidly Islamophobic individuals. The book shows how these key players worked with the ambassadors of the UAE and Saudi Arabia to bring a very influential Muslim ruler into power, Abdel Fattah el-Sisi of Egypt. Many leaders in the Muslim world receive their education in the U.S. and are trained in places like the National Defense University in Washington, D.C., which has a rabidly Islamophobic faculty. The understanding of Islam of people like MBS and Sisi, then, is deeply shaped by this Islamophobia.[66]

---

64 David D. Kirkpatrick, *Into the Hands of the Soldiers: Freedom and Chaos in Egypt and the Middle East* (New York: Penguin Books, 2019).

65 Michael Flynn and Michael Ledeen, *The Field of Fight: How We Can Win the Global War Against Radical Islam and Its Allies* (New York: St. Martin's Griffin Press, 2017).

66 See also Abou El Fadl, *The Prophet's Pulpit—Vol. 1*, 190.

Does this matter? Yes, in so many ways. Notice that Mohamed bin Zayed (MBZ) of the UAE last year hosted for the entire month of Ramadan the Muslim intellectual, Muhammad Shahrour (d. 1441/2019). Shahrour spent his entire career dismantling Islam from within. According to Shahrour, there are no five pillars, you do not have to fast in Ramadan, and *zina* is permissible so long as it is not in public. This so-called "intellectual" was hosted, celebrated, and awarded by MBZ.

Consider the following as we approach Ramadan and reflect on our faith. Think of the money that MBS spent on his yacht. If this money was given to a Muslim institution to fight Islamophobia, then the fate of our children around the world would be very different. Reflect on this. If the money spent on lavish parties was instead spent on organizations in the West to combat Islamophobia, then we would be living in a very different world. As you read these books, reflect on how the money spent on a single night of partying by MBZ and MBS could sustain ten, twenty, or thirty scholars for a lifetime.

Why focus on this issue at this time? I believe that the least we owe our children is an explanation for how we got to where we are. The least we owe our children is to tell them who the hypocrites are—those nominal Muslims who are, in truth, the sworn enemies of this religion and the cause of the present illness and malaise in Islam. In the Arab world, MBZ is widely known as "the devil of the Arabs" (*shaytan al-'arab*). It is true. But what matters is that these figures have empowered Islamophobes in the West in ways that will affect us for generations to come. Do not kid yourself. Regardless of how much you see yourself as a free and independent thinker, your psychological makeup is shaped by the mass media that surrounds you. This shapes everything. It affects your attitude toward things as simple as, "Do I think praying five times a day is a pleasure or a burden?"; "Do I think fasting is rational or irrational?"; "Do I want to get close to God or not?"; "Would I rather spend time learning about the life of the Prophet or playing video games?" And those who control this mass media are closely allied with MBS, MBZ, and Sisi.

In short, we owe our children an explanation. Why is it that whatever we say about our religion is not enough to combat the deluge of skepticism and doubt that is thrown at them from all sides about their Muslim identity? Most important of all is that we teach our children that what happens in Mecca and Medina and in the entire Muslim world is, in fact, their business. Teach them to dream of the day in which they become influential enough in U.S. politics to stop our government from supporting the likes of Sisi, MBZ, and MBS. Teach them that they owe it to their fellow Muslims to grow up to influence things in Washington, D.C., so that the U.S. supports those who are just, moral, and ethical. Teach them, at a minimum, that people like Michael Flynn and Steven Bannon should not get to decide U.S. policy vis-à-vis the Muslim world.

This is a difficult topic, but we cannot let yet another Ramadan pass without achieving some progress in honesty and transparency about our modern Muslim condition.

10 April 2020

14

How Do Our Youth
Make Sense of This World?

There are certain undeniable truths in our lives. We are all aware of the fragility of life. The reality of death and regeneration occurs in every single second of our lives. We could not exist if millions upon millions of cells in our body did not die and regenerate. Without that process, nothing would be. We are surrounded by living things that fly in the sky or crawl in the ground and that will soon expire. That is the logic of existence. Our children grow up to learn that the pets they love will die, the people they love will die, and while we are not quite sure what it means for our consciousness to expire, we know that we, too, will die. We are but a virus, heart attack, or accident away from expiration. Anything and everything could be the end of us.

This very logic testifies that our Lord, the Maker and Owner of existence, has created the logic of death and regeneration. But it is so easy for us to be oblivious to this. So many of us grow up believing that we are intelligent, sophisticated, and realistic human beings. We even place religion in the category of the "unrealistic." Yet, nothing is more unrealistic than to be oblivious to the logic of existence that surrounds us. This is the logic that everything dies, we will die, death can come at any moment, and regeneration persists despite death. What are the chances that this singular and universal logic of death and regeneration persists throughout the universe? Why does the entire universe follow laws of physics that seem ironclad and unbreakable? It is absurd to claim that it is all simply by chance. That is the greatest act of unrealism. It borders on the insane to believe that it just is, because it is. We must concede that the logic of existence is so tight, so profound, that if we have any level of intelligence, we are forced to pay attention.

Everything in our lives, however, is designed to distract us from death. Everything that results from industry, capital, and the logic of sales and profits; everything we watch, read, and buy; even the food we eat and the clothes we wear; in short, everything modernity has produced—it is all designed to distract us from the inevitability of death. We know that we will die and that we cannot escape it. We know that death can come at any time. But what happens after death? Do you simply live, die, and then disappear? If so, then your birth is meaningless, and your death is meaningless. Your entire existence is meaningless. If that is what you believe, then you cannot explain how this universe is the result of such remarkable universal laws. You cannot explain the symphony of existence. Ultimately, you have no answers as to why *you* matter. Coincidence created you and coincidence takes you away. You will be forgotten like the billions of other human beings that once lived and then disappeared. Even if you are remembered in the books of history, if death is truly the end, then memory does not matter. Ironically, the logic of atheism is that the memory of Hitler is equal to the memory of Mother Teresa. It is all the same. For once we die, Hitler is no more, and Mother Teresa is no more, just as you are no more. According to this logic, none of it really matters. If there is no meaning beyond death, then why does it matter if I am remembered as a serial killer or as a great moral teacher? For I am dead and the idea that my legacy "lives on" is crazy. That some people may remember me makes no difference.

The only way for anything to mean anything is if, after death, the story goes on. If, in fact, after death, there is resurrection and accountability. Only then is there meaning.

Our children love to think that they are independent, critical, and analytical thinkers. Our children search for a sense of self, dignity, and a reason for self-respect. What we, as Muslims, need to realize is the extent to which the cards are stacked against our children. For everything is designed to get them to never think about death. From their first day at school to the phones they carry, the computers they use, and the programs they watch, everything is designed to tell them to not think too deeply about death or about what happens after death; most importantly of all, to not reflect upon whether there are consequences for our actions in the Hereafter.

It is not an exaggeration to say that modernity structures itself around the logic of capital. We organize things so that those with capital can invest it and have a return on it. That is the logic of modernity. And for those with capital to have a return on their investments, our children cannot be allowed to think too deeply about the meaning of existence. The very logic of capitalism is the logic of distraction and heedlessness. That is precisely why everything in our world—including law, economics, and psychology—is organized around the idea that it is undesirable and unhealthy to think about death or the consequences after death. Except in very rare cases, our children never get an opportunity to understand this. It is not enough, then, that we simply communicate to our children the Qur'an, *hadiths*, prayer, fasting, and then tell them, "So off you go, be a good Muslim." We need to think deeply about our world, and we need to teach our children to think deeply about our world. We need to confront the simple question: what if, after death, you face accountability—are you ready? Thinking of what may happen to you in the future is precisely what it takes to be a realistic human being.

How do we help our children make sense of this world? What does this world mean to them? Muslim children, in particular, are supposed to understand that a critical part of their faith is to think of Muslims as a single *Ummah*. We are but one people, united by the belief that there is no god but God and that all the prophets, from Abraham to Moses, from Jesus to Muhammad, came with the same basic message. God does not need our worship, but God decreed worship for our own good because it teaches us to be moral and ethical beings. For this reason, if we teach our children to worship God but do not explain to them how worshipping God translates into an ethical, conscientious, and moral existence, then the very logic of Islam falls apart.

As Muslims, we confront this challenge more than any other group. Wherever we turn, we see a world that has become remarkably adept at persecuting, targeting, and tormenting Muslims, from Palestine to Bosnia, from the genocides in Myanmar and China to the rise of Islamophobia in the West. It is as if the devil himself looked upon the world and saw that Islam was the last bastion of logic, ethics, and morality, so it must be targeted.

It is remarkable that in the same way that there are those who can be surrounded by the logic of death and yet think of their own death as a remote possibility, there are those who can be surrounded by human suffering and yet remain oblivious to it. Islam is a bastion of morality, and the very logic of morality is how you treat others. How, then, can we have a moral order if we are not taught to think of others? If Islam is about morality, how do we raise our children to be true Muslims?

Think of the atrocious genocide taking place in China where Muslims are murdered, imprisoned, and tortured. Imagine raising a child to be Muslim, but never teaching this child to think of those suffering under this genocide. This child will learn to be oblivious to the suffering of others. This child will grow up thinking that their life is solely about them, their career, and their hobbies. This child will never learn that life is not about that; rather, it is about what you do for others, because *that* is the logic of morality. This child will never learn that it is, in fact, immoral to live solely for yourself and that there are consequences for that after death. Instead, this child is taught that God wants them to pray and fast. God wants them to do X and Y. But they are not taught what truly matters. They are not taught that the very logic of justice is that God supports those who are raised to serve a cause, i.e., to serve others.

It is extremely frustrating. I grew up watching Palestinians suffer under Israeli occupation. I saw how so many Muslims lived, died, and were completely oblivious or indifferent. I witnessed the gruesome details of Bosnian Muslim suffering and the horrors of the rape camps. So many Muslims, again, were oblivious. Add to this the plight of the Rohingya, Uyghurs, and, lest we forget, Chechen Muslims, all of whom have experienced genocides that many Muslims have largely forgotten or ignored. According to reports, a new genocide against Muslims is imminent. A detailed article titled, "Genocide Unfolding in India," addresses the 200 million Muslims in India.[67] The latest

---

67 See Hammad Sarfraz, "'Five-Alarm Fire': Genocide Unfolding in India," *The Express Tribune* (23 January 2022).

news is that Pooja Shakun Pandey, an influential Indian politician, has called for the immediate extermination of Muslims in India. This is in addition to many reports about escalating anti-Muslim rhetoric and violence in India and the ongoing genocide against Muslims in Kashmir. As I read an article like this, I am reminded of all the Muslims who have said to me, "Why are we so concerned with the Palestinians? We should move on. They are not the only people who suffer." They said the same thing about Bosnian Muslims. Eventually, they said the same about the Rohingya. Today, they say the same about the Uyghurs. Will they say the same about Indian Muslims?

Until when do we raise our children with the highly immoral logic that their lives are simply about themselves, their careers, and their successes? Until when do we continue to ignore the heart and soul of Islam, namely, that we are a single *Ummah* that feels and acts as one, that a single spirit emanates from us, flows within us, and through us? Until when do we continue to teach our children that their success is measured by their wage, zip code, and possessions, rather than their ability to do something good, just, ethical, and moral?

Many Muslims are oblivious, because Muslims are very good at being oblivious. Recently, the U.N. appointed a special rapporteur, Richard Falk, himself Jewish, to report on the conditions of Palestinians living under occupation in Israel. Falk described Israel as an "apartheid state" and Palestinians as living under "occupation." The public outcry and activism by those who raise their children very differently than how we raise ours was so deafening that the U.N. was forced to withdraw Falk's report. It was not highly influential people who accomplished this. It was common Jewish students on university campuses. Currently, the U.N., again responding to reports of Israeli violations, has appointed a panel of three human rights experts to report on the condition of Palestinians living under Israeli occupation. Israel has already launched a campaign to discredit whatever these experts are going to say. Yet Israel has gone even further. Israel has renewed another campaign that aims to spend anywhere between $40-80 million to support people in the West who do nothing but defend Israel, right or wrong.[68] Only a small part of this budget comes from the Israeli government. Most of the budget comes from Jewish donors. This campaign targets anyone who brings attention to the reality of Palestinian suffering or the Israeli apartheid state. This money recruits students, activists, and scholars to do nothing but defend and polish Israel's image.

I will give one example. As our children grow up to be selfish, self-absorbed, and self-centered, I want to share the plight of Deir Nidham, a small village in the West Bank that is like so many other Palestinian villages. Israelis confiscated the farms and land to build an illegal Israeli settlement called "Neve Tzuf." After stealing this land and building an illegal settlement—without compensating the Palestinians a single dime, of course—the Israelis brought 1500 Jewish settlers to live in it. Most of the settlers left their jobs in law, banking, and Wall Street to migrate from America. They came from the U.S. to displace Palestinians and settle on unlawfully stolen land. When local Palestinians protested, Israeli soldiers surrounded the village and laid siege. No one is allowed to enter or exit the village without going through numerous checkpoints, searches, and interrogations. I wish it stopped there. Most disturbing are the smuggled videos of Israeli soldiers storming schools under the pretense of searching for students who threw stones at the illegal Israeli settlement. One video shows Israeli soldiers beating a Palestinian student in 11th grade.

---

68 See Itamar Benzaquen and The Seventh Eye, "The new hasbara campaign Israel doesn't want you to know about," *+972 Magazine* (25 January 2022).

When his teacher tried to intervene, the soldiers beat the teacher. In under a year, Israeli soldiers have stormed the school 14 times, each time beating and harassing students and staff and arresting students without even notifying the parents.

Israel already suffocates Palestinians. There are no jobs in Palestine because Israel controls the economy. Wages are so low that most Palestinians must apply for a permit to work in Israel for low-paying jobs under horrible conditions in which they have to accept whatever their Israeli employer demands of them. In addition, work permits are extremely expensive. They must work from dawn till dusk, with half their wages paid to the middlemen who sell the work permit. Despite all of this, Israel is very well protected. Every time someone points to the obvious and says, "This is apartheid," there are those who rush to deny and erase this narrative. Israel has countless supporters who are willing to donate millions of dollars. Israel has so many students willing to dedicate their careers to propagating lies about "Israeli democracy," which, of course, does not benefit the Palestinians living under occupation.

To every Muslim in the West of immigrant parents: you could have been the Palestinian child beaten by Israeli soldiers on camera. Are you aware of that? There will soon be thousands of children in India whose parents will have been massacred. I am sure that there will be sexual assaults, imprisonments, and torture. Are our children aware that they could have been one of these suffering children in India? Do they grow up with this awareness?

Our children do not have a good moral example because they find that their parents follow the likes of Hamza Yusuf, who has sold out to the UAE, a country now in bed with the colonizers of Palestine. Even before the genocide occurs, the UAE has already sold out the Indian Muslims. The UAE gave its highest award to

Narendra Modi, the chief architect of the Hindu fascist state.[69] The UAE insists that any Muslim who speaks out about the plight of Palestinians or Indian Muslims are "Muslim Brotherhood," "terrorists," or advocates of "political Islam." The Islam of Hamza Yusuf and the UAE is an Islam that does not say a word. It is an Islam that chooses to stay silent in the face of injustice and betrayal. It is an irrelevant and immoral Islam. It is an Islam that tells us, "Numb yourself. Enjoy your life. Do not think too deeply. Do not think about anything other than feeling good." It is a capitalist version of Islam, identical to the hedonistic logic of capitalism. This UAE brand of Islam teaches us to be self-centered, hedonistic, and amoral. It tells us just to "feel good" about ourselves and our families. But this selfish "feel good" Islam is not true Islam. It is a fake Islam emptied of all morality, justice, and meaning.

Muslims with hearts have seen too many slaughters and atrocities against fellow Muslims. I still vividly recall the details of the Bosnian genocide and the rape camps. I still remember the details of the *Nakba*.[70] I cannot bear to watch yet another genocide take place against Muslims in India. Will we ever step up to the plate and make a difference? Will we ever teach our children that they must make a difference? Will we ever teach them that it does not matter if they go to medical school if, ultimately, all the money they earn is spent on themselves and their families, on prestige and appearances?

28 January 2022

---

69 On 24 August 2019, the UAE awarded the Order of Zayed medal, its highest civilian honor, to Modi. The move came weeks after Modi's Indian government stripped Kashmir of its special autonomy, sent thousands of troops to the region, and imposed a strict military curfew.

70 See footnote 61.

15

The Challenge of Commodification: What Can One Generation Say to Another?

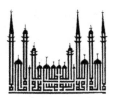

The biggest challenge in a *khutbah* is the attempt to achieve relevance. This is even more so when you speak across generations. A *khutbah* must be relevant not only to Muslims who are just like you. It must reach out to Muslims of different ages, backgrounds, and generations. What can one generation say to another? The older generation has gone through the various stages of life and entered its final years, with most of its opportunities and choices behind it, not ahead of it. As this generation prepares to exit the stage, what can it say to those who have, presumably, most of their lives still ahead of them? I say this not just as a teacher, but as a father. The challenge in these *khutbah*s is all the greater when my youngest son is in attendance. I always pause and think carefully about what I can possibly say that is relevant

to his life. For what is relevant to him is relevant to the lives of so
many young Muslims.

It is not just a generational gap. There are numerous cultural,
psychological, and other gaps between the generations. Many older
Muslims have lived through exceptional circumstances in which they
relocated, migrated, or were displaced from their homelands. Life
brought with it the struggle to assimilate, adapt, and be accepted
in new circumstances. These older generations experienced a deep
sense of disruption in their lives that they had to cope with and, to
the best of their ability, overcome. The experiences of Muslims born
and raised in the U.S., however, are often fundamentally different.

Often, the biggest challenge is the challenge of empathy. The
generations born in the U.S. understand and empathize with suffering very differently. It is not that this younger generation does
not witness suffering, but they see suffering of a different type.
They see the suffering that is induced by a loss of purpose, by the
restlessness and anxiety of asking, "What is the point? Why am I
in this world?"

Put simply, their challenge is often the challenge of nihilism. Their
challenge is that of the gravitational pull of apathy. Their challenge
is that of being born into a highly commodified world. They do not
realize this because it is not taught in schools. It is not taught in the
movies they watch or the video games they purchase. It is not taught
anywhere. But their challenge is that they were born into a world
that does not engage them as moral agents. Nor does it encourage or
nurture in them a sense of wisdom or morality. Rather, it is a world
that commodifies them. It is a world that engages them primarily
as consumers. It is a world that takes an interest in them solely to
the extent that they can purchase commodities. Again, this is not
taught to them, so it is not part of their consciousness.

Think of how we talk to this generation about their career prospects, job security, and earning potential. This normalizes for them a system that puts a dollar value on everything and that deals with people solely in terms of what they can produce by way of bottom-line profits.

The younger generation born and raised in the U.S. has never experienced disruption, displacement, or the trauma of explicit and barbaric ugliness. But it experiences a different type of barbarism and ugliness. It is an ugliness that is far more discrete, but still lethal. It is the ugliness of commodification. This generation lives between being a consumer and being consumed. Meanwhile, no one speaks to this generation about wisdom, inherited knowledge, philosophy, or ultimate truth and falsehood. They grow up being taught by the system to not even believe in the possibility of justice.

For this system to work, it needs generations of people who truly believe in their own powerlessness. The system raises our children to give up. It teaches them that the realities around them are so overwhelming that it is naive, uncool, and even idiotic to believe that they can make a difference. The system itself—through its many discreet methods of indoctrination—tells them that they either fall in line, or they are out of luck. It tells them to assign value to things that they consume and that, in turn, they will be assigned a value by those who consume them.

Our kids grow up wanting to be independent and cool. By natural impulse, they intuitively know that they are not just animals. Their instinct tells them that they should matter. Everything around them, however, says the opposite: that they matter only to the extent that they can assign a profit to something, or else they will be assigned a value in order to be consumed. So much of what ends up forming and shaping human psychology is designed to tell our sons and daughters that resistance is futile. It is akin to when the state sends a huge police or military force to apprehend a "deviant." The basic message the state wants to convey by this show of force is that resistance is futile.

We have failed to foster in this generation a humanitarian spirit of asking the deeper questions. How did this existence come to be, in all its fantastic complexity and multi-layered beauty? How can it be without a Creator? What does this Creator want from us? What does it mean to exist? What does it mean to have a relationship with our Creator? What does it mean to be an agent of beauty? What does it mean to have empathy for the other? What are our moral obligations toward those who suffer?

Many immigrants think that they faced the truly hard test. They immigrated, left their homelands, their loved ones, and struggled to adapt to a new life. But the sad truth is that the challenge their children face is much harder and more lethal. It is the challenge of a system that dehumanizes them, a system that teaches them to give up and be apathetic because there is no point to resistance. Comfort is one of the toughest and most lethal tests of all. Living in privilege is its own toxic challenge.

What do you say to your child? How do you convince your child to take their life seriously? How do you get them to think deeply about how they consume and how they are consumed? How do you communicate to them that it is insane not to believe in a Creator and to think that the universe is the result of happenstance? That it is insane not to ask the simple question: what does my Creator want from me? That it is absurd to ignore the reality of death and not think about what happens after death?

How do you communicate to your son or daughter that it is thoroughly uncool to live a life in which you are commodified, where you are just a consumer and, in turn, a commodity to be consumed? How do you explain to your child that for all their displays of coolness and individuality, it is the system that implants in them their sense of fashion, need, and desire? It is all given to them. None of it is innate. It is all part of a system of indoctrination. It is all designed to turn them into consumers and commodities.

Look at what young people post on social media. Reflect deeply enough, and you will see that the way young people pose and flaunt themselves online is communicating one thing: "I am a commodity." Often, this is through sexualized displays that appeal to people's animalistic desires. But we cannot blame them. How much blame can we put on someone who grew up in a world in which everyone posts and shares what they are doing, buying, wearing, and eating, a world in which the only way to receive positive reinforcement and "likes"—the only way to feel valued—is to pose and commodify yourself?

How do you reach through to this generation and tell them, "You deserve better than this. Do not believe the lie that resistance is futile. Do not believe that it is what it is, and so it shall be forever"? How do you tell them that they do matter, but not as a commodity or as a consumer—they matter as a powerful, holistic, and moral agent that exercises moral choices?

The Qur'an tells us about a wise man known as Luqman. Speaking to his child, Luqman starts with precisely what you wish you could communicate to your child: denying your Maker is a "great injustice" (Q 31:13). It is unjust not only toward your Maker, but also toward yourself. For without God, the path is open toward human beings consuming one another like animals. But for God, it is barbarism without restraint. Luqman tells his son that denying his Creator and failing to understand what his Creator wants from him is a great injustice because he will then live a heedless life. Without God, you end up at that juncture in life in which nothing makes sense. "Where am I going?" "What is the point of any of this?" "Who am I?" "What am I truly about?" How do you tell your child that, rest assured, this juncture in life will come, it is inevitable, and the only thing that can save them is their relationship with their Creator?

Only a relationship with your Creator can answer these questions and give you the confidence to defy the system to say, "I do not care what they tell me. I can make a difference because my God tells me, 'It is not up to them, it is up to God.' I have the greatest and most powerful ally in God, so my life can have meaning. My life is not just about commodities." How do you communicate any of that?

Luqman lived in a pre-capitalist society. In these societies, children were taught to look to their parents for guidance. Our capitalist society does not teach this. In fact, our society teaches our children not to listen to parents if their parents tell them to live a more meaningful life. Our society needs consumers, and a perfect consumer responds only to impulses, not to parents, not to wisdom, and not to ethics.

Younger generations will listen to a company or an influencer tell them what trends and styles they "need." But they will not listen to their uncool parents or to anything relating to wisdom. I truly feel sorry for our children. Their test is so difficult. I have said before that pain is a great educator. So many parents were lucky to be blessed with real pain in their lives. This pain woke them up and gave them clarity. When pain becomes a part of our children's reality, however, it is often too late. Pain is added to a sense of meaninglessness in life. Our children then go on to become depressed, alcoholics, or even drug addicts. They go through the kind of trauma from which it is truly difficult to recover.

Wisdom could have saved them. Faith could have saved them. We need to think very seriously about the plight of our children. We need to think very carefully about how we communicate to them that we are not here to judge them, but to be an agent toward their guidance. We sit not as judges, but as resources and, hopefully, as sources of wisdom.

Shortly before this *khutbah*, I became aware of a new report that has been released. The World Bank, through its organ, the International Finance Corporation, continues to fund Chinese companies that are directly involved in the Uyghur genocide.[71] These companies make products by exploiting Muslim labor in Chinese concentration camps. Muslim workers are forced to work in these camps, but the World Bank has for years done business with these companies, supporting them financially. The economic cycle goes on and on as human beings just like you and I—their only fault being that they are Muslim in China—are consumed and discarded.

At the same time, we know that some years ago the U.S. illegally invaded Afghanistan. The invasion and occupation of Afghanistan was against international law, leave alone moral law. In Afghanistan, we murdered, bombed, and obliterated. For twenty years, we slaughtered without the least degree of accountability. Not only that, but we created "black sites" where we arrested and tortured people. We also created an extremely corrupt government that abused the Afghan people.

The global system of trade is largely done through U.S. dollars because the U.S., as a superpower, does everything it can to ensure that people buy and sell products using the U.S. dollar. What this

---

71 See Laura T. Murphy, Kendyl Salcito, and Nyrola Elimä "Financing and Genocide: Development Finance and the Crisis in the Uyghur Region," *Atlantic Council* (16 February 2022).

means is that when countries deposit money in their central banking system, they do so in U.S. dollars. The Afghan government, through the Afghan central banking system, had a modest reserve of around $4 billion, a paltry sum for the U.S. We spend far more than that on bombs that kill people all over the Muslim world. For Afghanistan, however, this $4 billion is the difference between life and death. Although it is not our money, we insisted, as an occupying force, on controlling and determining what happens with this money—illegally and immorally. Why? Because we wanted to pay our cronies in Afghanistan. We wanted to ensure that they got money and that those who oppose us get nothing.

Now that the U.S. has withdrawn from Afghanistan, the Biden administration has decided to confiscate and seize the country's money. A headline in *The Intercept* reads, "Biden's decision on frozen Afghan money is tantamount to mass murder."[72] What this means in real terms is that Afghans who deposited money in the central bank have lost their money. If you saved a portion of your earnings for over twenty years, hoping to one day send your kids to college, for example, it is now gone. Uncle Sam decided to confiscate your money. It means that government workers, teachers, and doctors go without pay because the Afghan government does not have the money to pay them. It means that there is no hard currency for people to import food or medicine. What this means in real terms is that thousands upon thousands of Afghans will starve to death or die from disease and malnutrition. Criminality will explode. When people get desperate, what do they do? They sell drugs. The U.S., of course, knows this. Does the U.S. want to encourage the creation of a major drug industry and ensure that the

---

72 See Austin Ahlman "Biden's decision on frozen Afghan money is tantamount to mass murder," *The Intercept* (11 February 2022).

Taliban becomes drug producers and merchants? Whose interests are being served here?

The Biden administration recently sold a huge arms shipment to Saudi Arabia to continue slaughtering Yemenis. This comes as the United Nations warns, once again, that the funds needed to feed Yemeni children have run out. Eight million Yemenis now face starvation.[73] Why is it that when it comes to the perishing of eight million Yemenis, ten million Afghans, and millions of Uyghur Muslims, we do not care? Why are we such an immoral force in the world?

The biggest trick of the system is to teach our Muslim children that it is not their problem. Yemenis are dying, Afghans are dying, and Uyghur Muslims are dying, but the system tells our children to focus on going to *hajj* or *'umrah*, doing their prayers, and fasting in Ramadan. How do you convince the younger generation that things like the concentration camps in China do not just happen? That the World Bank doing business with companies complicit in the Uyghur genocide does not just happen? That it happens because people make decisions that allow it to happen? How do you convince this generation that it *should* be their business, and that they *can* make a difference? How do you convince them that Islam is about more than just rituals?

If there were moral human beings in influential positions in the World Bank, then perhaps the World Bank would not be funding a genocide against Muslims in China. Perhaps if we had greater leverage over the White House—if there were more Muslims in Congress who could pass laws to prohibit the President from stealing Afghan money and, in turn, murdering the Afghan people—then we could make a difference. Perhaps if we had more Muslim artists, writers,

---

73 See "U.N. Says 8 Million Yemenis Could Lose All Humanitarian Aid Next Month Due to Funding Shortages," *Democracy Now* (17 February 2022).

and singers, then Muslims could influence public opinion. These Muslims could create movies, documentaries, and art that would communicate the message that to be immoral is wrong, to slaughter people is wrong, and to be complicit in mass starvation is wrong.

The system teaches our children that resistance is futile and that they cannot make a difference, so they should not even try—"it is what it is." But it is human beings who create these institutions of ugliness. It is human beings who decide to commit crimes. And it is human beings who can make the principled decision to stop them. We always learn about the genocides committed, but we never learn about the genocides *averted*. Behind every genocide that was averted, you will find moral and principled human beings. This is what we should teach our children.

18 February 2022

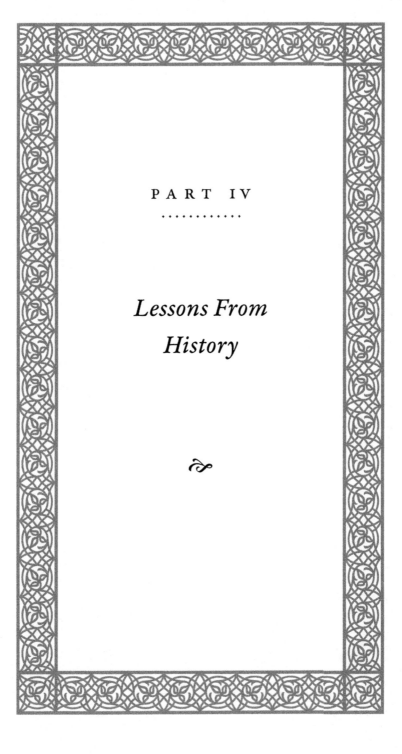

PART IV

. . . .

Lessons From
History

☙

16

The Islam of Dignity: Are You on the Right Side of History?

Islam should be the most important thing in the life of a Muslim. Islam should be the framework through which a Muslim sees and understands the world. It is critical that Muslims have a clear vision of what Islam means to them, and a clear understanding of the moral role of the Islamic message in the context of human history.

We have lived through a very interesting period of human history. We have seen the fall of communism and the rise of democracy in many countries around the world. With the fall of communism, we saw movements wherein people asserted their right to self-determination. Put aside all the sophisticated theories as to whether self-determination is umbilically linked to liberalism or some other socio-political philosophy. At their core, these movements were rooted in people's sense of their own dignity. But we have also lived

through periods of resistance to the rise of the notions of self-determination and human dignity. This resistance has taken the form of
various dictatorial, authoritarian, and totalitarian ways of thinking.
Sometimes this battle is so unequal. We see this in Russia, for example, where authoritarianism has returned. Or we see it in Palestine,
where people continue to live under occupation and their right to
self-determination and dignity has been frustrated. We see it also
in China, where a nascent movement toward greater freedom and
dignity has been frustrated through sheer power and force.

It is critical to understand that this is how history works. It is
critical that we understand the movement of history itself. Through
international momentum, for instance, we saw the movement against
slavery. This was long before our time. It sparked the American Civil
War. It sparked many political struggles all over Europe. There were
various nuances and permutations, of course, but the core idea is
that slavery lost its legitimacy and credibility all over the world. The
world moved against slavery as an institution.

Rest assured, however, that just as there was a movement against
slavery, there was also a reactionary movement that sought to preserve
slavery in its various forms. We see this in the Jim Crow laws in the
U.S., in various since-forgotten movements in Europe, and in various reactionary and conservative institutions around the world that
opposed the epistemological, moral, and theological changes that
would end the legitimacy of slavery as an institution. Yet a historical
movement arose against slavery and, despite considerable resistance,
eventually led to an official abolition of slavery. In later times, there was
momentum toward fascism and there were movements of resistance
against fascism. This ended with an at least official defeat of fascism.

This is the nature of human history. Certain ideas catch on
and spread like wildfire. Ideas become like a living organism. They

are absorbed by people and form part of their consciousness and awareness. And for every idea that catches on, there is a movement of resistance against it. Ultimately, however, it is very difficult to repress the movement of history.

Why do I say this? Our current problem is with racism. Our problem with racism in the U.S. is intimately tied to the historical movement that rejected slavery, and the reactionary movement that resisted the abolition of slavery. Our current problem with racism is but a continuation of the long human saga between despotism and, if you will, liberation. In Qur'anic terms, it is the constant saga between the oppressed (*al-mustad'afun*) and their natural inclination to resist their oppression, and the equally natural process—"natural" in that it occurs as if written in the laws of nature—by which a counter-movement resists the resistance to oppression.

It is a very old story. People oppress others because of deep moral flaws within. It is unrealistic to expect that, in any age, the problem of oppression and injustice will end. It won't. Human beings will always oppress other human beings. It is also unrealistic to expect that human beings will ever fully concede and accept a fair and just distribution of resources or live at peace with the idea of full individual rights, autonomy, and dignity. It is the nature of history. It is the nature of human society and psychology. There will always be oppressed people. But there will always be resistance to oppression. And there will always, also, be resistance to the resistance to oppression.

In this dynamic, certain momentums catch on and move humanity forward a step or two. But you do not have to be an expert in history to realize that every movement against oppression faces resistance. The story of history is the story of slow, incremental, and unequal progress. Slavery was formally abolished but continues to exist in many forms. Fascism was officially abolished but continues to exist in many forms. Communism officially fell in most parts of the world but continues to exist in many forms. But the recurring battle that we all witness, a battle both old and new, is racism.

This is why an understanding of Islam is so critical. God tells us that God sent this message to bring us from darkness to light (Q 2:257; 5:16; 14:1, 5; 33:43; 57:9; 65:11). But what does this mean? What does it mean in terms of how a human being should live their life, and in terms of the proper attitude of a Muslim toward the unfolding of history?

Take a step back to reflect upon a small but monumental event. Reflecting upon microevents in Muslim history often speaks volumes. Microhistory can be most revealing. Dihya al-Kalbi was a Companion whom the Prophet sent as a messenger to the king of the Ghassassina, a tribe of Christian Arabs allied to the Byzantine Empire, to invite the king to Islam. It is quite remarkable that this was the first time that Dihya had traveled to a royal court. He was not among the earlier Muslims who migrated from Mecca to Abyssinia to escape persecution and who entered the Abyssinian court. This was Dihya's first diplomatic mission. The Muslim *Ummah* itself was so inexperienced in diplomacy that the Prophet sent his message without an official seal with which to stamp his message. Muslims had to manufacture a seal for the Prophet after learning that the court would not read any message from a foreign dignitary unless it had an official stamp. This was their level of simplicity and inexperience.

Dihya traveled to the court of the Ghassassina and announced that he had a message from the Prophet Muhammad. He asked how he should present his message to the king. He was given a whole set of instructions. After entering, he was told to place the letter before the king, without directly handing it to him, and then take several steps back. He was told to stand at a certain distance. There was so much protocol and etiquette. A critical part of the protocol, however, was that Dihya was told to prostrate upon entering the king's presence. That is how they had long done things in the court. Dihya is not one of the most famous Companions. He is not one of those about whom there are so many stories. But I have always been struck by his immediate response: "Prostrate before the king? No. I cannot do that." He was told that if he did not prostrate, the king would not receive him. His response? "So be it. I will take my message and go back." He was also told that if he attempted to present the message without prostrating, the king may be so insulted as to have Dihya arrested and possibly executed. Dihya replied, "So be it. If that happens, it happens. My reward is with God." Every attempt by his fellow Arabs to get Dihya to observe courtly protocol by prostrating before the king failed.

This entire back-and-forth lasted for days, incidentally, because those at the court feared that if they presented Dihya to the king and he refused to prostrate, the king would blame and punish the court. The king may say, "How dare you bring someone who refuses to prostrate in my presence?" There were long debates about what to do. Should they refuse to let Dihya enter the king's presence, or should they take the message from him and present it to the king themselves? The one constant, however, was Dihya's stance. He would not prostrate. Note that he did not say, "I will not prostrate because I am a man of honor." His response was similar to the response of those Muslims who migrated to Abyssinia years earlier and who also refused similar courtly protocols, though not to the same extreme. Dihya's response was simple. "In Islam, we do not do that. Islam has liberated us from the need to worship other human beings." When people at the court told Dihya that he is not worshipping the king, only observing courtly protocol, he responded, "I am sorry, but what I understand from my religion is that when I prostrate to God, I prostrate to none other than God."[74]

Dihya al-Kalbi was not a theologian. He was not a great philosopher or a major jurist. How, then, did he have this innate understanding of what Islam is? How did he have this type of courage and rectitude? How did he gain such a fundamental understanding of what it means to take people from darkness to light?

Take another example, which is an oft-repeated statement from the *Sira*. We often find it when we read of the Companions interacting with each other or with the Prophet in the events surrounding the battles of Badr, Uhud, and Hunayn: "We, Muslims, cannot allow ourselves to be degraded or humiliated."[75] It is a striking phrase. It reveals a clear and innate understanding of Islam as a message of dignity. For the Companions to honor Islam and for Islam to honor them, they had to live dignified lives. Unless they were dignified human beings, the Islam within them would be defeated. We must look at these microelements to understand the truth of things.

Let us return to the idea of historical movements. The Islam of the Prophet Muhammad was, quite clearly, a movement of liberation and self-determination. For this very reason, it met a considerable amount of resistance. Much of this resistance, we should note, was internal to Islam itself. Many who converted to Islam did not necessarily hold any of these pristine ideals. Contrary to popular belief, it is not true that the first few decades of Islam were decades of liberation that were then followed by the long winter of authoritarianism, despotism, and

---

74 For more on Dihya al-Kalbi and the envoys sent by the Prophet see Ibn Hisham, *Kitab Sirat Rasul Allah*, ed. F. Wustenfeld (Gottingen: 1859-60), 1/975 and al-Waqidi, *Kitab al-Maghazi*, ed. J. Wellhausen (Berlin: 1882), 234. Also see al-Bukhari (4553) and Lings, *Muhammad*, 301-2.

75 See Muslim (1785) and al-Bukhari (2731, 2732, and 3182).

oppression. Rather, the dynamic between freedom and oppression within Islam has ebbed and flowed throughout Islamic history. The idea of human liberation and self-determination was eventually suffocated in the Muslim East while the Christian West embraced the idea and took it to new heights. I am referring to the defeat of the medieval Catholic church, the Reformation, and the radically modified church theology of Christianity. The idea of freedom in the Christian West became contagious and propelled the rise of Western civilization. From this emerged another huge historical moment in the movement to abolish slavery—which was, ironically, championed by the same people who brought colonialism to the world. By this time, however, Muslims had ceased to be a civilizational force. By this time, Muslims were simply on the receiving end, not the making end, of history. Muslims had entered their long winter and ceased to be an effective force in the world.

I submit to you that Muslims ceased to be an effective force because they forgot the simple intuitive knowledge of Dihya al-Kalbi. They forgot what it means to be Muslim, and the inherent dignity that Islam came to give human beings.

We are now living through a similar historical moment. This time, it is the long battle against racism. Racism is a very old illness. It is as old as the illness of poverty itself. Racism is intimately tied to the dynamics of oppression, dictatorship, and the unequal distribution of resources. It is tied to the ideas of class, domination, and hegemony. Racism is also the close demonic ally of slavery and colonialism. Early Islam clearly recognized racism as an immoral and intolerable illness. Muslims, however, as I say, have been in a state of slumber for a long time. So, in the same way that they were not at the forefront of the battles against slavery and despotism or for democracy in the modern age, Muslims have forgotten that what it means for Islam to take people "from darkness to light" is that God gives them the right to claim their human dignity, autonomy, and self-determination. God gives them the certitude to reject all blind allegiances, including that of racism. The Prophet taught that people are as equal as the teeth of a comb, and that there is no difference between an Arab and non-Arab.[76] But this pristine moral awareness has been in a state of slumber in Muslim civilization for a very long time.

God tells us that God has blessed us as a nation: "You are the best community brought forth unto mankind . . ." (SQ 3:110). But what is it that makes God bless a nation? It is not the amount of oil you have. It is not your wealth. It is not even your fasting or prayers. Nor is it because you make *du'a'* (supplication) during *laylat al-Qadr* (the Night of Power). It is not because you go to *hajj* or *'umrah*. Rather, it is because of a dynamic: ". . . enjoining right, forbidding wrong, and believing in God" (SQ 3:110). It is because, as a people, you enjoin what is good and resist what is evil. But this is impossible unless you first have an awareness of what "good" and "evil" mean. If you are confused about even this, then the idea that you can enjoin or forbid anything is idiotic. The premise upon which a nation is blessed in Islam is the awareness of goodness that precedes the actual act of enjoining what is good and forbidding what is evil. This is precisely like Dihya al-Kalbi. It is precisely the innate knowledge that Islam came as a message of liberation, self-determination, dignity, and freedom. That Islam came to condemn racism and oppressive institutions of power. This innate awareness must precede any act of enjoining the good and forbidding the evil.

I underscore that the Prophet taught the Companions that whoever stands in a broken and humble state before the rich and

---

76 See Shah Waliullah Dehlawi's (d. 1176/1762) collection of forty *hadith*s (16).

powerful, one-third of their Islam is null and void.[77] The Prophet was teaching the Companions the meaning of dignity. Even if you are poor or disadvantaged, as a Muslim, you cannot be undignified before the rich. Even in the presence of a prince or king, dignity is core to the identity of a Muslim. This is the kind of teaching that compelled Muslims to spread an entire civilization around the world. When human beings lose their sense of dignity, they become broken. They lose their creativity and sense of being. They cannot produce or think. They become like animals, terrified, cowering, searching for shelter. Take away their dignity, and human beings become the living dead.[78] That is precisely why the Qur'an rejects the idea of coercion (Q 2:256).

The Islamic message, in its pristine form, is that dignity is core to the identity of a Muslim. The lack of dignity teaches the heart and soul hypocrisy. A hypocrite is a liar, and a liar can never be a good Muslim or a moral human being. Learn this as a golden rule: you need dignity in order to avoid hypocrisy; you need to avoid hypocrisy because you cannot be a liar; if you are a liar, the aspiration of living in light is gone; there can be no light in a dishonest existence. It is this sense of dignity that made Muslims outliers at a time when the entire world would have never thought twice about prostrating before a king, prince, or person of nobility.

The battle today revolves around racism. We are witnessing once again a movement that rejects racism as fundamentally inconsistent with an innate awareness of human dignity. I mean "innate" in the sense that those protesting and resisting racism in the streets

---

77 See Shams al-Din al-Sakhawi, *al-Maqasid al-Husna fi bayan kathir min al-ahadith al-mushtahira 'ala al-alsina*, ed. Muhammad 'Uthman al-Kasht (Beirut: Dar al-Kitab al-'Arabi, 1405/1985), 1/763.

78 For more on the idea of Muslims as the "living dead," see The Usuli Institute, *Are You Alive? Justice, Necropolitics, and the Living Dead* (*Khutbah*, 18 March 2022).

do not need to be great philosophers. They know, intuitively, that we cannot be a moral people if we are a racist people. They know that a society that allows for systemic and institutional racism is an immoral society. They know that the claims to morality of such a society are deceitful and hypocritical. They know, intuitively, that if racism is systematic and institutionalized in society, it not only affects the victims but is a darkness that descends upon all of society. They know that the darkness that descends upon society after something like the murder of George Floyd is total and complete. They know that we cannot claim to be a nation of light, morality, and justice if we allow racism to exist, especially in egregious, unmitigated, and vulgar forms, as seen in the murder of so many African Americans.[79]

Rest assured, however, that just as there is a movement against racism, there is a movement that wants racism to survive. There was a movement that wanted colonialism to survive. There are movements that want fascism and communism to survive. There are, and will always be, reactionary movements that resist human progress. These are twisted souls, but they are a reality. For whatever reason, there are those who do not want others to enjoy full and equal dignity. To every action there is a reaction. To every progressive movement, there is a reactionary movement against it.

What concerns me is the position of Muslims in all of this. There is always a movement toward the light and a movement toward darkness. The question for you as a Muslim is simple: where do you stand? At the time of the Prophet, there was a pro-dignity movement and a counter-dignity movement. One of the main complaints of the Meccans against the Prophet Muhammad was that he caused

---

79 This *khutbah* was delivered several weeks after the murder of George Floyd at the hands of police officers in Minneapolis on 25 May 2020. For Professor Abou El Fadl's initial response in the immediate aftermath of the murder, see Chapter 21: *Jahiliyya and the Murder of George Floyd* in this volume.

slaves to rebel against their masters. Had you lived at the time of the Prophet, where would you have stood?

A common complaint against the early Muslims was that they were "too radical," integrating people of different races, ethnicities, and classes. According to the customs of the age, for example, a former slave could not marry a daughter of nobility. What did the Prophet do? He married his adopted son, Zayd, a former slave, to a daughter of nobility. In response to the outrage, the Prophet said that to resist the marriage was *jahiliyya* (a state of ignorance). At the time of the Prophet, then, there was a movement against the privileges of the nobility and a reactionary movement that sought to uphold these very privileges. Where would you have stood?

In recent centuries, there was a movement that sought to abolish slavery and a reactionary movement that sought to preserve slavery. Where would you have stood? More recently, there was a movement that upheld and defended fascism in Spain, Italy, and Germany, and a movement that rejected fascism as inherently oppressive. Where would you have stood? Today, there is a movement declaring, "Enough with racism in its various forms!" But rest assured that there are reactionaries—whether you see them or not—who are comfortable with the darkness of racism and who want to shelter racism in its various forms. Where do you stand?

Most critical of all is that Muslims have been outside the cycle of history. For too long, our position as Muslims has not mattered. This is what is most problematic. For far too long, Muslims have not been at the forefront of moral struggles in human history. This leads me to my final point. Throughout Islamic history, there have been those who understand Islam as a message of liberation that demands that Muslims be at the forefront of all moral and ethical struggles. For this group, Islam is a revolutionary doctrine that rejects lethargy, inanity, and ineffectiveness. Yet, there have also been those who resist this understanding of Islam and who want Islam to be an empty moral force, a void that does nothing but legitimize the status quo. In short, an Islam that is nothing more than rituals, without revolution. Where do you stand? Do you see Islam as irrelevant to any moral and ethical struggle? Or is it that you cannot *but* see Islam as a moral and ethical force in human life? This is the critical question.

Are you with the reactionaries of Islam or the revolutionaries of Islam? You will be asked this question in the Hereafter. It is wise, then, to ask it of yourself in the here and now. Do you understand the nature of darkness and light? Do you believe that Islam is, in fact, a vehicle for taking human beings from darkness to light? If so, how? Are you among those who are so morally lethargic as to not care whether it is dark or light; do you just want to do your prayers, fast, and otherwise be left alone? Will you be able to defend that before God in the Hereafter?

I pray that God has helped me express what is in my heart. For this is one of the most critical issues that we, as Muslims, have confronted and will continue to confront in the progress of human history.

19 June 2020

17

Our Character Is Built
on Our Stories

Our intellects and psyches are the product of numerous cumulative narratives that we receive at different points in our lives. Human consciousness is formed by narratives and stories. Stories from the past, and stories from the present. These stories shape our reality, how we understand things, and how we relate to values. Look at the present Muslim condition. What ails Muslims in our day and age? What has so injured the modern Muslim psyche and intellect that in the heart and soul of every Muslim is a sense of grievance and sadness about the world? This grievance is manifest in many layered and complex ways.

More fundamentally, what are the narratives that shape our consciousness? What are the narratives that make us feel confident about ourselves and our tradition, or not? What are the narratives that we pick up and absorb that make us clear about our purpose and goal in life, or not? As Muslims, it is critical that we understand

and actively construct our own narratives; in other words, that we study and understand our history and do so with a sense of urgency. We must understand that the way we comprehend and absorb our history defines our reality in the present and future. This is why I have increasingly turned, in my *khutbahs*, to sharing stories from the past. As a teacher, it dawns on you just how ill-informed most Muslims are about their own narratives.

What defines who you are as a person? It is your basic moral attitude toward the sum total of the past that created you. We are the by-products of our history—not, however, our history as it exists in some objective world. Rather, our history as we understand and comprehend it.

This *jumu'a*, I want to discuss some fairly minor events in Muslim history that ought to give us considerable pause and make us reflect upon what we know of our past, how we know it, why we know it, and what is needed for us to mend our relationship with our tradition. I pick these narratives because I am quite sure that most Muslims have never heard of them. Yet, we will see how these stories are significant for what defines us as Muslims and what could define our relationship with our tradition.

The first story is about a figure who is not famous in Islamic history but who played a very important role in the spread of the Islamic faith in its formative years. His name is Thumama ibn Uthal al-Hanafi. He has the title "al-Hanafi" not because he was a follower of the Hanafi school of thought, which came much later, but because he was from the tribe of Banu Hanifa. Thumama was a tribal chief in one of the important Arab tribes of al-Yamama, in today's Saudi Arabia. He lived at the time of the Prophet as a man of considerable wealth. His tribe was famous for farming and exporting wheat to Mecca. Because of these wheat exports, his tribe was, in many ways, the breadbasket of Mecca. Mecca had a close relationship with Thumama because of this long-established business relationship.

Our story takes place before the Treaty of Hudaybiyyah. At the time, an increasing number of Arab tribes that were allied to Mecca conspired to destroy the Prophet and the Muslim community in Medina. These tribes were alarmed at the spread of the Islamic message and formed various alliances to try to destroy the nascent Muslim community. At one point, Thumama started communicating with various tribes in and around Mecca. Plans were devised to launch a decisive stealth attack against Medina in the hope that it would finally finish the Islamic message once and for all.

The Prophet did not simply rely on his *iman*. He did his due diligence. Before asking God for help, the Prophet always exerted the effort that a Muslim must exert before daring to ask God for assistance. Part of this due diligence was that the Prophet had a fairly sophisticated network of informants that would convey news to Medina in order to know who was conspiring and planning military action against them. The news reached the Prophet that Thumama and his tribe were planning a surprise military campaign against Medina. In response, the Prophet created a military force to launch a preemptive strike to shock and neutralize his enemies before they could inflict any injury upon Muslims. So the Prophet sent Muhammad ibn Maslamah to launch a campaign against Thumama's tribe. The military campaign was short-lived, but wildly successful. So successful, in fact, that the tribal chief himself, Thumama, was captured and brought back to Medina.

Meanwhile, in Medina, there was a group of people who played a very important role in Islamic history that modern Muslims rarely hear about: the *ahl al-suffa*. These were the poorest Muslim converts in Medina. They were often, though not always, former slaves who did not have property, money, or trade, and who lived either in the central mosque in Medina or in very small and modest residences around the mosque. What distinguished the *ahl al-suffa* is that they turned their lack of wealth into a remarkable spiritual, moral, and intellectual force. They met in the mosque in Medina to pray, study the Qur'an, and supplicate to God. In fact, the Sufi tradition traces its roots to the *ahl al-suffa*. These are the real roots of Sufism in Islam. It goes back to the studious dedication of the *ahl al-suffa*, the modesty of their means, and the way they led lives in which they worked, prayed, and studied with very little else. The Prophet was known to spend a great amount of time with them. The Prophet loved them, and they loved him. He would often share his meals with them because they were hungry and lacked the means to feed themselves. The Prophet would go out of his way to ensure the *ahl al-suffa* had enough food. This group, of course, did not include people like 'Umar ibn al-Khattab, Abu Bakr, or 'Ali ibn Abi Talib. As modest as their means were, these Companions had homes. That meant they did not belong to the *ahl al-suffa*.

After Thumama was captured, it was decided to keep him in the main mosque in Medina where the *ahl al-suffa* spent most of their days. Thumama was tied to a pillar as a war captive. As a rich tribal chief, Thumama was, of course, unhappy with the fact that he had been captured. He was unhappy to be tied to a pillar in the mosque. But he was most unhappy with the fact that those who fed him were the poorest of society, the *ahl al-suffa*. Nor was Thumama used to their modest food. They fed him from what they ate. There are interesting reports that Thumama would look at the food he was served and scoff, "What is this? No meat? No spices? This is simple food. Do you expect me to eat this?" He refused to eat, at least for the first few days. The *ahl al-suffa* replied, "That is all we have. We are giving you from our own food." Thumama was in disbelief. "How can you live this way?" They ate only very simple food. In fact, one of the dishes that was presented to him consisted basically of wheat and milk.

Because he was tied to a pillar in the mosque, however, Thumama had the opportunity to watch the *ahl al-suffa* pray and do *dhikr*. He shared their very modest food, which he did not like, but he also observed how they spent their days. Thumama was struck by something that, as a tribal chief, he had not comprehended before. These people came from various tribal and ethnic backgrounds. They were of diverse races. There were Abyssinians, Yemenis, Romans, Egyptians, Basrans, and light-skinned Syrians from Aleppo. All these people would sit together, pray together, do *dhikr* together, and eat together. They seemed to be in the world of the *malakut*. They were happy—the type of happiness that Thumama had never seen before. They were tranquil and at peace with themselves in ways that Thumama did not understand. He would see the Prophet, who, for Thumama, was the equivalent of a tribal chief, sit, eat, joke, pray, and study with them in absolute humility and simplicity. No fanfare. No ostentation. Just human beings, in their simplest and purest form.

After a short period, the Prophet asked Thumama, "What do you think should be done with you?" The Arabic in the report is fascinating. Thumama replied, in effect, "If you kill me, then you have killed an honorable human being. If you release me, I will be grateful." As a typical tribal chief, however, he then got to the heart of the matter. "If you want money to release me, name your price. My tribe will pay whatever you want for my release." The Prophet said that he did not want to kill Thumama, nor did he want his money: "We are releasing you."

That was the final straw for Thumama. He was in disbelief. Upon capturing a tribal chief, were they to release him for nothing? Thumama's entire value system was in a state of shock. After a short period in which he did not leave Medina, he finally approached the Prophet and said, "I want to become Muslim. I want to live with you in Medina." The Prophet, of course, was very pleased with Thumama's conversion, but the Prophet added, "If you really want to serve this religion, do not live with us in Medina. Return to your tribe to teach them about Islam." Thumama reluctantly agreed. He knew that upon his return he would face considerable resistance. Ultimately, however, he understood that it is not just about him. He had seen a moral example, and it was now incumbent upon him to share that moral vision with his people. It is the vision of moving people from darkness to light (Q 2:257; 5:16; 14:1, 5; 33:43; 57:9; 65:11).

Our story does not end here. Thumama understood why the Prophet wanted him to return to his tribe. Thumama was also a famous businessman and well-known in Mecca. Thumama asked the Prophet if, before returning home, he could visit the Ka'ba. It would be his first time visiting the Ka'ba as a Muslim. The Prophet had no objection. So Thumama, now freed from captivity, traveled to Mecca, visited the Ka'ba, and supplicated. The Meccans did not yet know that he was Muslim, and when they overheard his supplications, they suspected that he had converted to Islam. The Meccan chiefs confronted Thumama, who responded, "Yes. I am now Muslim." The Meccans were outraged. So outraged, in fact, that they physically assaulted him.

Thumama took the beating and left Mecca. Upon returning to his tribe, however, the first thing he did was announce to his tribe that they will no longer sell wheat to Mecca. He had become a Muslim, yes, but he was also physically assaulted in Mecca. He was sufficiently upset and hostile to his former allies that he refused to sell them wheat. Thumama's decision caused huge upheaval in Mecca. The Meccans tried to find another source for their wheat other than his tribe of al-Yamama, but all alternative sources, such as Egypt, were too expensive and led to inflation. Thumama's decision, then, caused a serious economic problem. The Meccans met to discuss how to deal with the situation. They appealed to Thumama to change his mind and offered to pay a much higher price. Thumama refused. What, then, did the Meccans do? They decided to send a message to the Prophet, asking the Prophet to tell Thumama to end the economic boycott.

Understand that, at this time, Mecca and Medina were at war. Moreover, Mecca had previously imposed an economic boycott against Muslims that led to the near starvation of all Muslims and the actual deaths of several Muslims. The Meccan boycott against Muslims was horrendous and eventually led Muslims to leave their homes and businesses and migrate to Medina. The Meccan letter to the Prophet is also intriguing for it is haughty and arrogant. It tells the Prophet, "Don't you say that you were sent as a mercy to humankind? This issue is leading to the starvation of our children. You always claim to honor your family and kinship ties. If you see fit to ask Thumama to end his economic boycott, then do so." Look at the arrogance. It is a request, but not a request. It did not say, "Please, please have Thumama end the boycott." It says, "You *claim* to have been sent as a mercy to humankind . . ." Remarkably, in response to this letter, the Prophet asked Thumama to end the boycott, a request that Thumama knew he could not refuse. He let go of his grievances and restored the sale of wheat to Mecca.[80]

---

80 For a concise overview of this report, see Ibn Qayyim al-Jawziyya, *Zad al-Ma'ad*, 469. Various elements of the story are also captured in many *hadith* reports. See for example al-Bukhari (2422 and 4372), Muslim (1764), Abu Dawud (2679), and al-Nasa'i (189).

Pause and reflect upon the morality of that community that was able to impress an enemy stranger—a rich, haughty, and spoiled man—with its modesty, solidarity, and love for one another, so much so that this man became Muslim. Even with their worst enemies, there were moral limits to any conflict or hostility. The Prophet did not initiate the economic boycott against Mecca, and there are reports that he did not even know about it. The Meccan letter, however, appealed to Islamic morality: you have been sent as a mercy to humankind (Q 21:107). That has its own moral imperative. Muslims had themselves suffered an economic boycott, but they refused to inflict the same upon others because innocents like children, women, and non-combatants would likely suffer the consequences.

Ask yourself the question that I always go back to: what defines you as a person? You may have been raised a Muslim, but I am sure the vast majority of Muslims have never heard this story. You may have converted to Islam, but I am equally sure that, as a convert, you have never heard anyone talk about this story as part of the *Sunna* of the Prophet.

Let me give another short story. We have all at some point heard of the Companion of the Prophet, Abu Hurayrah. After converting to Islam, Abu Hurayrah was among the *ahl al-suffa*. He was very close to his mother and loved her dearly, but his mother remained an unbeliever. Abu Hurayrah consistently tried to convince his mother to become Muslim, but she would respond by insulting and attacking the Prophet. This would hurt Abu Hurayrah. He would complain about it to his friends. Remember that the *ahl al-suffa* were often very hungry. So hungry, in fact, that it is reported that the Prophet once saw Abu Hurayrah and asked him where he was going. "I do not actually know," he replied, "I am just trying to find food. The only thing that makes me roam the streets right now is hunger."

The Prophet smiled and said, "Well, the only thing making me roam the streets now is hunger as well." So, both were hungry and searching for food. Someone then delivered dates to the household of the Prophet. What did the Prophet do? He divided the dates and gave two to each member of the *ahl al-suffa*, two for each wife of the Prophet, and two for himself—just two dates. But the Prophet noticed that Abu Hurayrah took one date and put the other in his pocket. Look at the level of sensitivity. The Prophet noticed who actually consumed the two dates and who saved one. The Prophet asked Abu Hurayrah why he had saved one date. "O Prophet, it is for my mother." This is the same mother who was non-Muslim and who regularly cursed the Prophet. The Prophet smiled and said, "No, eat your two dates. We will give your mother two dates as well."

It is a very simple incident. The Prophet did not say, "Your mother is an unbeliever, she does not count." The Prophet did not say, "Your mother is an unbeliever, why is she living in Medina with us?" These people filled their stomachs not with a gourmet sandwich and fries. They filled their stomachs with two dates boiled in water. This is why they created the Islamic civilization.

You are either a servant of God, bonded in servitude to God, or you are bonded in servitude to material wealth. You are either bonded to moral values, or your god is materialism and the dollar. You either exist in a state of *tawhid* (monotheism) in which your life centers around God and the moral values that embody the Divine, or you exist in a state of *shirk* (associating partners with God) in which you worship material wealth and have a tenuous relationship with moral values, taking and leaving them as convenience dictates.

But the critical point to underscore is our relationship with our tradition. Again, I am sure that many of us have been Muslim all our lives but were never taught this very simple and straightforward narrative that could have constructed our entire moral being, our consciousness, and our relationship to our faith. Why? Why do we not know our tradition? Why do we have an arrogant attitude of presuming to know our tradition, and then feeling disappointed by it? If you are disappointed by it, it is because you do *not* know it. Even if it is not your fault that you do not know it, it *is* your fault that you have not committed yourself to finding the root cause of the disease of ignorance and its solutions.

Imagine if, thirty years ago, from at least the 1980s when, as a young man, I talked about these very issues, Muslims had devoted their wealth to funding the type of educational institutions that could have taught our youth, our children and grandchildren, about what the Islamic tradition really is. Imagine if we had brought qualified and competent teachers to teach our younger generations about our faith. Not engineers and doctors. Not people who teach Islam in their spare time. Imagine if, when we said thirty years ago that things needed to be fixed, we were honest and truly dedicated. Imagine if we had the type of dedication seen in the narratives of the early Companions, those who made Islam a moral force in the universe. Just imagine where we would be today. Our children would not be suffering the consequences of Islamophobia left and right. Their hearts, intellects, and psyches would not be so injured because of their not knowing their own tradition.

Morality is indivisible. Every time an evil occurs, something demonic occurs. Rest assured that the demonic leaves an imprint, and demonic imprints are like infections. They contaminate the atmosphere, poison the space, and turn the environment toxic. That is the nature of evil. Unless you clean it—unless evil finds those willing to confront it—it leaves an imprint. It poisons. It becomes toxic and will inflict further injury and claim more victims. That is

why God and the Prophet repeat so often the duty of moral upright-
ness, ethical vigilance, and the obligation to advocate, teach, and
act against moral failures.

I underscore this because of two major moral failures in our day
and age. The first is that of yet another evil, another toxicity, another
betrayal. Israel plans to confiscate more territory in the West Bank.
It is as if the Palestinians have not suffered enough. What struck
me was a recent release by the U.S. State Department that noted,
in effect, that Muslims did not do anything when the U.S. moved
its embassy to Jerusalem; the claims that there would be outrage in
the Muslim world were exaggerated. The sad truth is that the State
Department is right. Muslims have grown accustomed to meeting
evil with utter apathy. So Israel will claim more land, disinherit more
Palestinians, and Muslims will not do a thing.

Why do so many Jewish Americans—who are highly educated
and could make a fortune as doctors, lawyers, and bankers—choose
to become settlers in the West Bank, making a fraction of what they
could have made, living far more modest lives? It is because of their
commitment to an idea, a principle. In my view, it is an immoral
principle. It is a principle that they must colonize land even if it
means evicting Palestinians. But it is commitment and dedication,
nevertheless. On the other hand, there are Muslims asking why we
should care about the Palestinian cause. Even if Palestinians were
not Muslim, it is about the moral principle. These are people who
have had their land confiscated. They have become disinherited and
rendered homeless. This is to say nothing of Jerusalem and its critical
place in the Muslim psyche and Muslim morality.

The second major moral failure is the genocide that is being
committed against Uyghur Muslims by the Chinese government.
The former advisor to Trump, John Bolton, revealed in his recent

book that Trump told the Chinese President that it was a good idea to intern Muslims in concentration camps.[81] I do actually believe this, because Trump has made clear his hatred and disdain for Muslims. Yet Trump still finds Muslims around the world who celebrate and welcome him, from Egypt, to Saudi Arabia, to the UAE. This is someone who hates Islam. Yet, even in the U.S., there are still Muslims who say, "You are God's will. God let you be the President, so we have to accept you."[82]

Compare these Muslims to the Muslims of the past. Muslims of the past were layered. They had moral complexity. They waged war against and even captured the chief of a hostile tribe, but still observed moral limits in how they conducted conflict. They were strong, powerful, and resolute when it came to defending themselves against the enemy. Upon capturing the enemy, however, the enemy would see that they were moral human beings. So moral and beautiful, in fact, that the enemy would convert to Islam.

Let me tell you that China would not have built these concentration camps for Uyghur Muslims if, from the very beginning, China found that the U.S. and countries like Saudi Arabia, the UAE, Egypt, Turkey, Iran, and Qatar were resolute that you cannot do this to fellow Muslims; that if you do this to Muslims, there will be consequences. Is it because of racism? Is it because we do not think of the Uyghurs as real Muslims? I would be tempted to think so had we not done the same thing to the Palestinians, who are Arab. Are we, as Muslims, just losers across the board, then, or is there

---

81 John Bolton, *The Room Where It Happened: A White House Memoir* (New York: Simon & Schuster, 2020), 312. ("According to our interpreter, Trump said that Xi should go ahead with building the camps, which he thought was exactly the right thing to do.").

82 An allusion to comments made by Hamza Yusuf, who described Trump as "God's servant" and an agent of God's will. See Thomas Parker, "Hamza Yusuf may be the token Muslim Trump's administration needs," *TRT World* (11 July 2019).

an element of racism in how we think of the Uyghurs? Millions of Uyghurs have been placed in concentration camps. Uyghur women are raped. Uyghur men are executed and beaten. Uyghur organs are harvested. Yet, Muslims have not even succeeded in instituting an economic boycott of the products that come from these camps.

Trump recently signed the Uyghur Human Rights Policy Act. It turns out that this act is largely useless, because it only requires that Congress reports on the conditions of Uyghurs in the concentration camps where they are murdered and raped for saying the *Shahadah*, praying, or fasting, and where they are not even allowed to read the Qur'an. After Congress reports, the President then decides whether to impose sanctions. But there is already a statute that does what the executive order mandates, and Trump has chosen not to impose any economic sanctions upon China since coming to power, apparently citing U.S. economic interests.[83] Trump denies that he supported the Chinese President in building concentration camps for Muslims. He can now point to this executive order. But this order does nothing, for he chooses not to impose economic sanctions on China.

Think back to our relationship with narratives and the sense of injury to our psyche and soul. In one of its illustrious annual events, the American Jewish Committee (AJC) hosted a major conference. The Secretary of State, Mike Pompeo, gave the keynote address. Everyone at the conference talked about the security and safety of Israel. But what gave me pause was the attendance of the Head of the Muslim World League, Muhammad bin 'Abdul Karim al-Issa, who gave a nice plenary address. In Islam, he claimed, we do not have any problem with Jews. This is true. He stressed that the Holocaust was a moral abomination. Again, I agree. What, then, is the problem?

---

83 A likely allusion to the Global Magnitsky Human Rights Accountability Act.

The problem is that al-Issa, amid all the nice things he said about Israel and Jews, did not once mention the Palestinians. He did not even pay lip service to the Palestinians. It is as if they are a non-entity. Nor did he mention the Uyghurs. Al-Issa said, "The Holocaust must never be allowed to reoccur anywhere in the world," but it *is* occurring in China, against Muslims, at this very moment. Nor did al-Issa say anything about the Rohingya in Myanmar. Al-Issa went on to say in his speech, "Sadly, Jews and Muslims have in recent years had many misunderstandings, but there is no reason for Jews and Muslims to be hostile to one another." I agree. But he then said that the reason for this is because there are Muslims who are "confused" and who "mix religion and politics." Al-Issa is talking to the AJC, an organization that routinely mixes religion with politics. How about the Palestinians? How about the fact that al-Issa is talking to an organization that plays a role in promoting Islamophobia and demonizing those who defend Palestinian rights? An organization that regularly weaves religion, culture, and politics in complex ways that his draconian, dogmatic, and simple mind cannot quite imagine or understand?

See what Israel is doing in the West Bank and look at the position of countries like Egypt, the UAE, and Saudi Arabia. See what China is doing with its concentration camps against Muslims and look at the position of countries like Egypt, the UAE, and Saudi Arabia. Think of the moral illegitimacy of countries like these. I discount anything that comes from al-Azhar in Egypt today. I am not interested in anything they have to say about Islam. They have lost their legitimacy to speak for the Islamic tradition. What is far more serious is that I increasingly feel this way about the position of Saudi Arabia vis-à-vis the Hijaz. Saudi Arabia's guardianship over the Holy Sites is becoming illegitimate and unjustified. It has broken all the moral boundaries that could have justified Muslim silence vis-à-vis its custodianship of the Hijaz.

Re-orient yourself toward this religion. Take this religion seriously. It is a treasure trove of values, morality, sophistication, and ideas. Commit yourself to an Islamic education. Become a moral voice that speaks against the injustices and demonic toxicity that occurs in our modern world, especially when that immorality comes from fellow Muslims. If you do this, then you will no longer wonder why you were put on this earth. You will be too busy to worry about the purpose of your life or the meaning of your existence. You will live a meaningful life. Perhaps a difficult and challenging life, but a meaningful and a moral life that God will reward you for, and that you can honorably defend when you meet your Lord.

26 June 2020

18

Who Is the Better Muslim and What Would God Think?

$\mathcal{A}$s I was preparing for this *khutbah*, I watched a video that made the blood run cold in my veins. It unsettled me so much that I found it very challenging to organize my thoughts or focus on anything else. The video was of a woman from Egypt who turned out to be an orphan. She was married but her husband had died, so she is a widow. She is also a mother, with one child. In the video, this woman is pleading for help from anyone in a position of authority around the world. Her problem is that there is a police officer where she lives who started harassing her six months ago, demanding that she submit to him sexually. When she refused, he arrested her sister. Her sister has been in detention in this police station without charge for several weeks. He bluntly told this woman that unless she submits sexually, they will not release her sister and, according to this disgusting human being, they will continue sexually assaulting the sister in the police station.

It turns out that this younger sister is a divorcee. As far as I could tell, she does not have children. Of course, these two women, as orphans, are of disadvantaged social status. They are powerless. They have no connections or protection. This woman only dared to record her plea for help because she is brave.

The first thing you do when working in the field of human rights is verify the authenticity of events. You get as much information as you can on the victim, the offender, and the circumstances. And it turns out that this police station is notorious. There are numerous reports of its officers victimizing, abducting, and committing sexual offenses against women. As you would expect, the woman in the video pleads with the officer in charge of the police station. But what most affected me is that she also pleads with President Sisi to intervene. She pleads with the *Shaykh*s and scholars of al-Azhar to intervene. She then pleads with Muslims around the world to do something to help her because she does not want to submit to this man. She has gone everywhere seeking help. All she finds is abuse or neglect. She actually went to this man's superiors, who told her, basically, to get lost. They further abused her.

Let me emphasize that the problem of sexual abuse by those in power in a country like Egypt, sadly, is persistent and systematic. It is not rare. It is clear that the government has notice of this and simply does not care. The government sees it as yet another instrument of subjugation and control over the population. If you teach people that they have no dignity, should expect no honor, and have no rights, then these people will be broken and submissive.

Here is the problem. Muslims often wonder why their prayers are not answered, so consider this from the perspective of the Giver of mercy and beauty in the world. This is a Muslim woman who is begging because she is powerless, poor, and an orphan. She has no connections in society. As it turns out, she is not the exception. She is not an outlier. Nor, sadly, is the man victimizing her an exception. The problem of sexual abuse in a country like Egypt by those in authority is rampant. It is common in Egyptian prisons, police stations, and military units. It is everywhere. But the part that kept me up and tormented my soul is how easy it would be for this woman's fellow countrymen or fellow Muslims—her supposed sisters and brothers—to help her.

Imagine if you are an Egyptian with relatives in the higher ranks of the police or the military. You could call them and ask them to get their contacts to come to this woman's aid. Imagine if you are a wealthy businessman in Egypt. Everyone knows that money talks in Egypt. You could quite easily pick up the phone, call your friends and contacts in the military, the police, and the government, and say, "Help this woman." Not only this. There are so many rich expat Egyptians, including here in the U.S. They could see a video like this, pick up the phone, and call one of their contacts to get this woman protected. Not only that. If you work in the U.S. State Department, the Department of Defense, or Congress, you could quite easily call your contacts in Egypt or go through formal channels to protect this woman. Not only that. If you are just a regular American with a trip scheduled to visit the pyramids or the sphinx, you could see a video like this, write a letter to your travel agent, and cancel your visit. If the Egyptian government were to receive just ten such notices—visits canceled because of a woman's fear of sexual abuse—then, rest assured, the Egyptian government would do something about it overnight.

Not only that. Where is al-Azhar? This woman begs for the *Shaykh* of al-Azhar to come to her aid. She asks, "Do you want me to prostitute myself to the police officers?" All those *Shaykh*s in Egypt could pick up the phone, call their contacts, and ask, as a favor, that they help this woman. In Egypt, everything is done through *wasta*, meaning contacts and connections. Normally, when the *Shaykhs* of al-Azhar want something for their families or friends, they pick up the phone. Where are these *Shaykhs*?

Look at the magnitude of the failure by Muslims all over the world for this woman to be in the dire situation that she is in. Again, she dared to record a plea. But there are hundreds, if not thousands, of women who are victimized and destroyed and no one ever hears of them. Look at the magnitude of the failure. The failure of those with contacts in the Egyptian police or military. The failure of rich Egyptians at home and abroad. The failure of those with contacts in the U.S. government. Even the failure of wealthy Arabs who are not Egyptian. Everyone knows the Egyptian government will bend over backwards to do whatever Saudi, Emirati, or Kuwaiti investors want. You need only pick up the phone, call your friend in the military, say, "Help this woman," and that is it. This woman will be helped. But what chills me the most is the failure of al-Azhar. Where are the "illustrious" religious scholars? Not one of them thinks of lifting a finger to help this woman.

The problem is the level of apathy that plagues us as Muslims. Imagine if a woman reported a plea like this and, immediately, Muslims around the world felt offended and started tweeting or talking about it. Rest assured that the Egyptian government would help a woman like this immediately. It does not want the embarrassment. The problem is one of moral apathy and spiritual defeat. God sees a woman like this and her sister, who are both orphans, victimized, persecuted, and subjugated. God then looks upon Muslims and finds that wealthy Muslims are silent. God finds that politically active Muslims do not care. God finds that not one so-called "religious scholar" thinks this is worth mentioning in a *khutbah* all over the Muslim and non-Muslim world, including here in the U.S. I am sure that I am the only one giving a *khutbah* that mentions this.

I must therefore ask you, morally and ethically, what you think God's position should be vis-à-vis these people. Should God say, "Bravo, I am going to answer all your prayers"? Should God say, "You are wonderful and lovely people. I am going to be on your side"? If you pray to God in times of need, know that God remembers all the times in which you heard someone else begging for help and, though you could have done something, you failed to do so. Do you think God says, "No problem, I will help you even though you help no one but yourself"? I know so many rich Egyptians living in Los Angeles.[84] I know they have the cell phone numbers of people in the Ministry of Interior in the Sisi government. I know they call these contacts when their kids go to Egypt for a vacation to get the five-star treatment. With one phone call from LA, they could end the plight of this woman. But I know those rich LA Egyptians. I know they will rationalize the problem away. I know they will say, "It is a lie, a fabrication." They will not go through the steps of verification that I went through to find out who this woman is, who her family is, who the offender is, the offender's record, and what other reports we have about similar incidents in this police station. Even if they had an opportunity to learn any of this, they would not want to know.

How about those who continue to support the government of a man who started his reign by conducting virginity tests? When women demonstrated against Sisi, he had women arrested and his officers inspected these women to verify whether they were virgins.

---

84 Since January 2021, The Usuli Institute has relocated to Columbus, Ohio.

He admitted before the United Nations that he was responsible for this policy. Yet so many Muslims either support him or, like the Islamic Center of Southern California, do not want to condemn him.[85] How about a man who started his reign with the worst urban massacre in Egyptian history at Rabaa?[86]

Please understand that we Muslims are part of a single tapestry. We are interwoven like the threads of a single rug. God looks at us collectively, what we do with each other and for each other. Even if we cannot do anything, God looks, at a minimum, at how many Muslims cared and at least spent a few minutes feeling sad, condemning it in their hearts. If even this minimum is not fulfilled, then do not expect any blessings from God.

This episode reminds me of something that deserves pause. It reminds me of a story in the *Sira* about Umm Salama, her husband, Abu Salama, and their child, Salama. Compare the ethics and morality of the two episodes—not the religious affiliation, but the morality.

Umm Salama and her husband came from one of the important Arab tribes, Banu Makhzum, yet they were both poor. They were among the early converts to Islam who faced persecution in Mecca and migrated to Abyssinia. Later, of course, Abu Salama died, and Umm Salama married the Prophet. When Muslims started migrating to Medina, Umm Salama and Abu Salama traveled from Abyssinia to Mecca to then migrate onto Medina. In Mecca, they packed what little belongings they had. Their tribe discovered that they had escaped to Medina, however, and pursued and captured them. Umm Salama's family could not prevent Abu Salama from traveling

---

85 On the failure of the Islamic Center of Southern California to speak out against widespread human rights violations, injustices, and oppression in Sisi's Egypt and elsewhere, see Abou El Fadl, *The Prophet's Pulpit—Vol. 1*, 10, n.5.

86 See footnote 38.

to Medina, but they would not allow him to take his wife or son with him. Abu Salama knew the persecution in Mecca was intense and relentless. There was no point in staying, so he continued to Medina. Banu Makhzum, meanwhile, brought Umm Salama and her child back to Mecca. In Mecca, Umm Salama's family told her that they did not want the grandchild to be raised by a Muslim. So they separated her from her child.

Umm Salama was now without her husband, who had gone to Medina, and forcibly separated from her child. She begged her family to let her see her child. Umm Salama's family noticed that she stopped eating and cried constantly, but she would still not leave Islam. Umm Salama even went to the spot where she was forcibly separated from her husband. She sat in that spot, crying and praying. This situation lasted an entire year. After one year, her family realized that she was going to perish. Finally, they reunited her with her child. The minute Umm Salama was back with her child, she sought to travel to Medina to be with her beloved husband.

But there was a problem. Umm Salama had no means; no camel, no horse, no donkey, and no money. The only way she could travel to Medina was to walk. She did not want to wait until a caravan came along because she was worried that her family may change their mind and imprison her or separate her from her child again. What options did she have? The only option was to take her child and walk from Mecca to Medina, approximately 250 miles away in the heat of the desert.

Umm Salama took her child and started walking in the desert to Medina to be reunited with her husband and the Prophet. As a lone woman in the desert, however, the risks were huge. Anyone could come upon you in the desert and rape you. That was common. Any woman found in the desert, without protection, was at risk. More likely was for someone to find you, abduct you and your child, and sell you both into slavery. That, too, was common. Yet Umm Salama could not continue to live in Mecca and her passion for her husband, the Prophet, and the Muslim community led her to take the risk and walk from Mecca to Medina, despite all the dangers.

A man in the desert saw Umm Salama and her child. His name was Uthman ibn Talha. Uthman ibn Talha was, at this time, a *kafir* (unbeliever) and a sworn enemy of the Prophet. He hated Muslims. He would soon fight against Muslims in battle. When he saw a lone woman with her child in the desert, however, his sense of ethics moved him. He approached her and asked, "Where are you going?" Umm Salama answered, "I am walking to Medina to join Muhammad." He said, "Alone on your feet?" "Yes, I have no alternative." What did this *kafir*, Uthman ibn Talha, do? He got off his camel, put Umm Salama on the camel with her child, and walked in front of the camel, accompanying Umm Salama all the way from Mecca to Medina. When they got close to Medina, Umm Salama told Uthman ibn Talha, "I can come down now and you can have your camel back." He refused, saying, "No, you still have to walk about 20 miles to enter the boundaries of Medina." He eventually gave her his camel and walked back from Medina to Mecca by foot.

I often get asked the annoying question: why did God send Islam to the Arabs? It is because of people like Uthman ibn Talha. He was a *kafir*. He was a sworn enemy of Muslims. But his sense of dignity and pride could not stand the idea of a woman, even from the enemy's camp, traveling in the desert alone with her child. Out of sheer moral rectitude, he accompanied her all the way from Mecca to Medina and then walked back from Medina to Mecca after giving her his camel. At that time, to give someone your traveling camel was like giving someone your car. It took Uthman ibn Talha eight years to convert to Islam. He eventually converted with Khalid ibn al-Walid and Amr ibn al-'As. For eight years after this incident, he fought against Muslims.

These were the Arabs of the past. I assure you that the Arabs of today, if they were in Saudi Arabia and saw an Umm Salama in the desert, would ask, "Are you Saudi?" And even if she was from Saudi Arabia, "What family are you from?" If she was in Egypt, then I doubt anyone would care to help that woman. Ask yourself if the Arabs of today are worthy of God's message.

From the time that I saw this video and spent hours verifying its authenticity, I kept remembering the story of Umm Salama and Uthman ibn Talha. Ask yourself: is this man, in his state of *kufr*, closer to God, or are the Muslims of today closer, those like the *Shaykh*s of al-Azhar who can give the most beautiful *adhan* and recite the Qur'an perfectly, but who can see a poor woman like this and just move on, without doing anything?

What type of human being are you? Are you an Uthman ibn Talha, or are you like the Muslims of today who do not care that a sister is being threatened with subjugation, persecution, and exploitation? Are you like the Muslims of today who deny that there is racial persecution in the U.S,[87] who defend the Muslim ban,[88] and who tell us to only be concerned with our own problems, to perform our *salah* and wear the *hijab*, but not care about anyone else?

---

87 An allusion to comments made by Hamza Yusuf in 2016 in which he dismissed the Black Lives Matter movement. See "U.S. Muslim cleric Hamza Yusuf calls Trump 'a servant of God' during racist rant against Black Lives Matter," *Rabwah Times* (25 December 2016). Also see Dwayne Oxford, "This is not about Hamza Yusuf," *TRT World* (28 December 2016).

88 Abou El Fadl, *The Prophet's Pulpit—Vol. 1*, 127, n. 55.

Who is closer to God, and what type of God do you worship? That is the moral question.

As a Muslim, ask yourself why Muslims are not at the forefront of defending human rights. Why are Muslims not at the forefront of combating human trafficking, racial injustice, and poverty? Why is it that Muslims care more about the *hijab* or nail polish instead of working at every level of government for justice and equity around the world? Do you understand the power of the United States around the world? Do you understand that the police in Egypt would not dare to exploit this woman sexually if our President did not describe Sisi as his "favorite dictator"?[89] Do you understand that if our State Department told Sisi that it does not want Egyptian police officers sexually abusing women, then sexual abuse in police stations would end overnight because Sisi would tell his officers: "The U.S. warned me. They do not want this." Do you understand that we fund the instruments of oppression in countries like Egypt, Saudi Arabia, the UAE, Libya, and other countries around the world? We support the dictators. If you understand the power of the U.S., then how dare you say, "It is none of my business." Do you understand that when you vote for a President or a senator, you vote for a public official who will not only govern the U.S. but who will, in fact, rule the world? When you pick a senator or a President, you ought to think of the world, not just the U.S. Whether you like it or not, these are the facts. These are the realities.

What good faith effort have we shown God when in a country that has an institution like al-Azhar and thousands of religious scholars, not one of them lifts a finger to help this woman, an orphan,

---

89 See Michael C. Bender, Vivian Salama, and Nancy A. Youssef, "Trump, Awaiting Egyptian Counterpart at Summit, Called Out for 'My Favorite Dictator'," *The Wall Street Journal* (13 September 2019).

whose sister is being raped and who is herself in imminent danger of being raped? Not the *mufti* of Egypt. Not the former *mufti*. Nor the *Shaykh* of al-Azhar. No one lifts a finger to help.

I am sorry to be so vulgar and blunt, but I must ask: if you were in God's place, what would you do with these people? What would you do with their prayers? What would you do with their supplications when they catch the coronavirus, and say, "God, please help"? What would you do when you see them living in Beverly Hills, driving expensive cars, and flying to Egypt where they own expensive mansions and brag about their connections with the government and army? When they see a video like this, however, they say, "It cannot be true. It is all lies." If someone tells them, "There is an expert in human rights who verifies this stuff for a living. Call Khaled Abou El Fadl to find out if it is true," they say, "No, no, I do not want to know." What would you do with these people?

Here is another news item. "Federal authorities in New York seized a shipment of weaves and other beauty accessories suspected to be made out of human hair taken from people locked inside a Chinese internment camp. Thirteen tons of hair products worth an estimated $800,000 were in the shipment."[90] That is thirteen tons of hair from Muslim internment camps. This is not the first time that U.S. authorities have seized hair shipments from the camps that hold Uyghur Muslims. It is, in fact, the third time. Imagine how many human beings you need to control to cut thirteen tons of hair to then sell to hair salons and hair companies for a handsome profit. The U.S. confiscated the shipment because of a law that states the U.S. must not allow the entry or sale of products that are the

---

90 See "US seizes shipment of Chinese products over human rights fears," *Al Jazeera* (2 July 2020).

result of forced labor. These are our Muslim brothers and sisters in China! They are held in concentration camps, raped, killed, and not allowed to practice their religion. They are not even allowed to keep their own hair.

At a minimum, are you an ethical consumer? At a minimum, if you care about the rights of animals, do you also care about the rights of human beings when you go to a salon and look at hair products? As an American citizen, when you vote for a senator or a President, do you care about whether they will take a firm stand against the exploitation and abuse of your fellow Muslims in China? Many in the Muslim World League are keen to assure the world that they fully condemn the Holocaust, as they should.[91] But where are those same Muslims with regard to the genocide being committed against Muslims in China right now? These are not "re-education camps." These are camps that murder, rape, harvest organs, and harvest hair.

Do you see the connection between the women who are sexually exploited in China, this woman who is sexually exploited in Egypt, and the women who are sexually exploited all over the world? Do you see the connection with the woman who is sexually exploited by an LAPD or NYPD officer because she is poor, destitute, and without means? Have you researched the incidents of sexual abuse by our own police forces in the U.S. against the poor and powerless? Have you read how often the police will pull over a poor woman, a minority, just to demand sexual favors?[92] Do you have any clue about that?

---

91 See Chapter 11: *Why Our Youth Leave Islam: When Moses Will Not Confront the Pharaoh* and Chapter 17: *Our Character Is Built on Our Stories* in this volume.
92 See Isidoro Rodriguez, "Predators Behind the Badge: Confronting Police Sexual Misconduct," *The Crime Report* (12 March 2020).

Uthman ibn Talha walked in the desert for hundreds of miles, giving away his camel to Umm Salama just so that he could see a woman be safe. And he was a *kafir*. You may be a Muslim. You may even be a Muslim who prays and fasts. But which of you is better in God's eyes? Which of you is more worthy of God's blessings?

3 July 2020

19

On the Representation and Perception of Muslims

I want to talk in this *khutbah* about an urgent issue in the affairs of modern Muslims. This is the issue of representation and self-perception. It is the way that Muslims are represented and the way that Muslims perceive themselves. I will talk about this from perhaps a different angle. As always, I want to take into account our current moment in history. I always emphasize that Islam is a living religion. Islam is not about idols and dead symbolisms. It is not about artifacts. Islam is about a living God that accompanies us in all our affairs, a God that is ever-present with us. The minute we forget that God is with us in everything, we forget the core message of Islam. We forget the imperative of godliness and Divinity. We forget what God and Islam are all about.

I recall, many years ago, when I was very young, perhaps at the start of my teenage years, how American comic magazines were very popular. They were considered something of a luxury item.

I remember one of the comics that my friends and I would often read was called *Sgt. Rock*. It was about a U.S. war hero in World War II who fought the Nazis. Of course, the U.S. war hero would always win his battles. Like those who today play video games, it was these magazines back then that attracted us and got our attention. I remember how every now and then a few issues of the *Sgt. Rock* magazine would talk about a group of heroic Jewish resistance fighters. These resistance fighters aided the Allies against Nazi forces. After defeating the Nazis in battle, the Jewish heroes would wear their shawls and perform prayers as the U.S. soldiers stood by and watched them in admiration and gratitude.

At the time, young as I was, I had no clue that this magazine could have spoken about the many Muslim heroes who fought the Nazis and stood in prayer after battle. Of course, the magazine never did this. In fact, like so many others, well into adulthood it never occurred to me that a single Muslim had lost their life fighting Nazism or that Muslims had played any significant role in World War II.

Why is this important? It is because our global world order today is a post-World War II world order. The United Nations, the Universal Declaration of Human Rights, the International Covenant on Civil and Political Rights, the International Covenant on Economic, Social and Cultural Rights—in short, today's entire world order—was born out of the historical moment of World War II. And World War II had winners and losers. Like many Muslims, I always believed that Muslims were either non-participants in World War II or that they were implicitly on the side of the losers, with the fascists and Nazis.

The impression given by magazines like *Sgt. Rock* when I was young is a question of representation. This magazine had authors and publishers. There was an institution behind this magazine that made a conscious decision to influence young and impressionable minds with an assertion that Jews were on the right side of history in World War II. That impression has ramifications.

At the same time, I remember attending the American School of Kuwait in my teenage years. I had a social studies teacher, an American, who discussed World War II using an American textbook. This textbook never mentioned Muslims at all. Not only this, but I distinctly remember that this teacher gave us the impression that Muslims and Arabs supported the fascists and Nazis in World War II. This is even though the class was in Kuwait, an Arab Muslim country. We never admitted it or discussed it among ourselves, but, as young kids, we labored with an unspoken sense of shame that we were the descendants of those who supported fascists and Nazis in World War II.

Why is this important? Too often, in the age of Islamophobia, Muslims are unaware that their consciousness is a product of an engineered epistemology and an engineered awareness. Muslims know what they know because it was engineered for them to know it. Yet they are too often unaware of this fact. Therein is the problem. Indeed, there is a major and ongoing process of misrepresentation and false consciousness that gets to the heart of what is happening in our lives today.

Few people know that you can go to areas in Egypt and visit the graves of the hundreds, if not thousands, of Egyptian Muslim soldiers who lost their lives fighting with the Allies against the Nazis in World War II. You can go to Libya and visit the graves of Libyans who fought against Italian fascists and German Nazis in World War II. In Algeria, you can visit the graves of the thousands of Algerians who lost their lives fighting with the French against the Germans in World War II. In fact, it is often omitted from our textbooks and erased from our historical consciousness that countries like France were in desperate need of soldiers during both World War I and World War II. France had colonized numerous Muslim countries such as Algeria, Tunisia, Mali, and Senegal. France made a simple offer: Muslims who joined the French army and fought against the Germans would be given French citizenship. Many Muslims joined, thousands lost their lives, and those who survived were given French citizenship. But they were never treated as French citizens with equal rights. They were treated as a subservient class, always suspect, always marginalized.

After World War II, countries like France needed cheap labor to rebuild their destroyed countries. Once again, the cheapest labor was Muslim labor. Muslims were hard workers and silent about demanding their rights. Czech, Polish, and Italian workers were more expensive and conscious of their rights. So countries like France opened their doors and invited Muslim laborers from Senegal, Mali, Algeria, and Lebanon to rebuild the country and economy in return for residence and citizenship. Muslims thus rebuilt countries like France after World War II. [93] They gained citizenship but were once again treated like second-class citizens with few rights and few entitlements. We do not often hear about this long history of discrimination against Muslims in Europe, which led, for example, in 2005, to mass demonstrations by Muslims demanding equal pay and equal employment opportunities. We do not read the numerous studies about the impact of racism in countries like France and how it has led to the marginalization of Muslims, with Muslims in France treated similarly to African Americans in the United States.

---

93 The example used here could well extend to migration from the Indian subcontinent to the UK or Turkish migration to Germany. The emergence of a significant Muslim minority presence in Western Europe is a direct consequence of World War II.

When was the last time a Muslim was exposed to images of the graves of Muslims who paid with their lives fighting Nazism and fascism to create the world order that we live in today? How many of our children have seen or know enough to tell their school, class, and teachers that Muslims played a huge role in defeating Nazism in World War II? How many of our children have seen the videos of Senegalese, Malian, and Algerian soldiers praying in *jamaʿa* (congregation) in between battles?

The idea is that Jews were central and active participants in constructing the modern world order. So much so, in fact, that President-elect Biden says he is proud to be a "non-Jewish Zionist."[94] In saying this, he thinks he is on the right side of history. In his mind percolate all the images that have constructed his consciousness, images that have been instilled in him since his childhood by magazines like *Sgt. Rock* and the like.

Meanwhile, Muslims are absent. We are missing. Our children do not know about the videos of their grandparents praying in *jamaʿa* in between battles against the Nazis. They are unaware that without their grandparents, it is unlikely that Germany would have been defeated in North Africa. They do not know that without the sacrifices of their fellow Muslims, the fate of history would have been very different. Nor are they aware that a process of historical fraud is being perpetrated against them in the way that history is written, told, and taught. Many of our children, for example, will at some point hear about Imam al-Husseini of Palestine, who, having despaired that the British would ever treat Palestinians fairly, traveled to Germany to find a solution to the loss of Palestine by allying himself with Hitler. Many of our children will hear about

---

94 See CNN, *Biden: Were I a Jew I'd be a Zionist* (YouTube, 31 March 2016).

this, but they will not hear the other side of the story, that is, the thousands upon thousands of Muslims who fought and lost their lives playing a huge role in what became the global post-World War II world order.

Let us go back to France. It is myopic to think that what is happening in France today is simply an issue of freedom of expression or that of a misguided politician insulting the Prophet.[95] How many Muslims know that the first mosque in France dates back to 1856? That mosque, built in Marseilles, was destroyed by an Islam-hating mob during the French Revolution. After the Revolution, the French, despite all the talk of liberty and equality, could not tolerate Islam and did not allow the building of another mosque until the 1920s, when a mosque was built in Paris. Here I come to a very important point. How many of us know that this mosque in Paris saved the lives of hundreds of Jews under the Vichy regime at a time when Jews in France were being arrested and sent to concentration camps? Many Jews escaped to this mosque in Paris. The *imam* of this mosque gave false identity papers to these Jews, changing their status from Jewish to Muslim to avoid arrest. Thanks to this mosque in Paris, so many Jewish lives were saved. You can read the story in a book called *Among the Righteous*.[96] You can also read it in an article in *The New York Times*, called "Heroic Tale of Holocaust, With a Twist."[97] With a twist! What is the twist? It is that Muslims saved Jews. This,

---

95 A reference to comments made by French leader Emmanuel Macron that "Islam is a religion that is in crisis all over the world today" on 2 October 2020. Several weeks later, on October 23, offensive cartoon depictions of the Prophet Muhammad that were first published in the *Charlie Hebdo* satirical magazine were projected onto government buildings in France.

96 Robert Satloff, *Among the Righteous: Lost Stories From the Holocaust's Long Reach into Arab Lands* (New York: PublicAffairs, 2006).

97 See Elaine Sciolino, "Heroic Tale of Holocaust, With a Twist," *The New York Times* (3 October 2011).

again, reveals the issue of representation. The author is presenting it as an oddity, as something weird.

Why is it that when a mosque, like this mosque in Paris, plays a great historical role, we Muslims are not taught that this is from the heart and soul of our religion? The actions of this *imam* are instead portrayed as an outlier, the good deeds of a single person. Meanwhile, when a Chechen teenager kills a teacher, it is taken as representative of the entire Muslim world.[98]

It all goes back to the issue of representation.

In the recent attacks in Vienna, there was a Palestinian youth named Osama Khaled Judah, who, during the attacks, acted to save a police officer from the attacker.[99] The police officer was wounded. Osama Khaled Judah, a Palestinian, saved the policeman's life, risking his own. Another Muslim man, a Turk, saved the life of a non-Muslim woman. The actions of these two Muslims, the Turk and the Palestinian, were not taken as representative of a common Islamic impulse. They were not taken as a representation of what Muslim minorities contribute to European society at large. It was not taken as a sign of Muslim integration into European society. It was not taken as an expression of Muslim civic values that are well-integrated with the moral values of Europe. But the actions of the attacker *were* taken to represent the "Islamic danger," the "Islamist problem," and the ways in which Islam poses a "threat" to Europe.

Representation. And representation comes from awareness and power. You cannot have power if you do not have awareness. You could have all the means to power, such as a great deal of money,

---

98 A reference to the murder and beheading of a French school teacher, Samuel Paty, by an 18-year-old Chechen in France.

99 A reference to the so-called "Vienna attacks," a series of shootings that killed four civilians and injured 23, including one police officer, on 2 November 2020.

but without the awareness of knowing how to spend that money, that money will not yield any power. Awareness precedes everything.

A video emerged during the recent U.S. presidential election of Paula White, an inspirational figure for many Christians in the United States and a spiritual advisor to President Trump. This video is directly relevant to the issue of representation and self-perception. Paula White is seen shouting, "Strike, strike, strike against your enemies. I hear the sound of victory."[100] Imagine if this was a Muslim. Why is it that a Christian—a spiritual advisor to the President, no less—can do this and it does not become a controversy? Most non-Muslims will look at this and dismiss it as silly. If the same conduct came from a Muslim, however, it would never be attributed to silliness or to some type of psychological failure. It would be attributed to a failure of Islam itself. Notice, too, the blatant racism in the performance. She states that "there are angels coming from Africa." How do these angels express themselves? Through speaking in tongues. She cannot even be troubled to learn African languages. Instead, she utters gibberish. But even that racism does not raise an eyebrow. It does not make anyone pause. No one attributes that conduct to a defect in Christian theology, the Bible, the life of Jesus or the disciples, or the history of Christianity.

The minute we see any wrong committed by Muslims, however, even Muslims themselves start faulting the nature of Islam, the history of Islam, or the *Sira* of the Prophet. I cannot describe the number of people who email me, saying, "I am so troubled. My faith is shaken because I need an answer for this-or-that episode in the life of the Prophet." It is not enough for them that God says, "God and the angels pray on the Prophet, so you, believers, pray on the Prophet"

---

100 See NowThis News, *Donald Trump's Faith Advisor Leads Viral Sermon After Election Day* (YouTube, 5 Nov 2020).

(Q 33:56). It is not enough that God tells us the Prophet was a man of high moral character (Q 68:4). It is a sign of the psychological defeat of Muslims. Every little thing shakes the foundations of their faith. Every misconduct by fellow Muslims becomes representative of a larger defect in Islamic history and theology.

It is in our nature to think that we are independent free thinkers. But I am here to tell you that being a free thinker—a truly free thinker—requires hard work. It requires an enormous amount of deliberation and education. In fact, ninety-nine percent of Muslims are not free thinkers because they do not work hard enough to be sufficiently educated to know how to think freely and not have their world of ideas constructed for them by the other. They are as if robots. They only react to what the other wants them to react to. I pray to God that this remaining one-percent becomes five percent, ten percent, then twenty percent. For the day in which that one percent becomes five percent, the entire fate of the Muslim *Ummah* will start changing in material and foundational ways.

13 November 2020

20

The Islam of Sacrifice
and the Legacy of al-Husayn

Ａs human beings, our ability to recognize harm is embedded in our intellectual, moral, and even spiritual code. It is part of human nature. And the nature of our learning is experiential. At a minimum, we respond to what is pleasant and unpleasant. So much of what we know and how we know it comes from our own experiences of failure, displeasure, harm, or other unpleasant consequences. From this, we conclude that a particular act or option is not good. Much of what defines us is precisely this. We may like to think that we mold ourselves according to principles, but it requires a considerable amount of work to mold ourselves beyond the experiential.

To mold yourself through other than what is pleasant or unpleasant requires that you do not prioritize your own experiences of pleasure or harm. It requires living up to a principle that you believe in and pursue, despite your experiences. But the reality is that most people, most of the time, philosophize the experiential. They do not experience the philosophical. What most people, most of the time, experience in terms of pleasure or displeasure they then project onto society, onto the world, onto everything. They project it so that they can philosophize it. Few people want to admit that they, in fact, know nothing other than what they experience in life, and that what they experience in life is extremely limited. Most people, most of the time, do not want to admit that they only know lofty concepts such as justice, love, and truth through the extremely limited prism of their own pleasures and displeasures. In other words, they only know them experientially.

This is precisely why most people, most of the time, can read that the Qur'an demands that they testify for truth, even if against themselves (Q 4:135). They can read that the Qur'an demands that they sacrifice their lives, time, and money for God (Q 9:41). They can read the sacrifices of the prophets. They can read the entire moral universe of the Qur'an with all its lofty principles. When all is said and done, however, unless one is extremely conscientious and careful, the abstract will retreat into the background behind the experiential. In other words, whatever abstract concepts you find in the Qur'an, such as bearing witness to God, living in a state of *jihad*, and sacrificing for the sake of God, retreat into the background. Abstractions make most people uncomfortable. To realize them requires sacrifice and hard work. What most people do when they read the Qur'an, then, is gloss over these principles. They put Qur'anic concepts on the shelf and live according to a very convenient myth: "I am essentially good. I am okay." In addressing the Prophet and Companions, however, God teaches us a very basic lesson: "Do not commend yourself" (Q 53:32). In other words, do not blindly believe that you are, in fact, okay. But this is precisely what most people, most of the time, do. We tell ourselves, "I am fine. I do not live selfishly. I am a giving and caring person." For most people, most of the time, it is an absolute delusion. The challenge is to learn to get beyond the self and organize your life in the service of a principle.

Every civilization has a small percentage of people who get beyond the self and live in service to an idea or set of ideas. Not all of England became worldwide explorers. Yet, there was a small percentage among the English who dedicated their lives to exploring the world and traveling to remote lands where they put their lives and well-being at risk. Not all the Christian world committed to spreading the Gospel, but a small percentage of the British, French, and Dutch sacrificed their lives to live in remote lands in uncomfortable conditions to spread the teachings of Jesus. As a result, today, more than half of Africa is Christian. These people got beyond the experiential and understood that serving their principle necessarily meant forcing the self into the background and bringing to the foreground the principle itself.

Whatever mistakes were made in the course of Islamic history, whatever the failures, there was always a sufficient percentage that could assign the self to the background and live according to a principle. There were enough Ibn Battutas (d. 770-1/1368-9) to travel the world. There were enough Ibn Sinas (d. 428/1037) or al-Farrabis (d. 339/950-1) to imagine the truth. There were enough al-Ghazalis (d. 505/1111) or Ibn Rushds (d. 595/1198) to think about justice and beauty, and pursue them beyond the experiential, to cover the historical mistakes.

Let me put it more simply. Shortly after the death of the Prophet, the Muslim *Ummah* experienced a truly demonic moment that, in and of itself, could have been enough to destroy Islam forever. That demonic moment was the murder of al-Husayn (d. 61/680), the grandson of the Prophet, by the political authorities of the day. The first Muslim dynasty commenced its legacy with a truly atrocious and blasphemous act. They murdered the grandson of the Prophet! Even if you did nothing but this, it would still be enough to curse you until the end of time. But why was al-Husayn murdered? It was because the vast majority of people at that time put themselves first. Not the principle. Not the Prophet. Not the family of the Prophet. Not the grandson of the Prophet. Not justice, truth, or beauty. Most people knew very well that al-Husayn was the just party. They knew that they had an obligation to support al-Husayn. But they betrayed him, betrayed principles, and engaged in the utmost act of selfishness. Because of this betrayal, the first dynasty to rule Islam was a highly corrupting force. The Umayyad dynasty, like the later 'Abbasids, did everything within its power to corrupt and stymie Islam as an ethical revolution.

"And what ails you that you fight not in the way of God, and for the weak and oppressed—men, women, and children . . ." (SQ 4:75). God tells us in Surah al-Nisa' that we have an obligation to sacrifice and even go to war. Why? It is not for selfish goals. It is to empower the disempowered. The Islam of the Prophet and al-Husayn was an Islam of sacrifice. It was an Islam anchored in the belief that you are on this earth to sacrifice. You are on this earth to put yourself in the service of a higher cause. You have no grounds for selfish entitlement.

The Umayyad dynasty that murdered the grandson of the Prophet understood very well that this is a dangerous Islam. So they got to work. They invented an enormous number of *hadith*s about the duty of obedience that is owed to a ruler even if the ruler is unjust; children must obey parents even if parents are unjust; wives should obey husbands even if their husbands are unjust; slaves should obey masters even if their masters are unjust; people simply need to say the *Shahadah* to be Muslim; people need only perform ritual acts; they do not need to think about what the Prophet himself did, that is, sacrifice his best interests day in, day out. For that *is* what the Prophet did. The stellar Companions did it. 'Ali ibn Abi Talib, al-Husayn, and al-Hasan did it. The *ahl al-bayt* (family of the Prophet), generation after generation, did it.[101]

Umayyad Islam put into service generation after generation of corrupt scholars who invented, narrated, and collected *hadith*s, all to silence the Qur'an. What upheld the Islamic civilization, however, is that there was always a sufficient percentage of people—not a majority, but a sufficient percentage—who committed their lives to studying principles, comprehending principles, and implementing principles. This percentage is what constructed the glory of the Islamic civilization. The Islamic civilization crumbled because our historical mistakes eventually caught up with us, like racism caught up with the Roman Empire and will, eventually, catch up with the American civilization.

Learning selflessness is not as easy as you would think. This is especially true when we grow up under the Islam of the state, the same Islam that murdered the grandson of the Prophet. This is the Islam that we are all weaned on. It is the Islam that teaches us that we are fine so long as we pay our *zakah* (alms) of 2.5 percent of whatever is saved over a year. It is the Islam that teaches us that so long as we pray, fast, and take care of our families, we are fine. It is the Islam that does not get us to marvel at the fact that the greatest gift of God

---

101 For more, see The Usuli Institute, *Islamic Ethical Obligations, Umayyad Propaganda & Ahl al-Bayt* (Excerpt, 16 February 2022) and *Vending Machine Islam and Politically Motivated Traditions* (Excerpt, 15 March 2022). The difference between what Professor Abou El Fadl calls "Qur'anic Islam" and "Imperial Islam" is a key theme in the forthcoming Project Illumine *tafsir* publication.

is the intellect. Nor does it teach us how often God emphasizes the role of the intellect, moral conscience, and the place of justice in our lives. It is the Islam that does not teach us that if we do not live our lives in the service of a cause, then we are not truly Muslim. We are then like the hypocrites of Medina. And if we do not come to the aid of the disempowered and oppressed (*al-mustad'afun*), then we are like the hypocrites of Medina. Can you believe that the Islam we grew up learning is the Islam that murdered the grandson of the Prophet?

As Muslims, our reality is undeniable. We keep going from one misery to the next. Since the colonial era, Muslims have suffered tragedy after tragedy. We are like a people who keep putting their finger in an electric socket and—surprise—keep getting electrocuted. For centuries now, we keep doing the same thing, over and over. At what point do we say, "Enough is enough. We need to do a deep dive into our historical, moral, and intellectual framework"? At what point do we say, "Clearly, this is not working. Something is really wrong"? How insane it is that we keep going from one disaster to the next and yet we do not see any great change in the collective psychology and intellectual disposition of Muslims. When are Muslims going to wake up?

Another book has come out, titled *Worse Than Death: Reflections on the Uyghur Genocide*.[102] It is an extremely painful book written by a witness to the genocide. Yet another book, *The War on the Uyghurs*, documents how President Trump met with Xi Jinping, the President of China, and gave him the green light to build the internment camps.[103] Trump told him, in effect, that while the

---

102 Mamtimim Ala, *Worse Than Death: Reflections on the Uyghur Genocide* (London: Hamilton Book, 2021).
103 Sean Roberts, *The War on the Uyghurs: China's Campaign Against Xinjiang's Muslims* (Manchester: Manchester University Press, 2020). Also see footnote 81.

U.S. will condemn China in public, the holocaust against Uyghur Muslims is of no concern to the U.S. Will this awaken the conscience of Muslims? Will it awaken those Muslims who defend the Trump administration?[104] Will the fact that yet another extremely painful testimonial has come out make any difference? Moral vigilance is a habit. Do not get accustomed to putting your own comforts first. Be wary of having a sense of entitlement. Believe it or not, that is precisely what led to the murder of al-Husayn and the genocide against the Uyghur Muslims.

Yet another article has been published on the threat of another conflict and genocide in Bosnia.[105] This is extremely worrying. Serbian nationalism, Islamophobia, and talk of "finishing what we started" in the '90s, meaning the rape and murder of Muslims, is at an all-time high. Will this awaken Muslims?

There is yet another article detailing the ban on the *hijab* in India.[106] School after school is now banning *hijabs* in India. Sexually assaulting Muslim women has become a pastime for Hindu nationalists in India. Will this awaken Muslims? Will it convince Muslims not to put their own comforts first?

Listen to this new disaster. It has kept me awake for days. It is a new phenomenon that, had it happened to any other people, would have set the world alight. In Sweden, there is an intelligence agency that is supposed to focus on national security, known as SAPO. SAPO carefully monitors Muslims. According to public records, SAPO has logged with Swedish social services close to 300,000 complaints. The overwhelming majority of complaints, if not all, are directed at Muslim

---

104 An allusion to Hamza Yusuf and Zaytuna College. See footnotes 36 and 82.

105 See Jeremy Bowen, "Bosnia Shivers as Ghost of Nationalism Returns," *BBC News* (9 February 2022).

106 See "Court Says No to Religious Clothes Until Verdict Over India Hijab Ban," *TRT World* (11 February 2022).

refugee parents. What are the complaints? If you have a fight with your wife and yell at her, social services intervenes. If you do not allow your son or daughter to date, social services intervenes. If you object to your daughter wearing a bikini, social services intervenes. Article after article has shown that thousands of Muslim families have had their children taken away. Swedish social services have taken away the children of Syrian, Somali, and Moroccan families.[107]

Apparently, this is big business. It is not just about racism. Foster families are handsomely paid by the state, so there is a financial incentive. According to a recent book published in Sweden, however, social services in Sweden are not too discerning. Many of these foster families turn out to be sexual abusers. They serve the children alcohol and drugs. The percentage of these children that suffer sexual abuse is outrageous. Social services say that a judge will decide upon the eventual fate of the child. But even the U.N. has expressed concern that judges do not believe Muslim parents and do not honor the desires of Muslim children.

I watched a video of an 11-year-old who was taken from his parents. When he tried to run away, the police arrested him and even stepped on his head. The poor child was yelling the *Shahadah*. A Moroccan mother named Lena had her child forcibly taken from her. She tearfully recorded her story online. Later, she suffered a breakdown and killed herself. On YouTube, there is a video of her son shoveling earth onto her grave. I read of a 13-year-old girl, Yasmin, who was separated from her family and begged to be allowed to return to them. She, too, killed herself.

---

107 See Abdul Latif Haj Muhammad, "Sweden: Taking Syrian Children away from their Families," *Daraj* (19 November 2019), and Rayhan Uddin, "Sweden: Syrian parents plead to be reunited with children taken by authorities," *Middle East Eye* (28 January 2022). SAPO is an abbreviation of "Sakerhetspolisen," or the "Swedish Security Service."

Social services in Sweden are acting like the Gestapo, taking the children of Muslims, punishing Muslim families for being Muslim. If you tell your child that they ought to remain a virgin, it is cause for removal. If you tell your child that they cannot date or attend parties, it is cause for removal. If you tell them that they should pray five times a day or fast during Ramadan, it is cause for removal. If you tell them that they should wear the *hijab*, it is, of course, cause for removal. It is endemic, widespread, and unrestrained racism. Muslim families have lost their children in Italy, France, Germany, and Britain, but nothing on the scale of what is happening in Sweden.

But what do you do with a people who look at what is happening in China and carry on with their lives? Who look at what is emerging in Bosnia, India, and the widespread racism against Muslims all over the West, and still talk about what they are entitled to, their own wants and desires? To me, an act of selfishness brings down the curse of the unjust murder of al-Husayn. God has forced us to live under the shadow of this high act of immorality. It is as if God has said, "There is an event in history that should alert you to the price of egocentrism and selfishness. If you do not reflect and comprehend, then I will unleash the curse of this event upon you. But if you do reflect and understand, then you may belong to that minority that avoids hypocrisy in living as a Muslim on earth." Right now, what a small minority it is. What a small minority it is.

The answer, obviously, is not for someone to commit an act of violence. That only makes things worse. If nothing else—if you are incapable of doing anything, of giving money, of volunteering for legal representation, or of influencing politics—the answer is simply to get beyond yourself. It is to teach yourself not to be selfish. At a minimum, you can tell God, "God, You know I could not do anything about these children in Sweden, but the pain I felt pushed me to become a better Muslim, a Muslim like the Prophet and al-Husayn. It pushed me to live and die by a principle, not in the service of the self."

11 February 2022

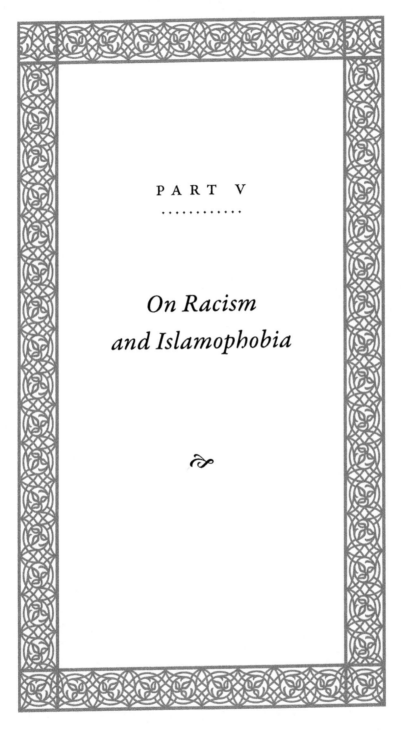

PART V
. . . .

*On Racism
and Islamophobia*

21

Jahiliyya and the Murder
of George Floyd

Islam came as a line of demarcation, a *furqan*, against the ethics, practices, rituals, lineages, affiliations, and prejudices of *jahiliyya*. The word *jahiliyya* is derived from the root *jahl*, meaning ignorance. In Islam, *jahiliyya* is wedded to notions of darkness and loss. It is a state in which Satan dwells. It is a state in which you are more in the realm of the demonic than the Divine. *Jahiliyya*, with all its connotations, is an ungodly state. It is a state in which you cannot claim to be close to the Divine.

The Qur'an time and again reminds human beings that Islam takes people from darkness to light (Q 2:257; 5:16; 14:1, 5; 33:43; 57:9; 65:11). A Muslim who understands what it means to walk in the company of the Divine must commit him or herself to emerging from a state of darkness to light. If not, then there is always the risk of drowning in *taghut*, which is the worst type of oppression. It is the oppression of bigotry, prejudice, and ignorance. Simply put, if you claim to be with the Divine, then your heart must be in the right place. Your heart must reject *taghut* and *jahiliyya* in all its forms. Imagine how many things fall under the category of *jahiliyya*. Your heart must reject blind affiliation. It must reject speaking out of ignorance. Slander, foul obscenities, treason, and cheating. Dishonesty, cowardliness, and miserliness. Materialism and a lack of empathy. Islam came as a clear demarcation from this state of darkness.

The enlightenment of Islam is founded on the principle of *iman*, and *iman* is not complete without fully rejecting the ethics of *jahiliyya*. God tells us in Surah al-Mutaffifin, for example, about those who cheat in business. God asks: do these people not know that they will meet their Lord (Q 83:4)? God underscores that cheating in business is like lying and cheating in anything. It is part of the world of *jahiliyya*. It cannot be part of the world of the Divine. A critical part of *iman* is to reject what is *jahili*, and this includes everything that is immoral and unethical. Every time we cheat, lie, act unfairly, hurt others, or act on bigotry and prejudice, it is *jahiliyya*.

There is a story that many Muslims often repeat. They know the story, but they forget the extent to which it conveys a morally transformative lesson.

> *He frowned and turned away, because the blind man*
> *came to him. And what would apprise thee? Perhaps*
> *he would purify himself, or be reminded, such that the*
> *reminder might benefit him. As for him who deems himself*
> *beyond need, to him dost thou attend, though thou art*
> *not answerable, should he not be purified. But as for him*
> *who came to thee striving earnestly while fearful, from*
> *him thou art diverted. Nay! Truly it is a reminder—so*
> *let whomsoever will, remember it—(SQ 80:1-11).*

228

Surah 'Abasa is perhaps one of the most famous chapters in the Qur'an. It relays an incident involving a poor blind man in Mecca by the name of 'Abdullah Ibn Umm Maktum, who was the cousin of Khadijah, the Prophet's wife. He had already converted to Islam. At the time, the Prophet was experiencing an increase in persecution. He had gone public with the Islamic message. He had announced to his people from Mount Safa that he is a prophet sent to them from God. On that day, however, of the forty-five heads of different tribes that attended the announcement, none converted. Shortly thereafter, the Prophet's close Companion, Abu Bakr, was severely beaten after preaching Islam openly. Other Companions who dared to pray or speak about Islam in public were assaulted. Those without tribal protection, especially slaves, were not just beaten, but tortured. In fact, Summayah bint Khayyat and her husband, Yasir ibn 'Amir, were murdered while their son, 'Ammar ibn Yasir, continued to be tortured before their eyes.

The Prophet was in a desperate situation. Many of the Companions were suffering egregious persecution and he was often unable to do anything to help them. Under these circumstances, it is entirely understandable that the Prophet eagerly wanted the elders of Mecca, figures like Walid ibn al-Mughira, to either become Muslim or to at least sympathize enough with Islam to moderate the persecution. If any persecution could be removed, it would be a great blessing. It is under these circumstances that the Prophet addressed several Meccan elders, fervently trying to earn their conversion or at least mitigate the suffering of his fellow Muslims. It is at this moment that Ibn Umm Maktum, the poor blind man, approached the Prophet and asked to speak with him. The Prophet asked him to wait while he talked to the elites of Mecca. "No, I want to talk to you. I have questions." Apparently, Ibn Umm Maktum was insistent enough for the Prophet to grow irritated. He was interrupting the Prophet, demanding priority over the Meccan elders. Remember that Ibn Umm Maktum was already Muslim. From a strategic point of view, one could say that the Prophet's time was better spent trying to earn the favor of these non-Muslim elites. According to reports, the Prophet was just irritated. Other reports say he was irritated and frowned. In any case, Ibn Umm Maktum could not see the Prophet's face because he was blind. Even if the Prophet did frown, Ibn Umm Maktum would not have seen it.

Look at the Qur'an. God reveals an entire chapter chiding the Prophet for that behavior. Surah 'Abasa is harsh in its criticism, although many of us would have done exactly what the Prophet did. Many of us, in fact, do it all the time. We give priority to important people. But there was a principle that the Qur'an had to anchor: in Islam, we do not play politics; in Islam, we do ethics.

Surah 'Abasa in its entirety came to say that in the eyes of God, the fact that these are powerful and wealthy people means nothing. In the eyes of God, that poor blind man is more important. As a Prophet of God, Muhammad should concern himself with the ethics of the process, not the results. The chapter asks: "How do you know?" (Q 80:3) The Prophet does not know whether the yield is better with the elites or the blind man. That is not the Prophet's business. To think of results is not his business. His business is the ethical process itself. Morally and ethically, the rich are not more entitled than the poor. The powerful do not take priority over the disempowered.

It is reported that every time the Prophet saw Ibn Umm Maktum after the revelation of 'Abasa, he greeted him as "the person on whose behalf God reprimanded me." Such amazing humility. The Prophet was taught a moral lesson and celebrated Ibn Umm Maktum as someone who became a vehicle for teaching him more humility, more principles, and for underscoring the difference between Islam and *jahiliyya*. In *jahiliyya*, we play politics. In *jahiliyya*, we give priority to the wealthy and powerful. In Islam, it is the principles and the ethics that matter.

Ibn Umm Maktum went on to become an important figure in Islamic history. When the Prophet left Medina, he often appointed him as his deputy. Many of us would be resentful of a man who caused a public embarrassment at a time when the Prophet was already being persecuted. Eventually, Ibn Umm Maktum's religious status rose until he became a significant moral figure in the Muslim community. He was eventually martyred in the Battle of al-Qadisiyyah (16/636). Although blind, he insisted on joining the battle as the flag bearer for the Muslim army.

The Prophet taught that human beings are equal like the teeth of a comb.[108] This was meant theoretically and practically. To discriminate between people on the basis of nationality, race, and even gender is *jahiliyya*. To treat people differently because of wealth, tribal affiliation, or ethnicity is part of the ethics of *jahiliyya*. This includes treating people differently on the basis of class, for that is the demonstrative example of 'Abasa. We too often forget that you can be a Muslim by name but, in substance, reflect the morality of *jahiliyya*. This is if you are a racist, a classist, or a bigot. It applies if you are full of hatred. It applies if you are a cheater or a liar. You are then Muslim by name, but in heart and mind you are *jahili*. You are part of *jahiliyya*.

Islam came as a moral and ethical revolution. It rebelled against the elite status of the clergy. It rebelled against the privileges and

---

108 See Shah Waliullah Dehlawi's (d. 1176/1762) collection of forty *hadith*s (16).

immunities of the rich. It rebelled against the ignorance of tribalism, lineage, and racism. It even rebelled against the classism of free versus slave. That is why the Prophet forbade us from referring to someone as a "slave" (*'abd*).[109] That is the Islamic ethical revolution. It is a rejection of *jahiliyya* in all its forms. This lesson is so important for us in the present moment. Yes, we are formally Muslims, but on so many levels we remain thoroughly *jahili* in nature.

We are all aware of the case of George Floyd, who was murdered by the police in Minneapolis.[110] The story of his killing has so many typical elements. A Black man enters a store and is suspected of criminal activity. The store calls the police. In what has become a common racist paradigm, the police arrive and see that this is a big man. As so often, the nature of racists is to be threatened by big African American men. As we saw in the video, they handcuffed him and one of the policemen put his knee on George Floyd's neck until he died. Incidentally, these same police officers had previously faced disciplinary action in cases involving police brutality. They escaped with a slap on the wrist.

Think of what this incident represents. Under no circumstances is it acceptable, whether in the U.S. or elsewhere, for the police to put their knee on someone's neck and ignore his pleas of "I cannot breathe" until he dies. This is the embodiment, the very essence, of police brutality. The main problem—what ignited the protests in Minneapolis and elsewhere—is that this is a repeated pattern against minority groups, especially African Americans. Had this incident

---

109 Muslim (2249).

110 Note that the date of this *khutbah* on 29 May 2020 was four days after the murder of George Floyd, on 25 May 2020. This *khutbah* was therefore Professor Abou El Fadl's first recorded response to the event. For more on the plague of racism in the U.S. as exemplified in the murder of George Floyd, see Chapter 16: *The Islam of Dignity: Are You on the Right Side of History?* in this volume.

not been filmed and led to mass protests, rest assured that nothing would have happened to these police officers. It happens all the time and the police officers involved are not disciplined, not fired, and certainly not charged. In fact, in Minneapolis itself, only last year, there was a shooting of another Black man under suspicious circumstances. Amy Klobuchar, who for a time was running for President, was at the time the prosecutor and declined to prosecute the police officers involved. It went to a grand jury and the grand jury did not indict.

The problem is that the *jahiliyya* of racism is endemic in our society. And it is endemic in so many of us, as Muslims. It is of course more lethal when it infects the police because the police are armed—not only with weapons, but the law. If you refuse to abide by their commands, the legal system could crush you. The police are meant to enforce the law, but their interpretation of the law is often unreviewed and not held to account. We write laws, but it is the police who implement the laws on the ground. In most cases, there is no way to hold those who enforce the law to account before they do so. And it is very difficult to hold them to account with hindsight. That is precisely why the ethics of society itself must change. It is because the police hold a very dangerous power. The ethics of society must change and the institutions that review the conduct of those who apply the law must be active, energetic, and empowered. The police cannot review themselves and hold themselves to account. That spells corruption.

Think of the endemic racism. Imagine the total number of African Americans who have been unjustly imprisoned, killed, or tortured from the time that the United States was established until today. Add to that the number of Native Americans and Latinos. Can you imagine how many volumes this would fill? An ethical human being cannot talk about democratic institutions, due process, and equality before the law in the U.S. without thinking of the sheer number of victims who bear testimony against those ideals.

Consider that until yesterday, when the policeman who murdered Floyd was charged, there had been several police shootings in Minneapolis over the years and none had led to a criminal charge, except one. The one exception is the exception that proves the rule. Why? Because the one exception was a Muslim police officer, named Muhammad Noor, a man of Somali origin, who shot and killed a White woman. He was charged with third degree murder and convicted. When a Black Muslim police officer shot a White woman, then, a grand jury did indict him, the prosecutor did prosecute, and no protests were needed. Everyone was against the police officer from the beginning.

There is no question that this is *jahili*. We cannot ignore the fact that the wonderful experiment in democracy and civil rights that emerged in the U.S. and Europe is under serious threat. It is threatened by bigotry, prejudice, and racism—a racism that includes Islamophobia. A recent study shows an alarming rise in White nativist movements in the U.S. that prefer dictatorial solutions and are not offended by Trump's erosion of democracy so long as it keeps minorities at bay.[111] In other words, these movements feel threatened by minority rights and see the Obama administration as an alarming moment that must never be repeated.

As Muslims, however, we cannot ignore another important point. In the U.S., people demonstrated and the police officer was finally charged with third degree murder. Meanwhile, all over the Muslim world, the police torture and kill people every single day and any

---

111 Rachel Kleinfeld, John Dickas. *Resisting the Call of Nativism: What U.S. Political Parties Can Learn From Other Democracies* (Carnegie Endowment for International Peace, 5 March 2020).

journalist who dares to say anything is arrested. Anyone who dares to protest is arrested. It is very rare, all over the Muslim world, for a police officer who tortures and kills to be held to account in any way. This is *jahiliyya*. It is pure *jahiliyya*. And as a Muslim, I am offended by the *jahiliyya* of Muslims far more than I am offended by the *jahiliyya* of non-Muslims. For when *jahiliyya* exists among Muslims, they should know better. They have no excuse.

In a *hadith* that, in my opinion, is erroneously categorized as weak, the Prophet said, "Let none of you stand by when someone is flogged unfairly. Let none of you stand by as someone is killed unjustly. God's curse will fall on those who tortured or killed, and on those who watched and did nothing."[112] In our day and age, who watches and does nothing? Previously, you had to be physically present to witness the incident. Not anymore. If you watched the video, read the news, saw the racism, and yet failed to act, do not complain when you find that blessings have been taken from your life. God does not bless the unjust. God does not bless *jahiliyya*. Understand that you can pray and fast all you want, but if your heart does not beat with a passion for justice, then do not ask God for blessings. For you have not held up your end of the bargain.

What pains me is that there are influential Muslims in the U.S. who de-emphasize the racial problem in this country. Who convince Muslims that their role in life is simply to learn how to pray correctly, get married, and have children. Who say things like "All lives matter" or "The police do not kill more African Americans than Whites. It is just that when the police kill Whites, we do not hear about it."[113]

---

112 See al-Tabarani, *al-Mu'jam al-Kabir*, ed. Hamdi bin 'Abdul Majid al-Salafi (Cairo: Maktaba Ibn Taymiyya, n.d), 11/260.

113 The comment on the police killing Whites refers to comments made by Hamza Yusuf. See footnote 87. On "All lives matter," see The Usuli Institute, *All Lives vs Black Lives and the Sin of Holy Rhetoric* (*Khutbah*, 28 August 2020).

These Muslims are on the payroll of the UAE, and they hold the positions of power in the U.S. They are *jahili* Muslims.

There are two types of Muslims. The first type responds to injustice—such as when a Black man is degraded and killed by the police—by saying, "Perform your *salah* correctly, then go home and raise your children. That is what the Prophet wants." The second type of Muslim tells you, "The Prophet is offended to the core by injustice! The Prophet wants you to protest. The Prophet wants you to say 'No!' to injustice, bigotry, and racism." Choose which type of Islam to follow. But the first, in my view, is not Islam at all. It is an Islamized *jahiliyya*. It is a thinly disguised *jahiliyya* with an Islamic veneer. Yet these are the dominant Muslim institutions in the U.S. I am not talking about groups like CAIR.[114] I am referring to those who receive money from the Emirati, Saudi, or Egyptian governments, governments that kill the soul of Islam with the soul of *jahiliyya*.

One final point. Las Vegas will reopen sooner rather than later. Las Vegas was in a real crisis. It had shut down and was suffering heavy financial losses due to the coronavirus pandemic. The problem was that Las Vegas needed coronavirus tests and nasal swabs, without which it was unable to reopen. The local government asked the federal government for nasal swabs and the federal government declined, saying that it will not be able to provide any support for several months. Who came to the rescue of Las Vegas? Mohamed bin Zayed (MBZ), the Crown Prince of Abu Dhabi. He sent two hundred thousand emergency test kits, costing Abu Dhabi and the UAE roughly $20 million. Because of MBZ's emergency relief, Las Vegas, with its gambling and prostitution, now has sufficient test

---

114 The Council on American-Islamic Relations.

kits and will reopen very soon. The article in the *Los Angeles Times* thanks MBZ for his generosity. [115]

Think of all those Muslims who pay their allegiance to the UAE. Many in the Arab world refer to MBZ as "the devil of the Arabs" (*shaytan al-ʿarab*). He truly is a demon. Wherever you find *jahiliyya*, including gambling, prostitution, and *kufr*, therein you find MBZ.

29 May 2020

---

115 See Anna M. Phillips, "Las Vegas Needed Help Testing for Coronavirus. Then a Crown Prince Stepped In," *Los Angeles Times* (21 May 2022).

22

Why Jerusalem Matters

A ceasefire has been agreed between Israel and Gaza.[116] It is a ceasefire that leaves the Palestinians with a monumental amount of destruction. Entire buildings have been razed to the ground. Families have been left homeless, losing homes for which they spent a lifetime working and saving. Hospitals have been hit. Governmental and civic infrastructure has been destroyed. Meanwhile, the blockade that suffocates Gaza continues so that more than two million Gazans in a small strip of land continue to suffer under gross and inhumane living conditions. After the ceasefire was announced, Palestinians poured into the streets to celebrate. The following day, shortly after *jumu'a* prayers, Israeli police once again attacked Palestinians gathered inside the al-Aqsa Mosque compound. It is as if the Israelis could not handle seeing the Palestinians waving the Palestinian flag and rejoicing. The clashes resulted in numerous Palestinians wounded and arrested. It was an

---

116 See footnote 12.

entirely avoidable clash. The Israeli police did not have to attack the Palestinians gathered and celebrating in the al-Aqsa Mosque after *jumuʻa*. Yet, they demanded that the area surrounding the mosque be evacuated immediately. When this did not happen, the police attacked the Palestinians.

We return to the status quo. It is a status quo that has been ongoing for over seventy years. It is a status quo in which Palestinians live in subhuman conditions and in refugee camps. It is a status quo that is an exception to international humanitarian law that has defined the global order since World War II. It is an exception to the right to self-determination. It is an exception to the right of an occupied people to resist occupation. It is an exception to the right of a native people under occupation to exercise self-defense against their subjugators and occupiers. International law states very clearly that those living under occupation have a right to resist their occupation. But this very right is, somehow, never recognized for the Palestinians. The United States, as it has done numerous times, prevents the U.N. Security Council from condemning Israeli aggression. As always, the U.S. makes sure at the level of the Security Council and other international organizations that the right of Palestinians to resist occupation is never acknowledged or recognized, and that the entire Western world speaks only of the right of Israel to defend itself. The occupier has the right to defend itself, then, but the occupied is expected to accept its subjugated status and to plead with the occupier to recognize its rights.

Since the Oslo Accords, Israel has confiscated most of the Palestinian land in the West Bank. What remains of the West Bank that has not been confiscated or annexed by Israeli settlers is a mere hodgepodge of small, isolated pockets of land. The Oslo Accords brought not a peace agreement but rather a license for Israel to further colonize and usurp Palestinian territory. Throughout, Palestinians are expected to accept their subjugated status. The last senior Israeli politician to talk of a Palestinian state and a two-state solution was Yitzhak Rabin, who was assassinated by a Jewish extremist in 1995. Many do not know that since Rabin's assassination, the idea of peace with the Palestinians has become a dirty word. None of the politicians who dominate Israeli politics talk about peace with Palestinians, leave alone the notion of a Palestinian state. The Israeli political left, which was considered relatively less racist, less colonial, and more accommodating, has all but disappeared. The only real forces that exist in Israeli politics are the right-wing and the extreme right-wing. It is as if the left has disappeared from the Israeli political landscape.

We in the U.S. engage in polite talk about Israel's right to self-defense. Meanwhile, Israeli discourse celebrates the normalization of relations with the UAE and Bahrain.[117] Israeli discourse also celebrates developments in Saudi Arabia and what it sees as the inevitable normalization of relations with Saudi Arabia. At the same time, Israeli discourse toward the Palestinians has become more extreme, more fascist, and more exclusionary with each passing year. It is as if, according to the Israeli political psyche, making peace with dictatorial rulers in the Gulf and Egypt—tyrants who thoroughly oppress their own people—means they no longer need to worry about the Palestinians as human beings, leave alone as people entitled to rights under natural and international law.

A particular development during this last confrontation caught my attention. Israel has adopted a very interesting discourse that

---

117 On 13 August 2020, the UAE announced its agreement to normalize ties with Israel. Bahrain's announcement followed shortly thereafter, on 11 September 2020. These agreements took place toward the end of President Trump's first term and were widely seen as an attempt by these countries to improve Trump's chances at re-election.

merits pause and reflection. It has adopted the practice of presenting designated spokesmen who present the Israeli perspective to the Muslim world and who speak in Arabic, not English or Hebrew. These representatives play a fascinating role. They often speak about what Islam requires of Muslims. On one occasion, several years ago, the Arabic-speaking representative of the Israeli army reminded the Muslim world that Muhammad ibn ʿAbd al-Wahhab (d. 1206/1792) was a "great reformer." That same spokesman claimed that the Ottomans had always oppressed Arabs and that Arabs should never be fooled by Turkey, a nation that intends to dominate and subjugate them exactly like the Ottomans had. Again, this is an Israeli spokesman talking to Arabs about the Ottomans. In other words, his message is: watch out for the Turks for they want to re-establish the Ottoman Caliphate. This Arabic-speaking Israeli spokesman often cites the Qur'an or *hadiths* to tell Muslims what Islam demands of them. When the bombardment of Gaza started, however, the Israeli army did something very interesting. It posted a tweet—since deleted—announcing the bombardment of Gaza by quoting, in full, from Surah al-Fil:

> *Hast thou not seen how thy Lord dealt with the masters*
> *of the elephant? Did He not make their scheming*
> *go astray, and send against them birds in swarms,*
> *pelting them with stones of baked clay, such that He*
> *made them like devoured husks? (SQ 105:1-5)*

This chapter refers to the attempts of Abrahah, a pre-Islamic Abyssinian general who ruled Yemen, to tear down the Kaʿba. God sent a swarm of birds that pelted the army of Abrahah with stones. The Israeli army cited this at the start of the bombardment of Gaza.

The implication is clear. The army is drawing a parallel between the birds that stoned the armies of Abrahah and the Israeli planes that are bombing Palestinians.

This raises the question of what the Israeli army meant by citing this chapter. Was the army claiming that it is similarly bombing heathens to uphold God's cause? Was the army mocking Muslims and saying, "Look, we are bombing you and there is nothing you can do about it"? Was the Israeli army mocking Muslims, then, or was it usurping the Qur'anic discourse to claim that it is the righteous party?

The ambiguity is not an accident. It is intentional. Let me mention another piece of the puzzle before putting it all together. There have been demonstrations in support of the Palestinians all over the world. However, there were no demonstrations in support of the Palestinians in the UAE, Saudi Arabia, and Egypt. This is not because the Emirati, Saudi, or Egyptian people do not support the Palestinians—they do. It is because supporting the Palestinians is not permissible in these authoritarian and totalitarian countries. In fact, in these countries, if you raise the Palestinian flag in the street, you could be promptly arrested and disappear, as has been happening in Egypt.

People often talk about the colonial nature of the Israeli state. Israel's supporters do not like that language, but look at the enormity of the price tag that comes with Israel. From the Israeli perspective, granting Palestinians their rights is a threat to the state of Israel. So, for Israel to feel safe and secure in the region while denying Palestinians their rights, we in the U.S. must ensure that we never deal with the masses of the countries that surround it. We must ensure that we never deal with the masses of Egypt, Saudi Arabia, UAE, Oman, or Jordan. For if we were to deal with these masses, the results would be unpredictable. If the masses were to exercise their autonomous will, we could not predict what they would decide vis-à-vis Israel.

What, then, is the solution? It is in Israel's highest interest that countries such as Egypt, the UAE, and Saudi Arabia are ruled by tyrants who ignore the rights and the will of their own people in the same way that Israel ignores the rights and the will of the Palestinians. These tyrants adopt the same racist attitude toward their own people that Israel adopts toward the Palestinians, namely, "Shut up and do what you are told. Don't interfere with our quality of life." It does not matter what the Saudi, Egyptian, or Emirati people think or want. The only people who matter are the tyrants who have extensive connections with the so-called democracies in the West and, of course, with Israel.

The very dynamic of a colonial state is to never deal with the masses of the natives. It is to deny the natives a will of their own. For that would be truly dangerous. In a colonial dynamic, we can deal with Arabs as a racial category represented by tyrannical figures like Mohammed bin Salman (MBS) or Abdel Fattah el-Sisi. In a democratic model, however, we would be forced to deal with the Egyptian people, the Palestinian people, the Saudi people, and the Emirati people themselves. The will of these people, if represented through democratic institutions, would be layered and complex. Israel's life would become infinitely more complicated.

Step one, then, is to ensure that the UAE continues to be ruled by Mohamed bin Zayed, Saudi Arabia by MBS, and Egypt, a country of over one hundred million people, by Sisi. At every level, these are thoroughly disgusting human beings. They are criminals who should be tried for crimes against humanity. Look at the crimes these tyrants have committed. Each of them should be in prison. Instead, we want them to rule over their natives and package the will of their natives so that Benjamin Netanyahu does not have to worry about the Saudis, Egyptians, Emiratis, or Palestinians as actual human beings. Instead, the U.S. government thanks Sisi for his efforts in ending the conflict and bringing a ceasefire. We elevate and honor these criminals so that they represent the will of the faceless Muslim masses in dealing with the only people that matter—ourselves. We are willing to overlook what we know to be true: that each of these rulers are thoroughly corrupt, tyrannical, and would not stay in power for one day if there were real democratic institutions in their countries. We know they are criminals who torture, murder, and rape.

The racist dynamic is that Arabs and Muslims only matter to the extent that their actions affect Israel. But there is another price tag that comes with Israel. It is not enough to ensure that we deal with tyrants instead of the Emirati, Saudi, or Egyptian people. We in the U.S. must do something else. We must change the Islamic tradition itself. We must demand that Saudi Arabia changes its school curricula, which it did. We must demand that Egypt and the UAE change their school curricula, which they did. We must recast Islamic theology and Islamic history so that the impulse within Muslims to resist tyranny, resist occupation, and demand their rights is snuffed out.[118] We must sanitize Islam from any discourse on *jihad*. We must ensure that Muslims remain confused about the institution of the Caliphate. We must ensure that Muslims collectively remember the Ottoman Caliphate as oppressive and destructive, even if they possess no real knowledge either way. And we must ensure that Muslims are confused about the importance of Jerusalem in their history and theology.

---

118 For more on attempts by despotic leaders in the Muslim world to eliminate "resistance Islam" and the notion that modern Muslims have been colonized informationally and intellectually, see Abou El Fadl, *The Prophet's Pulpit—Vol. 1*, 107-117.

We now hear Egyptian, Saudi, and Emirati intellectuals repeat the Israeli propaganda that Muslims should apologize for the battles of the Prophet, that the Prophet acted wrongfully when he fought his battles, and that Muslims should apologize for the expansion of Islam during the Umayyad era.[119] The genesis of this is with Israeli intellectuals. What this means is that we, as Muslims, must apologize for Islamic Spain. We must apologize for conquering Sicily and Greece and for the fall of the Byzantine Empire. This line of propaganda has even recently extended to claiming that these conquests do not represent Islamic but rather Arab expansionism. So Arabs must apologize for conquering Persia. If you apologize for the expansion of Islam into Persia, the Byzantine empire, or Spain, it means the Islam that was brought to these countries was flawed from its genesis. Suddenly, Islam becomes an alien phenomenon to Persian society. Islam becomes an artificial phenomenon even to Egypt or to the Amazigh of North Africa. Where is Islam not an artificial phenomenon? In the heart of Arabia. Islam simply becomes an Arab religion in the same way that Judaism is an Israelite religion.

For this to happen, however, one must sanitize Islam's relationship to the one spot on earth that affirms the universality of Islam: Jerusalem. I often tell my students that Jerusalem is not the third holy site of Islam. Rather, it is the first holy site of Islam. Jerusalem affirms Islam as the universal religion of Abraham, Moses, and Jesus. It symbolizes the primordial message of Islam that long pre-dates the prophecy of Muhammad. It represents that Islam is a gift to humanity, and not simply an Arabian peculiarity.

Why do so many Muslims repeat the ridiculous Israeli propaganda that Jerusalem never mattered until one hundred and thirty

---

119 On the role of these so-called "intellectuals" in the Muslim world, see Abou El Fadl, *The Prophet's Pulpit—Vol. 1*, 112-114.

years after the death of the Prophet? The Companions of the Prophet made Jerusalem part of the Islamic legacy. They understood that Islam is the sole representative of pure monotheism. Christianity is not a monotheistic religion, no matter how much it claims otherwise. Judaism has been usurped by a racial identity and a tribal history. This is precisely why the Companions knew that Jerusalem belonged in Muslim hands. It is because Jerusalem has always represented true monotheism. Despite this, we find ignorant Muslims who say the "al-Aqsa Mosque" in the Qur'an (Q 17:1) could not be a reference to Jerusalem because there was no mosque at that time in Jerusalem. You only say this if you rely on Israeli propaganda. The historical record is clear and cumulative: the area in which the al-Aqsa Mosque was built was a place of worship that was neither Israelite nor Christian, but represented the monotheism of Abraham. This is the site that 'Umar ibn al-Khattab reclaimed and rebuilt. The Companions of the Prophet agreed, acting on the instructions of the Prophet, that this is the location of the al-Aqsa Mosque. There is no historical evidence that the Dome of the Rock was built on the ruins of the First or Second Jewish Temple. Since 1948, Israel has been digging and excavating to find archeological remains that would prove it is the location of the Second Temple. It has found nothing. We have no archaeological evidence for it. One would, in fact, doubt the Second Temple ever existed, if not for the fact that the Bible talks about it and the Qur'an alludes to it.

History matters. It is not an exaggeration to say that people without history are without an identity and without a future. Israeli propaganda seeks to deconstruct Islamic history and make Muslims doubt everything about their history in order to neutralize what it perceives to be "dangerous" Muslim sentiments. So it does not matter that generations of Muslims lived, died, fought, sacrificed, and became martyrs for Jerusalem. We are told by Israeli propaganda and by its agents in Egypt, the UAE, and Saudi Arabia that all these Muslim sacrifices were for nothing. That the Prophet was wrong when he brought Islam to Persia and out of Arabia. That the Companions were wrong to bring Islam to Jerusalem. That everything about Islamic history is wrong, including the notions of the Caliphate and the *Ummah*. That even Muslim holy sites can be Westernized and commercialized and turned into materialistic entities that are solely about money and luxury. We are told by Israeli propaganda that Muslims have no right to say anything about anything because global powers deal not with them, but with their tyrannical rulers. It does not matter whether the Saudi people like what has happened in Mecca because global powers deal with MBS. Global powers do not care whether the Egyptian people are hurt by ongoing events in Gaza for they deal with Sisi, who prohibits the raising of a Palestinian flag.

Do you see how tyranny itself is racist? Do you see how any Muslim who defends authoritarianism and tyranny is a racist against their own people? Whites and Israelis are entitled to democracy, human rights, and civilization. Muslims, meanwhile, are treated like cattle. We are entitled to work, consume, and be led like a herd. Do you see how this is deeply racist, and how you can be a racist against your own people without even knowing it? Do you see how it is racist to ignore all the sacrifices and say to Muslims, "What is the big deal about Jerusalem?" In other words, forget your history. Forget your Companions. Forget your Prophet. Forget everything and be happy because nightclubs and music concerts are opening. Nicki Minaj has been invited to perform.[120] There was even a wine-tasting competition in the UAE this Ramadan. Do you see how it is racist

120 See footnote 24. See also The Usuli Institute, *The Price of Silence, Nicki Minaj, and the U.S. Human Rights Commission* (*Khutbah*, 12 July 2019).

to tell Muslims that this should be their happiness, and that they should leave sovereignty for the White race?

Muslims are even told that they should not talk about politics because "political Islam" is bad. Political Judaism, also known as Zionism, is good. Political Christianity, as in the Christian Democrats in Germany or the neocons in the U.S., is good. But "political Islam" is bad. It is as if Muslims exist only to consume, not to be politically engaged. In other words, Muslims exist to be cattle, because the claim that "political Islam is bad" condemns Muslims to be nothing but a consuming herd. Human beings have an intellect. If they use their intellect to solve problems, they are being political. No matter how you dress it up in fancy academic language, the truth is that condemning "political Islam" is racist. To insist that Muslims live under tyranny, consume commodities, and do as they are told is racist. It is racist to leave the exercise of the sovereign will to the Israelis, Germans, British, Americans, and Danish, but not Muslims. It is racist to demand that Muslims accept nothing but tyranny so that the tyrants ruling over them can package them up and deliver their will to global powers so that these powers have no need to worry.

Do you see the racism inherent in attempts to neutralize Muslims by taking away their history and theology? "*Shari'a*" becomes a dirty word. "Caliphate" becomes a dirty word. "*Jihad*" becomes a dirty word.[121] There is nothing about Islam that is good. Muslims are only good when they buy and consume products. The clear message to Muslims is to wear *hijab*s, so long as their *hijab*s are made in China. Use prayer rugs, so long as they are made in China. Pray with prayer beads, so long as they are made in China. Get a *zabiba* (prayer mark) on your forehead from regular *sujud* (prostration), so

---

121 See Abou El Fadl, *The Prophet's Pulpit—Vol. 1*, 108–110, 189–190.

long as you have no sovereign or political will. So long as you do not scream "O al-Aqsa!" or say anything about anything that matters.

Why am I telling you this? Because wherever we turn, we find Muslim *imams* and teachers who are fooling Muslims and delivering them as a herd. Listen to Hamza Yusuf's statement on Palestine.[122] He begins with the usual pietistic affectations that distract and dilute. He starts with a long series of "*Subhanallahs*" and "*Alhamdullilahs*," saying nothing about anything. This introduction numbs the intellect with religious jargon. It is not unintentional. It is a way of signaling to the audience that they should turn off their intellects: "I am going to talk about Islam, and I do not want you thinking while I do so." When Hamza Yusuf finally gets to the point, he says that Jerusalem is a sacred city, violence in Jerusalem is bad, and we must pray for "peace." Wow! His Emirati masters have really done a job on him. There is no talk of the aggressor. No mention of the offender. No reference to the fact that Israel has confiscated almost all Palestinian territory since the Oslo Accords. No mention of Israeli settler attempts to attack, abuse, and evict Palestinians living in Sheikh Jarrah. No mention of the sewage water used against worshippers at al-Aqsa. No condemnation of the Israeli soldiers who arrested the *imam* of the al-Aqsa Mosque and repeatedly beat worshippers during Ramadan. No condemnation of the disproportionate response by Israel in bombing Gaza and destroying civilization infrastructure. Nothing.

Of course, as is typical, Hamza Yusuf later removed the video. Someone must have told him how bad it looked, how it clearly showed the extent to which he is part of a colonial project. So he removed it.

You will meet your Lord. When you do, I am sure that God will not ask if you followed the *Sunna* in your beard, *hijab, miswak*, or

---

122 See The Interpreter, *Hamza Yusuf on Latest War on Palestine (Ramadan 2021)* (YouTube, 3 June 2021).

perfume. God will not ask whether you entered the bathroom with your left foot and exited with your right foot. God will not ask about any of that. Rather, God will ask whether you followed the *Sunna* in upholding the dignity of the Prophet and the *Ummah*. Have you lived in ʿ*izza* (dignity)? Have you testified on God's behalf? Or have you betrayed everything and turned Islam into a colorless, odorless, and tasteless phenomenon that is solely about appearances and affectations? Of this, I am sure. I hope my fellow Muslims come to the same belief before it is too late.

21 May 2021

23

The Tyranny of the Nervous System and the Muslim Betrayal of the Uyghur Muslims

The challenge for Muslims and perhaps all human beings is to live a life anchored in Divine values. The values that God taught human beings are core to our moral existence. It is elementary, but necessary, to say that all beings have been given consciousness. The nervous system is part of this consciousness. It responds to stimuli and allows us to experience emotions. Some emotions are pleasant, others are unpleasant. This is the nature of consciousness and the nervous system. So many of God's creatures live and die, and that is the extent of their existence. These creatures were granted consciousness and a working nervous system that induced them to feel moments of pleasure and displeasure, only for it all to end as mysteriously as it began. Yet, a creature that is endowed with a reactive nervous system from the beginning to the end of its life is not worshipping God.

God tells us in the Qur'an, "I have only created human beings and *jinn* to worship Me" (Q 51:56). To worship is to reflect or ponder upon something. To worship God, according to Ja'far al-Sadiq (d. 148/765), is to come to know God. Coming to know God, however, does not mean that we simply intersperse ritual acts into our daily life. If rituals do not impact our nervous system, then the nervous system will not be guided. Ritual is not simply a time-filler. Ritual is not simply one of the many chores that we must perform to feel that we have a fully lived existence. To come to know God is to understand the attributes and characteristics of Divinity. It is to come to know the realm of values. Values are determinations about what is good and bad as a matter of principle, regardless of how it impacts our individual nervous system. To live according to values is to say, "Yes, I have a nervous system, but that nervous system does not define me as a human being. I am more than that. I am not simply an animal that responds to the stimuli of pleasure and pain."

To say "I am more than that" is to tell the nervous system, "I know certain things make you happy and others make you unhappy, but you, nervous system, are not me. I am something beyond you. I can think in terms of values and Divine objectives, and because I think, reflect, and comprehend the way I approach you, nervous system, I can tell you that your feelings about this matter are right, and your feelings about that matter are wrong."

This is stating the obvious, but the truth is often obvious. So many of us claim to believe. So many of us claim to be Muslim. So many of us even perform our rituals. Yet, values have little to do with what we feel and even less to do with how we conduct ourselves on a daily basis. The very point of values is to acknowledge that just because you feel something does not necessarily make it right. The very point of values is to demand that you live a principled life.

To worship God is to liberate the self from the tyranny of the senses. It is to not simply live as a slave to the ego; to what the ego demands, how and when it demands it. It is to live within the guiding light of your Lord, and your Lord has made the path of guidance so clear. God commands you first and foremost to pursue justice, goodness, and the ties of kinship. God commands you to steer away from all that is corrupt and immoral (Q 16:90). That is the Divine command. One of the names of God is "The Just" (*al-'Adl*), but justice requires a soul that responds to something other than the stimuli of the nervous system. If you do not care about justice, then there is simply no possible way that you care about your Lord. God has described God's own self as "Just" and informed us in no uncertain terms that we are charged with understanding and pursuing justice and goodness. God has willed for us the demands of a reflective life. It is remarkable that Muslims today are not at the forefront of discourses on justice, nor are they at the forefront of thinking about what a reflective and moral life means or looks like. Again, ritual is beautiful, but only if it is something other than a chore. Ritual is beautiful only if it affirms and strengthens the bond that you have with your Lord, and only if you understand the moral values of the Divine.

It is simply obscene for a person to perform rituals while, in all other regards, they simply respond to the stimuli of their nervous system, nothing more. Yet this applies to most people in our age. They can pray, but their prayer does not affect whether they are happy or sad. They can fast, but their fast does not affect how their nervous system responds to any situation. To them, rituals are simply acts.

Is this worship? Did God gaze upon us and say, "With all My Glory, I have created you so that I can see you five times a day standing up, bowing down, prostrating, then standing up"? Is this why God created us? Do you think that God created us and said, "What I care about is how many *tahmids* (praise) and *takbirs* (glorification of God) you say during the day, otherwise you can live in the heart of injustice, immorality, and ugliness"? This is an offense against Divinity itself. It makes the Divine so petty as to only care about optics such as beards and *hijabs*, the formulaic language of *tahmid* and *takbir*, and the physical movements of prostration. Did God create the magnanimity and complexity of the human intellect for us to imitate the optics of a bygone age? So many people think that living a reflective life means living a depressed and sad life. Nothing is further from the truth. Living a reflective life means living beyond the vagaries and tyranny of the nervous system, the way that it takes you up one moment and down the next. Living a reflective life means learning to find happiness and pleasure in the moral values of Divinity. It means learning to find happiness and pleasure every time you render aid, see goodness prevail, or do anything to help anyone. It is when you say, "Yes, that is what I was created for. That is what God wants me to do."

Since the colonial period, non-Muslims have carried the intellectual project of defining Muslims. The Western world has spoken of Muslim "fanatics," "extremists," "fundamentalists," "militants," "jihadists," and, most recently, of "political Islam." In these dynamics, Muslims are not defining themselves and thinking about their own theological orientations. Rather, it is non-Muslims who have gone beyond the trap of their nervous systems. It is non-Muslims with an intellectual project—a project that is, sadly, usually hostile toward Islam—who are defining Muslims for themselves. And because Muslims have been largely absent from the intellectual arena for much of recent history, we find that Muslims have followed these intellectual projects blindly, simply repeating what they are told.

When the West talks about "militants" in Islam, Muslims do the same. When the West talks about "jihadists," "extremists," and "fundamentalists" in Islam, Muslims do the same. Even when the West talks about "moderates" in Islam, Muslims do the same. And now, everywhere we turn, we find Muslims, like parrots, are repeating the language of "political Islam."

I have previously spoken about the incoherence of the concept of "political Islam."[123] Since then, God sent my way an example of the dangers of this incoherence. Last year, the Austrian government raided the homes of up to sixty prominent Muslims. There were no charges. There were no real accusations. The only accusation was that, in the eyes of the Austrian government, these Muslims could have followed "political Islam." More recently, the Austrian government decided to go beyond this and conduct several surveys. It first created The Documentation Center for Political Islam, which surveyed all mosques in Austria and decided that six hundred mosques—almost all the mosques in the country—were frequented by practitioners of so-called "political Islam." It does not stop there. The same center then published a map of these mosques in Austria. The Austrian government erected signs at each of these six hundred mosques that feature an image of an angry-looking Arab man with the warning: "This is a dangerous area because 'political Islam' is present."[124] Of course, since the government did this, bigoted attacks against Muslims in Austria have skyrocketed. Throughout it all, no one truly understands the Austrian government's definition of "political Islam." The Center is, of course, staffed with Islamophobes. But this

---

123 See The Usuli Institute, *The Qur'anic Impulse and the Fallacy of Political Islam* (*Khutbah*, 4 June 2021). Also see Chapter 22: *Why Jerusalem Matters* in this volume.
124 See "Anger as Racist Signboards Erected Close to Vienna Mosques," *TRT World* (2 June 2021).

is the nature of the thing. Any mosque that opposed the banning of the *hijab* in Austrian primary schools was branded as "political Islam." Any mosque that called for reasonable accommodations at work for Ramadan was branded as "political Islam." Any mosque that was unhappy with Israeli actions in the West Bank and Gaza was branded as "political Islam." Any mosque that said anything about Jerusalem was branded as "political Islam."

People like me know what the label "political Islam" has done in countries like the UAE, Saudi Arabia, and Egypt. These are countries in which anyone, at any time, if they say the wrong word, look the wrong way, or fight with someone connected to the military or police is immediately accused of "political Islam." They are promptly arrested and disappeared. This is the nature of a people who have delegated the task of thinking for themselves to others. When Muslims lose sight of the obvious point that God commands us to pursue justice and goodness (Q 16:90), forget what that means, and come to believe that Islam is all about optics, prayer, and fasting, they get defined by the other. When you get defined by the other, this is the world that you create.

Who would have imagined that Austria, a country that after World War II was imagined as a bastion of democracy and civil liberties, has turned out to be so fragile when it came to the racial challenge of dealing with the Muslim other? I can at least understand this intolerance toward the Muslim other. I do not forgive, but I understand. What I cannot understand, however, are those among us who raise the next generation of Muslims just as they were raised: unintelligent, uneducated, and oblivious. How can we raise intelligent Muslims if we teach our children, "Be a Muslim, but do not be a political Muslim"? Before you use this kind of language, ask yourself who defines the language. When it comes to "political

Islam," it is Islamophobes in the U.S. who define the language. Racists and bigots in the French and Austrian governments define the language. The fascist ruler of Egypt, Sisi, defines the language. The psychotic rulers of Saudi Arabia and the UAE define the language. You are using language that is defined, utilized, and circulated by bigots, racists, and psychotic tyrants.

The least we can do as Muslims is teach our children to think for themselves and to live reflective lives. Lives in which they pursue meaning. Lives in which ritual helps them to achieve meaning. Lives in which they are not distracted from the pursuit of meaning. That is the least we can do.

I want to share the opening of an article about our Muslim brothers and sisters in China. It relates to what happened to a Uyghur family in Dubai. The article reads as follows:

Amannisa Abdullah and her husband, Ahmad Talip, were on their way to shop for baby clothes in Dubai when the message that changed both their lives came through. Ahmad read it and announced an abrupt change of plan: He had to report to a police station immediately. Ahmad dropped Amannisa off at a friend's house that day, promising to pick her up later, but Ahmad never came back. In their Dubai apartment, a sleepless Amannisa prayed and cried through the night, watching the hours pass as her repeated calls to Ahmad went unanswered. The next morning, the heavily pregnant 29-year-old shuffled out of the door, hugging her five-year-old son close. They hailed a taxi to the police station where she tried to explain her predicament to a police officer. As she spoke, her little boy tugged at her hand. Quietly, he pointed towards a jail cell where Ahmad was sitting.

*For 13 days, Amannisa shuttled back and forth between
her home and the jail, pleading with law enforcement in
Dubai to release Ahmad. With each visit, her husband
looked more dejected. He told her he was convinced that
the long reach of China had reached his Uyghur family in
the United Arab Emirates. "It's not safe here. You must
take our boy and go to Turkey," he told Amannisa in their
last conversation. "If our new baby is a girl, please call her
Amina. If it is a boy, please call him Abdullah." A week
later, Ahmad was sent to the UAE capital in Abu Dhabi.
Five days later, Amannisa said the Abu Dhabi authorities
told her that he had been extradited to China. Ahmad went
to a concentration camp where he never reappeared.*[125]

This is from a news article about how Uyghur Muslims are
extradited from the UAE to China so that China can place them in
concentration camps where they are forced to eat pork, drink alcohol,
and learn Mandarin Chinese. Even if they survive or their organs
are not harvested, their sense of Islam is wiped out.[126] Ahmad Talip,
of course, is not the exception. The UAE has long been sending to
China any Uyghur who visits Dubai or Abu Dhabi.

Egypt has rounded up Uyghur students studying at al-Azhar
and forcibly sent them back to China, where they disappear into
concentration camps.[127] These are fellow Muslims who escaped to

---

125 See Jomana Karadsheh and Gul Tuysuz, "Uyghurs are Being Deported From Muslim
Countries, Raising Concerns About China's Growing Reach," *CNN* (8 June 2021).

126 For more on reports of organ harvesting of Muslims detained by China, See
Abou El Fadl, *The Prophet's Pulpit—Vol. 1*, 19, n. 12 and 74, n. 32.

127 See "'Nightmare' as Egypt aided China to detain Uighurs," *France 24* (18 August
2019) and Areeb Ullah, "Egypt aided Chinese officials to detain and 'interrogate'
Uighur students," *Middle East Eye* (18 August 2019).

a Muslim country and enrolled at al-Azhar to become theologians and jurists! The Egyptian government sent them back to China to be destroyed. There has not been a word of protest or condemnation from the Rector of al-Azhar.

It does not stop there. The Saudis have seized Uyghur Muslims performing *hajj* or *ʿumrah* and handed them over to the Chinese government.[128] If you are a Uyghur living in the U.S., Europe, or Turkey, do not go to Saudi Arabia for pilgrimage. You are at risk of being arrested and turned over to the Chinese government. In the same way that the Egyptian government has long blockaded and strangled Gaza to death, Muslims are now complicit in handing over disempowered and helpless Uyghur Muslims to the Chinese government so that the Chinese government can kill them off.

What do you think God will do with a people like that? People tell me that I am too pessimistic. My response is simple: do you want me to lie to God? I know there are Muslim brothers and sisters whose misfortune is that they are Uyghurs who have been seized and turned over to concentration camps by their fellow Muslims. Look at what Jewish communities have done about the plight of their fellow Jews in concentration camps, and then look at what Muslims are doing. Muslim governments are fully complicit in the genocide committed against the Uyghur Muslims. The immorality and evil of these governments must be recognized.

It cannot be that a so-called *imam* like Hamza Yusuf has a cozy relationship with the UAE. We cannot listen to those *imams* who enjoy a close relationship with the Saudis. We cannot listen to those *imams* who ignore the immorality and criminal conduct of the Egyptian government. We cannot simply do whatever we want,

---

128 See Jilil Kashgary, "Four Uyghurs Facing Persecution After Deportation by Saudi Arabia to China Identified," *Radio Free Asia* (16 October 2020).

whatever makes us feel warm and fuzzy, simply responding to the call of our nervous systems, instead of living principled and moral lives that recognize right from wrong. Sending people to perish in concentration camps is wrong. Being friendly with governments that do so is wrong. And being friendly with those who are friendly with these governments is also wrong. I have given up on people like Hamza Yusuf. I do not think they will ever wake up. But how about you? If you do not recognize immorality, then you are immoral. It is as simple as that. Are you a moral or an immoral human being?

American Muslims often choose to be silent. When the devil is present, however, and you do not have the nerve to acknowledge him as the devil, then you are also a devil.[129] If you choose to remain silent, then you are part of an immoral enterprise. You are immoral. If you want to call this "political Islam," do so. But if you want to call this "moral Islam" or "ethical Islam," that is my terminology. For there is no other type of Islam. It is either an Islam that makes ethical sense, or it is not Islam at all.

11 June 2021

---

129 See footnote 51.

24

Intimacy with God and the Truth of the World Laid Bare

There are those who understand that their relationship with God, their Lord, is the most personal thing in the universe. It is the most central and valuable thing. It cannot be replicated, compared, or reproduced. The relationship of a believer with their Maker is extremely personal. It is as individual as our genetic code, or even more so. It is the most truthful, honest, and sincere thing in existence. Yet, at the same time, it is the thing we most easily falsify. It is the most easily ignored, corrupted, and misunderstood thing in our existence. God reminds us that God is closer to us than our jugular vein (Q 50:16). Wherever we are, God is with us. Try to exist anywhere without your jugular vein. If you are stressed, excited, or moved, the first thing you feel is the flow of blood in your body. Our existence with God can be as intimate and personal as the flow of blood in our bodies. The remarkable thing is that our blood does not have a choice as it flows through our veins, but we do have a choice whether we acknowledge God in our spirit, in our intellect, and in the very flow of our blood.

Remarkably, so many people choose an escape route. They objectify their relationship with their Maker into a set of laws. They imagine that God is reducible to a set of hard and fast truths. They make their relationship with God solely about prayers, fasting, and other certain acts that define and bracket the role of God. They are, of course, delusional. They live the heart of a lie. God cannot be locked within simple performative acts. We cannot lie to God. If you do not feel God's company, then you cannot lie to God and say, "Indeed, I feel Your company." If you do not acknowledge God's constant presence in all your affairs—in the very breath you take, in every move, every thought, and in every molecule that surrounds you—then you cannot claim otherwise to God. The blood that flows within does not flow sometimes and stop flowing at other times. God is more intimate, more essential, and more pervasive than the blood that flows within.

We either choose to live in the full gaze of this truth, dealing with the challenges of this truth, or we deceive ourselves. There is no deceiving God. We either choose to live in the full gaze of this truth, or we acknowledge God's constant presence only when it suits us, when we are tested, or when the mood takes us there.

Blessed are those who testify to the truth of their Lord. For we live in a truly challenging world. We live in a world in which a Muslim must be anchored and fully conscious of their personal relationship with their Maker. We live in a world that, through centuries of malfeasance, negligence, error, and ignorance, challenges the intellect and soul of every Muslim, at every moment. In this world, Muslims need to be fully aware that their relationship with God is not contingent or somehow derivative. It depends not on what other human beings, especially other Muslims, do. If you lose sight of the fact that your relationship with God is fully your own, and allow for the contingencies of this world, especially the actions of other Muslims, to influence you and perhaps even define your relationship with God, then you have fallen in the abyss of *fitna*. The Prophet warned us about *fitna*. In a typically misogynistic way, however, we have made *fitna* all about women. Or, in a typically oligarchical way, we have made *fitna* about those who rebel against unjust rulers. However, *fitna* is what alienates you from your Lord. It is all the things that make you unable to feel God. From this, all types of unhealthy things unfold.

Recent events involving the Russian invasion of Ukraine have been among the most challenging in my life. These events present us with a hard truth. These events are like an act from God, stripping bare the truth of the world we live in and confronting us with an ugly picture—but only for those who see. At a basic level, as I touched upon in my last *khutbah*, these events reveal an uncompromisingly racist world.[130] Someone sent me an email about my last *khutbah*, agreeing that the coverage of Ukraine is racist, sharing clips from various news agencies. On *NBC*, someone commented on events in Ukraine, saying, "These are not refugees from Syria. They are Christian and White," implying that our response should be different. On the *BBC*, someone said, "These are European people with blue eyes and blond hair who are being killed." On *Al Jazeera*, someone said, "These are prosperous middle class European people, not refugees from the Middle East. They look just like those who live next door to us." On *CBS*, someone said, "This is not Iraq or Afghanistan. This is

---

130 See The Usuli Institute, *The Plight of the Individual and the Sunna of the Maker* (*Khutbah*, 25 February 2022).

a civilized and European country." Yes, these events expose an amazingly racist Europe.[131]

It is not just the different response to refugees from Ukraine as opposed to those from Syria. It is not just the fact that Romanian and Polish authorities have forced African, Middle Eastern, and Asian students who are studying in Ukraine and fleeing the war to give up their seats to White Ukrainians, and further mistreat these students at the border. There have been many reports of mistreatment.

It is not only this clear racial discrimination. It is the very narrative itself. When it comes to so-called civilized, Christian, White, blue-eyed, and blond-haired people, we recognize and celebrate that they love and heroically defend their country. We do not do what we did in Bosnia, imposing a weapons embargo that allowed the Serbs to slaughter Bosnian Muslims with ease. We do not do what we did in Iraq and Afghanistan, describing those who resist the occupation of their country as "fanatics" and "extremists." We do not say, "Why are they resisting? We are there to civilize them, after all." This is typical colonial discourse. It is deeply racist. But it is not only this. Remember that we criminalized any Muslim who thought to come to the aid of their fellow Muslims in Iraq, Afghanistan, or anywhere. This includes any Muslim who thought to volunteer to fight the Russians in Syria or join the resistance in Chechnya or Kashmir. All those Muslims who thought of coming to the aid of their fellow Muslims ended up in prisons, on designated watchlists, or in Guantanamo. All such Muslims were designated as "terrorists." People endlessly wrote books about the dangers of "*jihadi* ideology."

Meanwhile, amid reports that volunteers from all over the Western world are traveling to Ukraine to fight, we clap and admire. There

---

131 See H. A. Hellyer. "Coverage of Ukraine Has Exposed Long-Standing Racist Biases in Western Media," *The Washington Post* (28 February 2022).

is no talk of "Christian fanaticism." There are no documentaries about the role of Jesus for those who volunteer for war. There are no reports about those who believe that if they die fighting the Russians, they die as martyrs with Jesus at the gates of heaven to receive them. There is none of that. It is as if we are living in the heart of the 18th and 19th centuries, surrounded by such blatant, bare-faced racism.

To be clear, I am not offended by how we are standing up for Ukraine. But I *am* offended that we do not apply the same standards for Palestine, Iraq, Afghanistan, or any other Muslim population. When it comes to Muslims and Muslim countries, we see typical colonial and racist tropes. A good Muslim is a Muslim who informs upon their own people. A good Muslim is a Muslim who is ashamed of their fellow Muslims. A good Muslim is a Muslim who recognizes that they are fundamentally flawed. A good Muslim is, essentially, a traitor to their own people. These are not, of course, the standards we apply to Ukraine.

Even this is not the true *fitna*. It is old news that we live in a racist, colonial, and imperial world that has not changed in centuries. God has simply allowed the masks to slip, if only Muslims would notice and learn. The true *fitna* is what all this exposes and says about us.

Look at how Europe reacted to the situation in Ukraine. As I saw the reaction of Britain, France, the Netherlands, and Germany, my mind went to the *hadith* of the Prophet that states that the Muslim *Ummah* is a single body; if one part is hurt, the entire body reacts.[132] Article V of the North Atlantic Treaty, the founding treaty of NATO, states that to attack one member is an attack against all. There is a discussion that Ukraine is not, technically, a member of NATO.

---

132 Al-Bukhari (6011) and Muslim (2586).

But if you dare to attack any member of NATO, then all bets are off. Did they attend a seminary in Qom, Najaf, or al-Azhar to learn this? Where did they learn how to translate what the Prophet said about the unity of a single *Ummah*? These are non-believers declaring *jihad*, coming to the aid of their fellow non-believers.

The real *fitna* is that, suddenly, all the pretense that political realism governs international relations, not ideology, has come to an end. Major businesses immediately withdrew from Russia, taking huge financial losses. Companies rushed to announce that they were divesting from Russia. What happened to political realism and pragmatism? Here we see thoroughly ideological people acting at a thoroughly ideological level. They are prepared to sacrifice and take huge financial losses because of what they believe in. Disney has canceled the release of movies. Facebook has decided to withdraw. European sports teams have refused to play Russian teams. Artists have canceled their performances. I then think back to us, Muslims. When the UAE announced that it would have sporting events with the Israelis, we asked, "What about Jerusalem and the Palestinians?" and were told by a chorus of Muslim pseudo-intellectuals that it is "uncivilized" to mix politics with sports; politics is one thing, sports another. When we talked about imposing financial sanctions against those who support the annexation of Jerusalem, we were lectured ad nauseam about political realism; how politics is one thing, business another. We were told that only "religious fanatics" and "fundamentalists" do not understand the world of political realism.

The entire world expresses outrage about what is happening in Ukraine and rushes to divest from Russia, throwing realpolitik out the window. On Ukraine, the entire world says, "We are about principles. Even if you raise the price of oil or wheat, we stand for principles. We may lose money, but we stand by principles." But at the same time, when it comes to Jerusalem and al-Aqsa, the entire world says, "Be realistic. Civilized people are about political realism."

What are we going to say to God, who is closer to us than our jugular vein? Compare the reaction of non-believing Europeans toward their fellow non-believers in Ukraine with the reaction of Muslims toward their fellow Muslims in Palestine, Myanmar, Bosnia, China, and Kashmir. If that does not wake you up, then, in my view, there is no hope for you as a Muslim. If this does not shape your world, if it does it make you say, "*Alhamdullilah* that I lived to see the lies exposed in my lifetime," then there is no hope for you as a Muslim.

Banks divest not because of political realism, but because of principle—the type of principled action that we, Muslims, could not bring to bear for al-Aqsa. I have lost faith in Muslim institutions and organizations. I have lost faith in al-Azhar and every institution like it. I am now at a point of certitude about the *fisq* (immorality) and *fujur* (depravity) of every government in the Muslim world. I have even lost faith in law, because law is the refuge of the hypocrite and the cowardly. Everyone who wants to feel like a good Muslim finds refuge in the law. So long as they follow the law, they can ignore the foul corruption and stink of their soul. It stinks to high heaven, but it does not matter, so long as they can hide behind the ostentation of the law.

What was the response of these Muslim institutions when Muslims talked about boycotting France after it insulted the Prophet? "Be civilized. Think of freedom of speech." Freedom of speech! Europe has just banned *RT*, the Russian news agency, from broadcasting in Europe because of its offensive lies. Where are all those who lecture Muslims ad nauseam about the need to respect freedom of speech? We hear not a peep from them.

We live in a world in which the UAE abstained from condemning the invasion of Ukraine in the U.N. Security Council, which upset the U.S. But the U.S. knew it did not carry as much weight with the UAE as the Israelis. The White House asked Israel to speak to the UAE to get the UAE not to abstain in the General Assembly vote against the invasion of Ukraine. This is why the UAE voted to condemn the invasion in the General Assembly, but not in the Security Council.[133] Israel! Not values. Not principles. Not fellow Muslims. Not even America, but Israel.

One media channel showed a report about a brave Ukrainian child who stood up to a Russian soldier, hurling insults at the Russian soldier and even threatening to punch him. As I watched this, it triggered something in my memory. "Where have I seen this image before?" Lo and behold, God sent an article my way that nearly made me cry. I was right. There was a Palestinian girl, Ahed Tamimi, who, when she was 11 years old, in 2012, challenged an Israeli soldier. This same girl was later sentenced to prison in Palestine. Of course, the world did not care about her as an 11-year-old Palestinian challenging an Israeli. The world did not care about her when she was later thrown in prison. The world only cared about usurping the image of a brave child against a fully armed soldier, co-opting it for Ukraine, not Palestine.[134] Why can the forces of lies and deception do that? It is because Muslims sit idly by, arguing about law, hiding behind law, camouflaging behind law. It is because Muslims see immorality but do not stand up to the immorality of their fellow Muslims. It is because Muslims are very good at saying, "Brothers

---

133 See Ali Abbas Ahmadi, "UAE does about turn and finally condemns Russian invasion of Ukraine," *The New Arab* (3 March 2022).

134 See Peter Oborne, "Let's Call Out the West's Bias Over Ukraine for What it is - Blatant Racism," *Middle East Eye* (1 March 2022).

and sisters, donate to help us build the *masjid* (mosque)." That is what Muslims are good for. But will Muslims build the type of institutions that empower the truth and speak truth to power? No. Instead, we build *masjids*, so that we can segregate women to one side and men to the other side.

It is remarkable that when an 11-year-old Palestinian girl challenged an Israeli soldier in 2012, no one admired the nationalism of Palestinians. No one cared about how Palestinians love freedom and their homeland. When the same girl was jailed a few years later, no one cared. She is not White. She is not Christian. She *is* blue-eyed and blonde, incidentally, so she "passes." So the world can steal her image and leverage it, knowing that they can get away with it, because Muslims do not matter.

Another article tells us that since President Biden came to power in 2021, Israel has demolished over 1,000 Palestinian homes.[135] More demolitions have taken place since Biden came to power than during the entire Trump era. Trump is complicit, of course, because without his decision to move the U.S. Embassy and force "the deal of the century," and without Jared Kushner and his foul friendship with Mohammed bin Salman (MBS), none of this would have been possible. Nevertheless, Israel has demolished more than 1,000 homes since Biden came to power, and what is the reaction of Saudi Arabia, the "Guardian of the Two Holy Sites"? Nothing. It is to seek closer relations with Israel. What is the reaction of Egypt? Nothing. Sisi praises the Israelis at every turn. What is the reaction of other Muslims? Israel has a peace treaty with Sudan, Morocco, Oman, Bahrain, and the mother of them all, the UAE, a country that cannot get into bed quickly enough with any force that is hostile to Muslims and Islam.

---

135 See Austin Ahlman, "Israel Surpasses 1,000 Demolitions in the Occupied West Bank Since Joe Biden Took Office," *The Intercept* (25 February 2022).

What truly breaks my heart is this: do those on the payroll of the UAE in the West feel any blowback from their fellow Muslims about being agents of a country that has dedicated itself to the deconstruction of Muslim causes everywhere, from China, to India, to Jerusalem? No. They can live on the payroll of the UAE. They can enjoy UAE largesse. They can pretend to be pious Muslims, and their popularity is not affected one iota. Tell me: how does that affect your personal relationship with God? To the Muslims who admire the scholars and *imams* who have sold their souls to the UAE: how does this affect your personal relationship with God? May God protect us from the *fitna*.

I talked in my last *khutbah* about a man named Adnan Ibrahim.[136] Listen to the lectures this man gave in 2011 and 2012. He condemned the dictators of Egypt and Saudi Arabia and spoke about how authoritarianism and dictatorship have corrupted the soul of Islam. Fast forward to today, and something has happened that caused him to sell himself to the Saudis and the UAE. He now praises MBS and Mohamed bin Zayed (MBZ). He used to praise the scholarship of Hasan Farhan al-Maliki. Since the imprisonment of al-Maliki, however, Ibrahim has not said a word. This is even though he lives in Vienna, not in the UAE or Saudi Arabia. You cannot but wonder what happened. Are they blackmailing him somehow? Is it just about cash? If so, why do so many Muslims sell out for cash? Is it because the law allows them the comfort of deception and camouflage? Is it because they can hide behind the law and pretend that they are good Muslims?

As I watched old videos of Adnan Ibrahim on YouTube, I was struck by how many commercials kept interrupting these videos.

---

136 See The Usuli Institute, *The Plight of the Individual and the Sunna of the Maker* (*Khutbah*, 25 February 2022).

What appeared in video after video was a commercial by an organization called Know The Truth, which is, amazingly, a missionary organization dedicated to converting Muslims to Christianity. These commercials are well-produced and well-financed. They look extremely professional. They feature people who claim to have been Muslim who then saw the light of Jesus and converted to Christianity. Look at the level of insult. Are we so powerless, so ineffective in this world? It is already problematic that a missionary group dedicated to converting Muslims to Christianity—its content consisting of people testifying to the evils of Islam—is all over YouTube. But for this group to invade the space of internal Muslim discourses and for Muslims, including those responsible for Adnan Ibrahim's channel, to be either unaware or unable to do anything about it, is absurd. It is a true *fitna*.

I watched every video on Know the Truth's site. I listened to the testimony of those who claim to have been Muslim who converted to Christianity. The amazing thing is that I can imagine its impact upon Muslims who are simply exhausted by the lies, the hypocrisy, and the weakness. The common theme is not a rational and deep discourse about the mystery and nature of the Trinity. No video addresses anything of substance. Rather, all they talk about, in video after video, is how "Jesus loves us" and how, "As a Muslim, I was unhappy, but when I met Christians, they loved on me." I have researched this idea. Like so many Muslims who convert to Christianity, they did not do their homework. They do not understand that missionaries are taught that the way to convert Muslims is to "love on them." You find this in missionary manuals on how to convert Muslims. It is not out of the generosity of their heart. It is not a natural impulse. It is, in fact, a training technique. When they find a Muslim, they are told, "Pour love on them. Give them food. Give them gifts. Constantly ask about them. Constantly call and text them. Do everything. Pour it on." In every video, I heard the same thing. "As a Muslim, I could not feel God. But then Jesus and the Holy Spirit came upon me, and I am so happy now because Jesus is always with me. Jesus loves me." Jesus, of course, lets the Palestinians, Uyghurs, and Rohingya suffer no end. Jesus does not seem to have much love for those who are not his followers. Nor does he seem bothered by the hypocrisy, racism, and colonialism of his missionaries.

This is precisely why your *iman* is such a personal thing. If your *iman* is affected by what the UAE or Adnan Ibrahim do, by the imprisonment of Hasan Farhan al-Maliki, by the ugliness and hypocrisy of MBS and MBZ, then you have been walking down the wrong path. That is not what a relationship with God is about. My heart can break as I see the way Muslims have betrayed al-Aqsa and Jerusalem. It enrages me. It angers me. I may even cry about it. But it does not touch my *iman,* just as the existence of viruses and bacteria all around me does not make me scared of my own blood.

My relationship to my blood is so intimate and so personal. It is what sustains me. It is what gives me life. My relationship with God is even more personal, more essential, and more unique. I do not hide behind law. Discharging or violating the law does not define my relationship with God. What defines my relationship with God is the way that I feel God within, in every heartbeat, in every thought. It is the way I truly feel God's step next to mine, feel God's breath with my breath, in every second, in every instant. In an age of deception, when we steal the images of brave Palestinian girls; in an age of hypocrisy, when we cry for some people because they are blond and White, while ignoring the misery of others; in an age of treachery, when scholars sell their souls for money and prestige; in an age of true *fitna*, we must hurry up and discover our personal relationship with God. For if we do not, the *fitna* will soon catch up with us.

4 March 2022

25

Why Despair Is Not an Option

Life on earth only makes sense if it is a temporary abode with ultimate consequences, an abode that has been ordained by something bigger, something that understands its objectives and purposes. It is very tempting to lose sight of the fact that this is a purposeful existence that is measured by justice. For justice to be the premise of existence, there must be a Lord and Creator, a Maker and Owner. Otherwise, we live in a whimsical, purposeless, and pointless world in which all is fair game; there are no morals, no values, and no virtues. A world in which nothing, ultimately, makes sense.

We have just passed the twenty-fifth anniversary of the Srebrenica massacre in Bosnia in which 8,000 Muslims were killed.[137] This was but one massacre in a war that saw the slaughter of thousands of Muslims. The saddest thing is that the Bosnian genocide became

---

137 The Srebrenica Massacre took place between 11–22 July 1995. This massacre of Bosnian Muslims by Serb forces occurred in a U.N. declared "safe zone" and in the presence of U.N. peacekeepers. It was the bloodiest episode in Europe's most recent genocide.

simply a prelude to a whole number of massacres against Muslims. The Bosnian genocide was a harbinger. It was a clarion call for the birth of what we now know as Islamophobia.

What produced the Bosnian genocide was a sustained racist discourse about Muslims as a dangerous other. Muslims were seen as possessing alien qualities that were incompatible with civilized existence. This is the thesis of Muslim exceptionalism. During the birth of what we now identify as Islamophobia, this genre of racism was directed at Muslims. Muslims, as a religious group, were given specific racial attributes. They were then demonized in a systematic way. The saddest thing is that instead of the Srebrenica massacre becoming a turning point for the world to wake up to the danger, ugliness, and genocidal tendencies of Islamophobia, we find, twenty-five years later, that Islamophobia has in fact exploded. It has swept the entire world. In addition to the Bosnian genocide, we are now witnessing the plight of the Rohingya, Uyghur, and Kashmiri Muslims. Islamophobia has only become more firmly rooted in the world. It has managed to weave itself into the mainstream. It presents itself as an intellectualized discourse, camouflaging its racism and fooling a good number of intellectuals and otherwise decent people. But it gets even worse than this. What is worse is that many of the theses and premises of Islamophobia, and even much of the racism, has come to be internalized by Muslims themselves.

Just because you belong to a racialized and oppressed minority does not mean that you cannot be a racist yourself. Many people do not realize this. Simply put, it is possible for a Black person to be racist against his or her own race. It is possible for an Asian person to be racist against his or her own race. And it is also possible for a Muslim to become a racist, to racialize Islam and then adopt bigoted, stereotypical, and superficial attitudes toward that Islam.

Sadly, much of the racist, bigoted, and stereotypical discourse of Islamophobia has come to be adopted and repeated by Muslims themselves. These Muslims are oblivious to the racial and ignorant overtones of what they are saying. We see this when Muslims who hardly know anything about Islamic history—for most Muslims know nothing about Islamic history—repeat claims about the role of despotism in Islam, tarnishing the entire Muslim experience as a despotic experience. We see this when Muslims say that Muslims are not yet ready for democracy or cannot coexist with liberty. These Muslims do not realize the extent to which they are bigoted and racist against their own selves.

Twenty-five years since Srebrenica, so much more Muslim blood has been shed. The moral issue of Islamophobia and racism has worsened. It is as if the blood spilled in genocides and massacres has only whetted the appetite of human beings around the world to become even more racist and more bigoted. In my view, however, the worst is when we find that racism or Islamophobia has penetrated to the heart of the Muslim world. Much of what we hear coming out of countries like Egypt, Saudi Arabia, or the UAE is resoundingly Islamophobic, racist, and ignorant.[138]

You may be tempted in this situation to adopt an air of pessimism and despair. You may be tempted to say, "Things keep going from bad to worse. It does not seem like we can make a difference." This is precisely why I begin this *khutbah* by reminding all of us, including myself, that justice is the premise of this world. For God is the premise of this world, and God is justice. For a Muslim, despair is not an option. Despair is an attitude of *kufr* because despair is premised on an attitude that things cannot be changed, although they ought to be

---

138 For more on internalized racism and Islamophobia within Muslim cultures, see Abou El Fadl, *The Prophet's Pulpit – Vol. 1*, 101–117 and 188–194.

changed. That takes God out of the equation, the Owner and Maker of all who, if God so willed, would change everything in an instant.

Throughout the Qur'an, God reminds the Prophet Muhammad of the stories and legacies of other prophets. But I have always been struck by the fact that the first prophet that God ever mentions to the Prophet Muhammad is Jonah (Q 68:48-50). One would think, logically, that it would perhaps be Adam, Noah, or even Abraham. We are called "Muslims" because of the Prophet Abraham (Q 22:78). Or it would be the prophet of the law, Moses. Or the Prophet Jesus, who was closest in time to the Prophet Muhammad. Instead, the first prophet that God mentions is Jonah in Surah al-Qalam, one of the earliest revelations in the Qur'an. More specifically, God tells the Prophet Muhammad to *not* be like the "companion of the fish" (Q 68:48), a reference to Jonah. God then gives a brief reminder of the story of the Prophet Jonah, with an emphasis to the Prophet Muhammad to reflect upon the lessons from the legacy of Jonah.

> *So be patient with thy Lord's Judgment and be not like*
> *the companion of the fish, who cried out while choking*
> *with anguish. Had not the blessing from his Lord*
> *reached him, he would surely have been cast upon the*
> *barren shore still blameworthy. But his Lord chose him*
> *and made him among the righteous. (SQ 68:48-50)*

What is the moral behind the story of the Prophet Jonah that makes it so pressing for the Prophet Muhammad, for us, and for humanity forever?

Remember that this is at the very beginning of the Qur'anic revelation. The Prophet has a long road of persecution and suffering ahead of him. He will face at least a decade of suffering in Mecca, a migration to Medina, and then another decade of intense persecution. God is preparing the Prophet for this long road ahead, and God chooses to first instruct the Prophet Muhammad with the legacy of the Prophet Jonah.

The most credible reports say that Jonah was an Israelite prophet sent to an area that is now in Mosul, in Nineveh, Iraq, during the Assyrian dynasty. Reportedly, he spent a very long time—we do not know how long exactly—inviting the people of Nineveh to the path of truth, to believe in one God, abandon the worship of idols, and refrain from the unjust and oppressive practices that were the hallmark of Assyrian culture and laws. There are reports in the Torah that the Assyrians persecuted the Israelites and that Jonah sought for the Assyrians to scale back their oppressive and racist practices against the Israelites. The Torah, however, makes everything about the Israelites. In Islam, Jonah is portrayed as a universal prophet just like Jesus, Moses, and all the prophets. Jonah finds the people of Nineveh unresponsive and unreceptive. Very few people follow him and respond to his call for justice, decency, morality, and truth. Like the Islamophobes of today, the people of Nineveh become even more hostile. There are those who, when you call them to their conscience, become even more defiant and augment their bad behavior.

Eventually, Jonah gives up. Depending on the report we read, either Jonah prays to God to punish the people of Nineveh and God answers the prayer, saying that they will be destroyed in three days, or God decides that the people of Nineveh will be destroyed and informs the Prophet Jonah. In any case, Jonah receives notice that the people of Nineveh will be destroyed and decides to leave. The Qur'an profoundly describes the scene. This is in Surah al-Anbiya':

And [remember] Dhu'l-Nun, when he went away in
anger, and thought We had no power over him. Then
he cried out in the darkness, "There is no god but
Thee! Glory be to Thee! Truly I have been among the
wrongdoers." So We answered him, and saved him from
grief. Thus do We save the believers. (SQ 21:87-88).

"Dhu'l-Nun" means "the man of the whale," an epithet for Jonah.
Jonah is angry, upset, and leaves the people of Nineveh. At that
point, he boards a ship to get as far away from Nineveh as possible,
having lost hope in its people. The people on the ship, through rumor
and reputation, recognize Jonah as a stranger, a monotheist. They
do not recognize him as a prophet. The ship is then hit by a storm.
According to the customs of the age, people would offer sacrifices to
the gods during trials and tribulations, hoping that the gods would
provide relief, in this case by allowing them to survive the storm.
Those onboard the ship therefore decide to throw the Prophet Jonah
overboard to drown in the ocean. When Jonah is thrown overboard,
a whale appears in the ocean and swallows him. Jonah remains in
the belly of the whale for a period (Q 37:139-148). One day? Two
or three? One week? No one knows. Through a miracle of God,
however, Jonah survives and is eventually expelled from the belly
of the whale onto a seashore (Q 37:145-6).

The crux of the matter is this: when Jonah is swallowed by the
whale, he recognizes, at that point, that he erred. He realizes that
he did something wrong and that he is now expiating for his sin.
He utters a famous *du'a'*: "God, there is no God but You. Praised,
be You. I have been among the unjust" (Q 21:87).

What was the sin of Prophet Jonah? Why did he need to be
thrown overboard, swallowed by a whale, and supplicate to God

intensely about his own injustice before God saved him? Think of his horrible suffering. The stories about the appearance of Jonah, his illness, and the condition of his skin after he is released from the belly of the whale are horrible. The man suffered—and suffered intensely. But what was his sin? The lesson comes full circle when we realize what happened to the people of Nineveh after the Prophet Jonah left them.

Were they destroyed? As the Prophet Jonah recuperated under a fig tree (Q 37:145), he thought so. But they were not destroyed, nor were they punished. After Jonah left, the people of Nineveh noticed the skies darkening. They grew terrified. One of the followers of Jonah—we do not know exactly who—told them, "This may be your last chance. Why don't we all gather, beg God for forgiveness, and plead with God not to curse us?" In other words, this follower managed to get them to change their minds at the very last second. So they pleaded with the Lord, and the Lord, in fact, forgave them (Q 10:98). After Jonah recuperated and returned to the people of Nineveh, he found that in his absence they were not only saved, but that many of them, if not most, now followed his message.

What was Jonah's sin? Despair.

Even after being told that they had three days before being destroyed, it was still not right for Jonah to give up on his people. In the very last moments, a follower who stayed behind made all the difference. Jonah's sin was so grave that he had to go through an excruciatingly painful lesson. He had to leave the city of Nineveh, confront another group of ignorant people, be thrown overboard, and swallowed by a whale. He had to find himself despairing in the belly of the whale. He had to be scorched by the acid in the whale's stomach. It is said that Jonah's skin became raw and red like a newborn baby. He had to be in a horrible state of suffering, eventually nursing himself back to health under a fig tree. He had to return to the people of Nineveh to learn the lesson that if you believe in God, then you must believe in justice, and if you believe in both God and justice, then the results are in God's hands.

Our job is to speak to the truth until the very last second of our lives. Even if all the indicators are that we have failed or that our prayers have not been answered, we must persist. That is why Jonah was the first prophet to be mentioned to the Prophet Muhammad.

It is not a coincidence that some of the worst persecution the Prophet Muhammad experienced was in Ta'if. Having suffered enormously in Mecca, the Prophet travelled to Ta'if to try to convince the people of Ta'if to protect him and give him amnesty and shelter. Instead, they turned on him and threw rocks at him, pelting the Prophet so much that he bled. The Prophet was insulted and assaulted. He fled to a point outside of Ta'if to rest, collapsing in exhaustion, bleeding and hurt.

At that point, a slave boy saw him, took pity on him, and approached the Prophet to offer him some grapes. The Prophet Muhammad asked the boy where he was from. "I am from Nineveh," he replied. The Prophet Muhammad smiled and said, "You are from the city of the Prophet Jonah." And the Prophet was reminded, at that very moment, of the revelation in Surah al-Qalam, one of the earliest revelations, that warned him to learn from and not repeat the mistake of the Prophet Jonah.

Despair is not an option.

It is as if that boy who gave the grapes to the Prophet in Ta'if was a little mercy from God. If we are not alert to these mercies and the ways that God communicates with us, we could easily miss them. How often in life could something appear completely happenstance and coincidental, but it is, in fact, God speaking to us? That little boy with a few grapes that he offered to a bleeding Muhammad, in pain after being insulted and humiliated by an entire town, was God's reminder to the Prophet that despair is not an option.

I focus on the theme of despair because of the nature of immorality and sin. Most people do not decide to become immoral. Most people do not decide to do what is wrong. Most people slip into immoral or sinful situations because they simply give up. Most people have a sense of idealism at some point in their lives. They want to do what is right, but then Satan tells them, "You have been doing what is right all your life. Has it really made a difference? Until when will you keep doing what is right? Does it make a difference if you believe in justice, if you speak the truth, if you are a nice human being, or if you obey God? Why does God care? God really does not care about you. You do not really matter. So, really, if you follow this, do that, or believe in this, will it really make a difference?" Most people allow Satan to convince them that it really does not make a difference, so they start slipping. They do not slip in one fell swoop. Rather, they slip in baby steps, little by little, until they get to a point where they do not like themselves anymore. Then they give up. They start to feel like hypocrites, so they give up.

The biggest ally of Islamophobia is Muslim despair. It is for Muslims to feel like nothing they do makes a difference. The biggest victory that Islamophobes have achieved is to convince Muslims that their Islamic values and ethics do not make a difference, so they may as well give them up. That is precisely what has happened. I distinctly remember the Bosnian genocide. They were my prime years. When Srebrenica happened, there was total outrage. Today, however, Jerusalem has been taken, and we do not even care anymore. We gave up. We despaired. The Rohingya and Uyghurs are being slaughtered, and we do not care anymore. We gave up. We despaired. That is the biggest gift to the Islamophobes and racists. The racist truly wins only when the racialized and oppressed accept their oppression and philosophize the racism inflicted against them. The racist does not win so long as you resist. The racist wins only when you philosophize the racism as something other than unjust, immoral, and disgusting. That is the racist's true victory.

If you believe in God, then there is no room for despair. You must still do your part. The Prophet Jonah was told by God that the people of Nineveh will be destroyed in three days and yet, even then, he still did not have the right to despair. He did not have the right to give up and leave. God taught him a very painful lesson. Jonah should have kept trying until the very last second.

Reflect upon this. The stories of the prophets in the Qur'an are not mere stories. If God chose to tell us these stories, God has a point. But the point is not to entertain us. Nor should we think, "But we are not prophets." The stories of the prophets teach us moral lessons about *our* lives. Reflect upon this.

10 July 2020

GLOSSARY OF TERMS

Adhan
A call to prayer recited five times a day before each of the communal prayers.

Ahl al-bayt
Lit., "the family of the house." The term refers to the family of the Prophet Muhammad, particularly his daughter Fatima, her husband 'Ali, who was also the Prophet's cousin, their sons al-Husayn and al-Hasan, and their descendants. The Shi'a tradition holds the *ahl al-bayt* to be the rightful leaders of the Muslim community.

Ahl al-suffa
An appellation applied to certain persons who were the "guests" of Muslims in Medina, i.e., supported by the charity of the Muslims. These were poor refugees and houseless men who passed the nights in the *"suffa"* of the Prophet's mosque in Medina, which was an appurtenance of the mosque roofed with palm sticks.

Alhamdulillah
Often used expression that means "thank God," my gratitude be to God.

Al-Sirat al-Mustaqim
The straight path which is tread by prophets, the truthful, martyrs, and the righteous (Q 4:68-69).

Astaghfirullah

Often used expression that means "I seek forgiveness from God."

Azhar

Lit., the brilliant or the radiant. A mosque and university in Cairo established by the Fatimids in 358/969. The Azhar has graduated many religious scholars in the Muslim world.

'Abbasid

The second ruling dynasty of the Muslim empire after the Umayyads. Flourished in Baghdad from 132/750 to 656/1258. Thereafter, it survived as a shadow Caliphate until 923/1517.

'Aql

Mind, intellect, rationality, reason.

'Awra

Areas of the human body that are considered private and to be covered in the presence of others. A modest man or woman would cover these parts of the body with loose-fitting cloth. The parts that should be covered are different for men and women. Cultural norms should be considered in defining modesty.

Caliph

Arabic: *Khalifa* (pl. *khulafa'*) lit., successor or deputy. Refers to the head of the Islamic state after the death of the Prophet. Also see *Caliphate*.

Caliphate

The term literally means "government under a Caliphate." It refers to the Islamic state that emerged after the death of the Prophet Muhammad in 632 and that came to represent the global Muslim community and govern the people and lands under its control. Major caliphates included the Umayyad and 'Abbasid Caliphates. The last major caliphate, the Ottoman Caliphate, claimed caliphal authority from 1517 to 1924 CE. The word stems from the Arabic *khalifa*, meaning successor, deputy, or viceroy. See also *Khalifa*.

Constitution of Medina

A document drawn up by the Prophet Muhammad shortly after his arrival in Medina that formed the basis of a multi-religious Islamic state in Medina. The document brought to an end the bitter tribal fighting between the rival clans of Banu Aws and Banu Khazraj in Medina and established the Muslim *Ummah* as a community united across tribal divisions.

Dhikr

Remembrance of God.

Du'a'

A supplication or prayer.

Fahisha (pl. Fawahish)

A vile deed often involving sexual misconduct. A grave sin.

Faqih

A jurist, one learned in jurisprudence *(fiqh)*.

Fasad

An Arabic term denoting a sense of corruption, depravity, and rottenness. The condemnation of the spread of *fasad* on earth is a major ethical theme of the Qur'an.

Fatwa (pl. fatawa)

A non-binding legal opinion issued in response to a legal problem.

Fiqh

Lit., the word implies "an understanding." Islamic law: the process of jurisprudence by which the rules of Islamic law are derived. The word is also used to refer generally to positive law.

Fisq

Immorality, sinfulness. The condemnation of the "*fasiqun,*" a term derived from the same trilateral root of *f-s-q,* is a key ethical theme in the Qur'an.

Fitna

Calamity, corruption, civil discord. Also refers to enticement or seduction.

Fujur

Depravity, wickedness. The term conveys the sense of committing abhorrent deeds without any inclination toward repentance.

Furqan

Lit., "criterion," usually said to denote the criterion between truth and falsehood. In this vein, "*al-Furqan*" is another name for the Qur'an (Q 25:1) and chapter 25 of the Qur'an is called Surah al-Furqan.

Ghayb

The realm of the unseen, including the realm of angels, demons, and *jinn*. The term can also extend to knowledge of future events. The Qur'an affirms that a key constituent of belief in God is a belief in the unseen (Q 2:3).

Hadith Qudsi

A special category of *hadith* said to be unique because their content is attributed to God while the actual wording is credited to the Prophet Muhammad.

Hajj

The fifth pillar of Islam; pilgrimage to Mecca at least once in a person's lifetime, if physically and financially able to do so.

Halal

Islamic law: the permitted, allowed. Most schools hold that everything is permitted unless there is evidence requiring that it be prohibited. Most schools adhere to a presumption of permissibility, and so, the burden of proof is against the person who is arguing for a prohibition. *Halal* meat is meat slaughtered according to the specifications of Islamic law.

Hanafi

An adherent of the Sunni juristic school of thought named after its eponym Abu Hanifa (d. 150/767). The school developed in Kufa and Basra but spread in the Middle East and the Indian subcontinent. The Hanafi school is one of the four main surviving Sunni jurisprudential schools in the modern age.

Haqq

In Islamic contexts, the term can have a variety of meanings, including truth, justice, morality, and righteousness. One of the 99 names of God in the Islamic tradition is "*al-Haqq*," which affirms God as the ultimate source of truth. The term also translates as "right," and Muslim scholars accordingly speak of two types of rights: the *haqq al-'ibad* ("the rights of people") and *haqq Allah* ("the rights of God").

Haram

Islamic law: what is forbidden, the sinful, the prohibited. One of the five categories or values of *Shari'a,* connoting that which is forbidden or sinful.

Haram (pl. Haramayn)

Holy site. Used to refer to two of the three holiest sites in Islam, Mecca and Medina, also referred to as "The Two Holy Sites" (*al-haramayn*). The third holiest site, and the most significant in the view of some scholars, is Jerusalem, which signifies Islam's intimate connection to all of the Abrahamic faiths.

Hasan

Lit., good, desirable. Islamic law: refers to that which is considered beautiful and moral as opposed to the ugly and immoral *(qabih)*.

Hijab

Lit., obstruction, shield, shelter, protection, cover, screen, seclusion, obscure, and hide. The veil with which a Muslim woman covers her head, except her face. The face veil is called *niqab*.

Hijra

Lit., migrate, desert, or abandon. The historical migration of Prophet Muhammad and his Companions from Mecca to Medina in the year 622 C.E. The *Hijra* marks the beginning of the Islamic lunar calendar.

Hijaz

A geographical region comprising most of the west of modern-day Saudi Arabia, including the two holy sites of Islam, Mecca and Medina.

Iftar

The evening meal with which Muslims break their fast after sunset during the month of Ramadan.

Ihsan

Lit., kindness, goodness, compassion. That which is commonly known to be good and moral. In a tradition, the Prophet defined it as fulfillment of the Divine Will as though one sees God at all times.

Imam

Lit., one who stands out in front. Islamic law: leader of prayer or of a congregation. In common usage it often means a religious leader.

Iman

Belief, faith, right belief. Also, belief in God, the Messengers including Muhammad, angels, and the revealed books including the Qur'an.

'Izza

A key ethical term in the Qur'an with connotations of dignity, honor, self-esteem, and pride. The Qur'an contrasts the true *'izza* of the believer who derives their sense of worth and honor from God (Q 35:10) with the false and arrogant *'izza* of the unbelievers (Q 38:2).

Jahiliyya

A state of ignorance, a state of misguidance. These terms are used to refer to the pre-Islamic period in Arabia. Often used to connote paganism or a state of darkness.

Jalabiyya

The cultural dress of the Arabs, a one-piece garment that usually extends down to the ankles.

Jama'a

Congregation, grouping, the majority, the righteous group.

Jinn

A species of creation mentioned in the Qur'an. Reportedly, the *jinn* share certain attributes with human beings, such as free will, belief and disbelief, morality and immorality, procreation, and so forth. Satan was from this species of creation. Both humans and *jinn* differ from the angels insofar as the angels do not have free will to choose between right and wrong. Hence, Satan is not a "fallen angel" in Islamic theology.

Jumu'a

Friday; the day of congregation in which Muslims gather at noon to hear a sermon (*khutbah*) in the mosque and offer the noon prayer.

Unlike the Jewish or Christian Sabbath, Muslims are not required to refrain from work or rest on Friday or any other day. Although Muslims believe in six periods of creation, they do not believe that God needed to rest on the seventh period.

Kafir

A non-believer, someone who does not believe in God or in Islam. Someone who is ungrateful toward God. See also *Kufr*.

Ka'ba

Lit., cube. Refers to the house of worship built by Abraham and his older son, Ishmael, in the desert of Mecca. Muslims face the Ka'ba in their daily prayers as a symbol of their global unity.

Khalifa (pl. khulafa')

Successor, deputy, or viceroy. According to the Qur'an, human beings are the *khulafa'* of God on earth. Also see *Caliph*.

Khatib

Lit., a speaker. Usually, the term refers to the one who delivers the sermon (*khutbah*) before the noon prayer on Friday (*jumu'a*).

Khutbah

Lit., a speech or lecture. Usually, the term refers to the sermon delivered on Friday (*jumu'a*) before the noon prayer.

Kufr

Lit., to cover over something. In this sense, the term is found in the Qur'an in its plural form as a reference to farmers (Q 57:20). Islamic law: covering over the truth once one has recognized it as true, i.e., rejecting the message of Islam. Also means ingratitude or infidelity, not believing in God or being ungrateful toward God.

Laylat al-Qadr

Variously referred to as the "Night of Power" or "Night of Decree," the term refers to the holiest night in the Islamic calendar that occurs during the last ten nights of the month of Ramadan. This is the night in which the Qur'an was first revealed to the Prophet Muhammad. The Qur'an describes the significance of this night as superior to one thousand months of worship (Q 97:3). Its exact date is uncertain.

Malakut

Lit., "the realm of dominion," an invisible realm close to God. See also *Ghayb.*

Masjid

Mosque, Muslim place of worship.

Masjid al-Haram

The Great Mosque of Mecca.

Miswak

Tooth-stick; a piece of stick with which the teeth are polished and cleaned, the end being made like a brush by chewing it so as to separate its fibers.

Mizan

Lit., "balance," a core Qur'anic term that has connotations of justice, equity, and fairness in all aspects of life. The term is also understood as "measure" or "scale," and signifies the weighing of one's deeds on the Day of Judgment.

Mufti

Muslim legal scholar who is qualified to issue legal *responsa*. See *fatwa*.

Mujahid

Lit., "person of *jihad*." The term describes the believer who commits to a life of *jihad*, that is, a life in which one strives and struggles in pursuit of a noble aim. The term *jihad* has a more expansive meaning than military combat. The Qur'an, for example, often praises those who perform *jihad* "with their wealth" (Q 4:95; 9:20; 49:15; 61:11).

Niqab

A piece of cloth that covers the face.

Qaramita

An Isma'ili Shi'i movement that rebelled against the Fatimid and 'Abbasid Caliphates and flourished in Iraq, Yemen, and Bahrain between the 9th and 11th centuries. The Qaramita launched many raids into 'Abbasid territory. In 930 CE, they sacked the city of Mecca and stole the Black Stone of the Ka'ba, an act for which they became notorious in Islamic history.

Qubh

Lit., "ugliness" or "the bad." Medieval Muslim theologians and philosophers debated the nature of *qubh* and its opposite, *husn* (beauty or the good). This debate hinged on the question of whether *husn* and *qubh* were objective ethical principles that human beings, through reason, could understand (known as "ethical objectivism"), or whether acts were only ugly or beautiful because God had decreed them so ("Divine command theory").

Ramadan

The ninth month of the Islamic calendar. It is the month of fasting for Muslims in which the devotee abstains from food, drink, conjugal relations, and all sins and indecencies from dawn to sunset each day.

Rak'ah

A prescribed unit of the five daily prayers. A single unit consists of a ritual of bows, prostrations, and the recitation of prayers.

Sahih

Valid, authentic. Often refers to a *hadith* report or tradition considered to be authentic.

Salaf

The word *salaf* means "predecessors" and usually refers to the period of the Prophet and the Companions. The term invokes the authenticity and legitimacy of this archetypal generation. What it means to be a Salafi, however, is far from clear. The term has historically invoked a wide spectrum of quite contradictory thinkers and movements, each claiming to be an authentic representation of the beliefs and practices of the Prophet and Companions. Since the 1970s, the term has become increasingly associated, even interchangeable, with the Wahhabi school.

Salah

Prayer. One of the five pillars of Islam, prayer is a prescribed ritual performed by observant Muslims five times per day.

Sawm

Fasting, especially during the month of Ramadan. Fasting during the month of Ramadan constitutes one of the five pillars of Islam. See also *Ramadan*.

Shahadah

Lit., derives from the verb *shahadah* which means to witness, see, or testify. Islamic theology: a testament of faith, to bear witness that there is but one God and that Muhammad is God's Messenger. This is the first of five pillars of Islam (namely, the five are *shahadah*, *salah* (prayer), *sawm* (fasting), *zakah* (almsgiving) and *hajj* (pilgrimage).

Shari'a

Lit., the water source, the way, the path. In Islamic theology and law, the path or way given by God to human beings, the path by which human beings search God's Will. Commonly misinterpreted as "Islamic law," *Shari'a* carries a much broader meaning. It is the sum total of categorizations of all human actions. These categories are mandatory (*fard* or *wajib*), encouraged (*mustahabb*), permissible (*halal* or *mubah*), discouraged (*makruh*), and forbidden (*haram*). *Shari'a* is not restricted to positive law per se but includes moral and ethical values, and includes the jurisprudential process itself.

Shaykh

Lit., old man, master, leader. The title is often used to describe a learned man or religious scholar.

Shirk

Polytheism or the association of partners with God. Believing in gods other than the One God. For Muslims, *shirk* could mean placing the importance of things like wealth, power, and prestige on the same level as or even higher than God, such that they become an object of "worship" or one's own "god".

Sira

Lit., this word derives from the verbal "*sara*" meaning, "to walk." Islamic theology: the biography of the Prophet (i.e., how he "walked" through life).

Sunna

Lit., the way or course or conduct of life. Islamic law: the example of the Prophet embodied in his statements, actions, and those matters that he silently approved or disapproved as reported in *hadith* literature. The *Sunna* of the Companions means the precedent or the conduct of the Companions of the Prophet. *Sunna* is also the name used to describe the main branch of Islam.

Taghut

A word of Aramaic and Syriac origin connoting injustice, inequity, false deities, idolatry, oppression, tyranny, and despotism. *Taghut* is the very antithesis of the Qur'an's moral and ethical worldview.

Tahmid

Praise of God. Also see *Alhamdullilah*.

Takbir

The declaration of "Allahu Akbar," which means God is greater than all.

Talaq
An Islamic divorce.

Taqwa
God consciousness; piety; caution; being religiously cautious; the precaution of piety.

Taraf
An Arabic term connoting luxury, indulgence, and opulence. The Qur'an draws a close link between *taraf* and injustice in that it is often because of *taraf* that people fail to challenge or even contribute to corruption on earth (Q 11:116; 17:16; 23:33; 34:34; 43:23; 56:45).

Tariqa
Lit., "path" or "way." The term commonly refers to a Sufi school or order.

Tawhid
Lit., unification, oneness. The Islamic doctrine of monotheism, *tawhid* connotes more than just numerical oneness. It is the idea that God is singularly unique, that all prayers and worship are due to God alone, and that God alone is the source of all that there is. The doctrine of *tawhid* rejects Christian Trinitarianism. Debates over the meaning and implications of professing *tawhid* underpin the diversity of Islamic thought. The various branches of the Islamic sciences, including philosophy, Sufism, and theology, all seek to explain the idea of God's oneness and unity.

Treaty of Hudaybiyya
A treaty agreed between the Prophet Muhammad, representing the Muslim state of Medina, and the Qurayshi tribe of Mecca in the

year 6/628. The treaty guaranteed a ceasefire between the Muslims and Meccans for a period of 10 years and allowed Muslims to return the following year in a peaceful pilgrimage to Mecca. Despite initial misgivings by some of the Companions over what were seen as unfavorable terms, the Qur'an vindicated the Prophet and heralded the Treaty of Hudaybiyya as a "manifest victory" (Q 48:1). Indeed, the Treaty soon paved the way for the eventual Muslim conquest of Mecca, which took place only two years later.

Ummah
The global community of Muslims.

Umayyad
First Islamic dynasty after the death of the Rightly Guided Caliphs. Established by Mu'awiya Ibn Sufyan after the death of 'Ali Ibn Abi Talib, and lasted from 41/661 to 132/750.

'Umrah
Pilgrimage to Mecca that can be undertaken at any time of the year, unlike the *Hajj*, which falls during the Islamic month of *Dhul-Hijjah*. See *Hajj*.

Wahhabi
Follower of the strict puritanical teachings of Muhammad Ibn 'Abd al-Wahhab. Wahhabis are hostile to the intercession of saints, visiting of tombs of saints, Sufism, Shi'ism, and rational methods of deducing laws. The Wahhabi creed is very restrictive of women and until the ascension of Crown Prince Mohammed bin Salman (MBS), was dominant in Saudi Arabia.

Wasta

Lit., "intermediary." The term refers to use of one's social influence or personal connections to get things done. The use of *wasta* is a common practice and social norm throughout the Arab world. A loose equivalent would be the English phrase of "It is not what you know, but who you know."

Wudu'

Ablution with water in preparation for prayer.

Zabiba

Prayer mark that appears on the forehead of those who engage in regular prostration.

Zakah

One of the five pillars of Islam; the required almsgiving of Muslims. In the Qur'an, the term is used to convey charity in the broadest sense, which extends far beyond the 2.5% surplus savings that many modern Muslims cite as the required percentage. Some modern scholars argue that Muslims should regularly give 20% of their regular income. The root of the term in Arabic connotes a sense of "purification." As such, the act of donating to the poor and needy is said to "purify" the giver of their sins, an idea affirmed in the Qur'an (Q 92:18).

Zina

Fornication or adultery.

Selected Biographies

Abu Bakr al-Siddiq (d. 22/634)

His full name was 'Abdullah Ibn 'Uthman Ibn 'Amir Ibn Abi Quhafa. He was the first noble and rich man to believe in the Prophet in Mecca and among the closest Companions to the Prophet. Abu Bakr spent all of his wealth supporting the persecuted Muslims in Mecca, and he was in the Prophet's company when the Prophet migrated to Medina. Upon the Prophet's death, Abu Bakr was appointed to lead the Muslim nation and became the first Caliph in Islam.

Abu Hurayrah (d. 58/678)

His full name was 'Abd al-Rahman Ibn Sakr al-Dawsi, and he was called Abu Hurayrah because of his fondness for kittens. He was a late convert to Islam. Abu Hurayrah joined the Muslims in Medina around the time of the Battle of Khaybar in 7/629. Although he was with the Prophet for less than four years, Abu Hurayrah has transmitted more traditions from the Prophet than most other Companions. Knowing that he was criticized for this, he would often respond that he spent all his time with the Prophet and made a conscious effort to memorize as much as he could from him. Abu Hurayrah died in Medina.

Alodah, Salman (b. 1376/1956 -)

An influential Saudi religious scholar and jurist with a mass following in the Arab world, Alodah is the author of numerous works, including a 2013 reflection on the Arab Spring, entitled *As'ilat al-Thawra* ("Questions Around the Revolution"), which argued that political despotism and tyranny were incompatible with Islamic theology. As of September 2017, Alodah has been in prison in Saudi Arabia for alleged "terrorism and conspiracy against the state."

Al-Albani, Nasir al-Din (d. 1420/1999)

An Albanian-born Islamic scholar who became a famous *Salafi hadith* scholar. Largely self-taught, he spent much of his life critically re-evaluating the *hadith* literature. He criticized the four mainstream schools of Islamic law. He is widely considered one of the most influential figures in the 20th century *Salafi* movement.

Al-Bukhari, Abu 'Abdullah Muhammad Ibn Isma'il Ibn Ibrahim Ibn al-Mughira Ibn Bardizbah (d. 256/870)

He compiled the collection of *hadith* known as *Sahih al-Bukhari*. He began studying *hadith* at an early age. Bukhari spent sixteen years gathering reports about the Prophet, traveling widely between Egypt and Khurasan. Reportedly, he collected more than 600,000 traditions, of which only 7,397 found their way into his collection of *hadith*. Although he held that the Qur'an was uncreated, he adhered to the view that the recitation of it was created. As a result, he was accused of heterodoxy and was exiled from his home in Nishapur. He moved to Bukhara, but after encountering more political problems, he was again expelled. He lived the rest of his life with relatives in a village near Samarqand. Bukhari's collection of traditions is considered by Sunni Muslims to be one of the six canonical works on *hadith.* Some modern Muslims claim that all the traditions documented in Bukhari are absolutely authentic and are not susceptible to criticism.

Al-Farsi, Salman (d. 32/652 or 653)

A close Companion of the Prophet Muhammad and the first Persian to convert to Islam. He is credited with the idea of digging a trench around Medina, a Persian military technique, when it was attacked by Meccan forces during the Battle of the Trench. Along with other Companions, such as Abu Dharr al-Ghifari and 'Ammar ibn Yasir, Salman has a prominent place in Shi'i tradition on account of his reported support for 'Ali's leadership of the Muslim community in the years after the Prophet's death.

Al-Ghazali, Abu Hamid Muhammad Ibn Muhammad (d. 505/1111)

A famous Shafi'i jurist, theologian, philosopher, and mystic. He was a distinguished student of the prominent jurist al-Juwayni, and was appointed to a teaching position at the Nizamiyya School in Baghdad while fairly young. His fame as a jurist and philosopher spread widely. Troubled by his fame, al-Ghazali resigned his prestigious post and traveled to Jerusalem and then Damascus, seeking spiritual purification. His spiritual journey lasted ten years, after which he wrote some of his most influential works. His works of law and jurisprudence, such as *al-Wajiz* and *al-Mustasfa,* are reference sources for Shafi'i *fiqh* and jurisprudence. His monumental work *lhya' 'Ulum al-Din* was an attempt to revitalize religious sciences among the laity. Al-Ghazali also tried to integrate and reconcile between juristic and spiritual sciences. He wrote a famous work about his own spiritual journey, a pseudo-autobiography named *al-Munqidh min al-Dalal* ("Deliverance from Error"). He also wrote a refutation of philosophers named *Tahafot al-Falasifa,* which is translated into English as *The Incoherence of the Philosophers.* He died in Tabiran.

Al-Ghazali, Muhammad (d. 1416/1996)

An author of numerous works and one of the greatest Muslim jurists in the contemporary age. He challenged essentialist and apologetic Islamic reform efforts by reinvigorating inquiry and investigation into the classical sources. He wrote a scathing critique of essentialist *hadith* methodologies and of Wahhabi thought. This became his most controversial work, leading to a ban in some Muslim countries.

Al-Husseini, Muhammad Amin (d. 1394/1974)

A Palestinian-Arab nationalist and Muslim religious leader who served as the Grand Mufti of Jerusalem in British Mandate Palestine between 1921 and 1948. Al-Husseini was initially considered an ally of the British but later became known for collaborating with both Italy and Germany and calling for Muslims to join the side of the Nazis during World War II. An early critic of Zionism, upon meeting Adolf Hitler in Berlin, he requested Hitler's support in opposing the establishment of a Jewish national home in Palestine. Opponents of Palestinian nationalism today make use of his example and activities to associate the Palestinian national movement in general with anti-Semitism and the genocidal campaign of the Nazis.

Al-Khattab, 'Umar ibn (d. 23/644)

An early convert to Islam who migrated from Mecca to Medina and was a close Companion of the Prophet. 'Umar was a very important figure during the Prophet's life and after his death. His daughter Hafsa was married to the Prophet, and he often served as the Prophet's confidant. 'Umar became the Caliph after Abu Bakr and ruled for about ten years. 'Umar played a critical role in the development of Islamic law, and his legal precedents remain very influential. He is also the source of many reports from and about the Prophet. He was assassinated by a mentally unstable slave.

Al-Maliki, Hassan Farhan (b. 1389-90/1970 -)

A reformist Saudi cleric who remains in prison in Saudi Arabia where he faces the death penalty after his arrest by Saudi authorities in September 2017. Among the charges that he faces is that of "insulting the country's rulers and the Supreme Council of Religious Scholars." Al-Maliki has challenged the intolerant and ahistorical theology of the Wahhabi school and criticized the selective use of weak *hadith* reports to justify silence and quietism before unjust rulers. He has also challenged the veneration of figures such as the first Umayyad Caliph, Mu'awiyah ibn Abi Sufyan, in the Sunni tradition, and sought to re-assert the moral, social, and political role of the Prophet's household, the *ahl al-bayt*, in Islamic history.

Al-Nawawi, Muhyi al-Din Abu Zakariyya Ibn Muri (d. 676/1277)

A prominent Shafi'i jurist. At first, al-Nawawi studied medicine in al-Rawahiyya School in Damascus, but he soon switched to the study of law. He was appointed to the Ashrafiyya School of *hadith* as a professor, but when he refused to sanction unjust taxes imposed by Sultan Baybars, he was fired and expelled from Damascus. He was appointed as chief judge in Egypt where he was, in time, fired again and imprisoned. Al-Nawawi died in his father's home in Nawa south of Damascus. Al-Nawawi's works on law and *hadith* became very influential in Islamic legal history and remain influential today.

Al-Nasa'i, Ahmad Ibn 'Ali Ibn Shu'ayb Ibn 'Ali (d. 303/915)

A *hadith* scholar whose collection, *Sunan al-Nasa'i,* is considered one of the six authoritative works on *hadith,* alongside *Sahih al-Bukhari* and *Sahih Muslim.* Originally from Khurasan, he moved to Egypt where he resided. However, because of petty jealousies he was forced to leave Egypt for Palestine. In Palestine, he was suspected of not believing in Mu'awiya Ibn Abi Sufyan's merits. Reportedly, he was asked about the merits of Mu'awiya, but when he refused to respond, he was badly beaten in the mosque. He sustained injuries and later died. Some reports indicate, however, that he died in Mecca while performing *hajj.*

Al-Qaradawi, Yusuf (d. 1444/2022)

He was an Egyptian Islamic scholar and jurist based in Qatar, chairman of the International Union of Muslim Scholars, and widely known as a "global mufti" on account of his worldwide influence and reach. Qaradawi is perhaps best known for his television program on the Arabic *Al Jazeera* network, entitled *al-Shari'a wa-l-Hayah* ("Shari'a and Life"), which regularly attracted audiences in the millions.

Al-Sadiq, Ja'far ibn Muhammad ibn 'Ali (d. 148/765)

A highly distinguished Muslim scholar, jurist, and theologian, he was the founder of the Ja'fari school of Islamic jurisprudence and the sixth Imam of the Twelver and Ismaili denominations of Shi'i Islam. He features prominently in the spiritual genealogies of many Sufi orders and is also revered in the Sunni tradition as a teacher of both Abu Hanifa and Malik ibn Anas, eponymous founders of the Hanafi and Maliki Sunni legal schools, respectively.

Al-Tabari, Muhammad Ibn Jarir Ibn Yazid (d. 310/923)

A famous jurist and historian, al-Tabari was considered to be the founder of his own school of thought. He was first trained in Shafi'i law, however, his extensive learning enabled him to develop an independent school of thought. Unfortunately, much of his legal writings have not survived. What have survived are his Qur'anic commentary and his historical chronicle. Nearly the entire chronicle has been translated into English. He was offered many government appointments during his life but consistently refused all of them. Through much of his life, he was persecuted by members of the Hanbali school in Baghdad, who considered al-Tabari disrespectful to the founder of their school. In fact, their persecution was so great that people could not visit al-Tabari even if they wanted to, due to the efforts of the Hanbalis to keep him isolated. It is even reported that upon al-Tabari's death, the Hanbali students burned his books and buried his body in an unmarked grave in a Christian cemetery. His school of thought did not survive long, and apparently vanished a few centuries after his death. Notably, he was one of the few jurists who held that women may lead men in prayer.

Al-Wahhab, Muhammad ibn 'Abd (d. 1206/1792)

Founder of the strict puritanical creed known as Wahhabism. Wahhabis are hostile to the intercession of saints, visiting of tombs of saints, Sufism, Shi'ism, and rational methods of deducing laws. The Wahhabi creed is very restrictive of women and until the ascension of Crown Prince Mohammed bin Salman (MBS), was dominant in Saudi Arabia.

'Ali Ibn Abi Talib (d. 40/661)

Cousin, son-in-law, and a close Companion of the Prophet, 'Ali was one of the first converts to Islam in Mecca. 'Ali was, according to Sunnis, the fourth Rightly Guided Caliph (*rashidun*). During 'Ali's Caliphate, Mu'awiyah, the governor of Syria, rebelled against him, and this insurrection led to the Battle of Siffin in 657. After 'Ali was assassinated by a member of the Khawarij rebels, Mu'awiyah declared himself Caliph. The supporters of 'Ali, *shi'at Ali* (the party of 'Ali), asserted the right of the 'Alid branch of the Prophet's family to the Caliphate, and led several rebellions against the Umayyads. This conflict eventually led to the sectarian division between Sunni and Shi'a. 'Ali was married to the Prophet's daughter, Fatima, and fathered the Prophet's two grandsons, Hassan and Husayn.

Gomaa, Ali (b. 1371/1952 -)

A prominent Egyptian Islamic jurist, he served as the Grand Mufti of Egypt between 2003—2013 and is a notorious supporter of authoritarian government in the Muslim world. Gomaa initially condemned the Arab Spring protests that erupted in Egypt and across the Middle East in 2011. He then gave his support to the 2013 military coup in Egypt and encouraged Egyptian security forces to kill those protesting against the coup. A leaked video recording cited Gomaa as lending religious sanction to mass murder by the Egyptian state. In harsh and uncompromising terms, Gomaa told an audience of Egyptian military and police officials to "shoot to kill" the protestors, whom he also described as "trash." The resulting Rabaa Massacre of August 2013 has been described by *Human Rights Watch* as a crime against humanity and "one of the world's largest killings of demonstrators in a single day in recent history."

Husayn Ibn 'Ali Ibn Abi Talib (d. 61/680)

Grandson of the Prophet Muhammad. He is the son of the Prophet's daughter Fatima and the Prophet's cousin 'Ali. He was born in Medina before the Prophet died. Husayn was extremely pious and particularly influential in the development of Islamic law. Upon the death of Mu'awiya (d. 60/680), the first Umayyad caliph, al-Husayn refused to give the *bay'a* (oath of allegiance) to Mu'awiya's son and successor, Yazid. Thereafter, al-Husayn sought help from his supporters in Kufa to start a revolt against the Umayyads. Upon his journey to Kufa from the Hijaz, he was met by Yazid's forces at Karbala in modern-day Iraq. Betrayed by many of his supporters, al-Husayn's small forces were defeated by the much larger Umayyad army, and al-Husayn was killed. The battle of Karbala is of central importance in Shi'i theology, and passion plays *(ta'ziya)* are performed regularly in Iran in remembrance of the events leading to al-Husayn's death.

Ibn 'Affan, Uthman (d. 35/656)

A Companion of the Prophet who was an early convert to Islam and later appointed as the third Rightly Guided Caliph after the death of 'Umar Ibn al-Khattab in 23/644. Uthman was married to

Ruqayya, the Prophet's daughter, and upon her death, married Umm Kulthum, another daughter of the Prophet. His twelve-year reign as Caliph saw the consolidation of the text of the Qur'an and the expansion of the Islamic Empire. As his reign progressed, however, an increasing number of Muslims, including other Companions of the Prophet, came to criticize Uthman's policies. His Caliphate ended in revolt, and his death at the hands of rebels led to a civil war that was to later eventually contribute to the split between Sunni and Shi'i Islam.

Khadijah bint Khuwaylid (d. 3 years before *Hijra*/619)

She was the first wife of the Prophet and the first convert to Islam. A wealthy woman, she hired the Prophet before his calling and then proposed to him in marriage. She spent all her wealth supporting the persecuted Muslims in Mecca and died before the migration to Medina. The Prophet loved her dearly and was married to her for more than twenty-five years before she died.

Umm Kulthum bint Muhammad (d. 9/630)

A daughter of the Prophet from his wife Khadijah. Upon her sister Ruqayya's death, she married 'Uthman Ibn 'Affan, who would later become the third Caliph. She died during the Prophet's lifetime.

Umm Salama, Hind bint Suhayl (d. 62/681)

One of the wives of the Prophet. Before her marriage to the Prophet, she was married to a man named Abu Salama. She and Abu Salama migrated to Abyssinia before joining the rest of the Muslims in Medina. When her husband died in Medina, she was a widow with four children. When the Prophet wanted to marry her, she told him that she was old, given to jealousy, and had young children. After marrying the Prophet, she played an important role in the Muslim community in Medina. She continued to live in Medina after the Prophet's death, where she taught and transmitted traditions from the Prophet.

Further Reading

Works by Khaled Abou El Fadl

And God Knows the Soldiers: The Authoritative and Authoritarian in Islamic Discourses (Lanham, Md: University Press of America, 2001) analyzes the case study of a *fatwa* that supported a Muslim basketball player's refusal to stand up for the American national anthem. The book documents the rise of authoritarian, as opposed to authoritative, methodologies in modern Islam. The book is a revised and expanded edition of an earlier work; see *The Authoritative and Authoritarian in Islamic Discourses: A Contemporary Case Study*, 3rd edition (Al-Saadawi Publications, 2002).

Speaking in God's Name: Islamic Law, Authority, and Women (Oxford: Oneworld, 2001) analyzes the interplay between author, text, and reader in the construction of meaning. With a particular focus on Islamic law and women, the book explores the demise of the juristic tradition and the rise of authoritarian discourses in modern Islam by examining a range of *fatwas* by leading Wahhabi clerics.

Rebellion and Violence in Islamic Law (Cambridge: Cambridge University Press, 2001) is the first systematic study of the idea of political resistance and rebellion in Islamic law. The book uncovers a highly technical and sophisticated discourse on the legality of rebellion, rebutting Orientalist notions that medieval Islamic political thought was characterized by political quietism and a doctrine of strict obedience to rulers.

The Great Theft: Wrestling Islam from the Extremists (New York: HarperOne, 2005) offers a primer on modern Muslim thought and exposes the hypocrisies, inconsistencies, and intolerance intrinsic to Wahhabi Islam.

The Search for Beauty in Islam: A Conference of the Books (Lanham, Md: Rowman & Littlefield, 2006) is a collection of essays inspired by the search for what is beautiful in Islam, about Islam, and among those who practice Islam. This search is often negotiated through an unflinching look at the ugly realities of modern Islam. A landmark publication that has since become a classic in the field.

Reasoning with God: Reclaiming Shari'ah in the Modern Age (Lanham, Md: Rowman & Littlefield, 2014) explores the true meaning of *Shari'a* and the way it can revitalize modern Islam. The book calls upon Muslims to re-engage the ethical tradition of their faith and explore the Qur'an's moral trajectory in the modern world.

The Prophet's Pulpit: Commentaries on the State of Islam—Volume I, ed. Josef Linnhoff (Dublin, Oh: Usuli Press, 2022) comprises a collection of twenty-two Islamic sermons that deliver incisive commentaries on the current state of the Muslim world from the symbolic pulpit of the Prophet of Islam.

Other Works

Darren Byler, *Terror Capitalism: Uyghur Dispossession and Masculinity in a Chinese City* (Durham, NC: Duke University Press, 2022), examines the mass detention of over one million Uyghurs in "re-education camps" in the northwest autonomous region of Xinjiang as part of a process of resource extraction in Uyghur lands, what the author calls "terror capitalism." The work shows in vivid detail the ongoing genocide against the Uyghurs and how mass surveillance, mass incarceration, and the state imposition of "Chinese values" contribute to Uyghur dispossession.

David Motadel, *Islam and Nazi Germany's War* (Cambridge, Ma: Harvard University Press, 2014) offers a detailed account of the largely unsuccessful attempt by Nazi Germany to build an alliance with the Islamic world. The book examines the Nazi perception of Islam and, in particular, how Nazi Germany saw Islam as a potential ally with the same enemies as Germany: Jews, the Soviet Union, and the British and French Empires. The book also examines the tactics used by the Allies to rally Muslims against Hitler.

John J. Mearsheimer and Stephen M. Walt, *The Israel Lobby and U.S. Foreign Policy* (New York: Farrar, Straus, Giroux, 2007) demonstrates how the remarkable level of economic, military, and political support that the U.S. provides to Israel is largely due to the influence of a loose coalition of pro-Israel lobbying groups, the largest of which is the American Israel Public Affairs Committee (AIPAC). The book gives a vivid account of the extent to which a committed and well-funded lobbying movement can buy political influence in the U.S.

The authors also note that this influence is greatly enhanced by the lack of an equally well-organized and well-funded pro-Palestine counter-lobby.

Michael A Sells, *The Bridge Betrayed: Religion and Genocide in Bosnia* (Berkeley: University of California Press, 1996) documents how the conflict in Bosnia in the 1990s was not just a civil war but an anti-Islamic genocide sustained by Christian holy war religious mythology. The book examines how "Christo-Slavic" extremism played a key role in the tragedy, which included the common depiction of Muslims as "Christ-killers" and the stereotyping of all Bosnian Muslims as foreign "Turks."

Seyyed Hossein Nasr, *A Young Muslim's Guide to the Modern World* (Chicago: Kazi Publications, 1994), is a work written specifically for young Muslims to familiarize them with the Islamic tradition, gain an understanding of the modern world from the Islamic point of view, and provide an outline of the Western intellectual tradition.

Usaama al-Azami, *Islam and the Arab Revolutions: The Ulama Between Democracy and Autocracy* (London: Hurst & Company, 2021) explores the Arab revolutions of 2011 and the counter-revolutionary coup in Egypt in 2013, examining how key religious figures like Ali Gomaa justified authoritarian regimes and lent religious backing for repression, even to the point of legitimating the murder of unarmed protestors. The work includes translations of Ali Gomaa's pre- and post-Rabaa private lectures to the Egyptian security forces in which Gomaa encouraged Egyptian security forces to "shoot to kill" those protesting the 2013 counter-revolutionary coup.

Index

321

ABOUT THE AUTHOR

*D*r. **Khaled Abou El Fadl** is the Omar and Azmeralda Alfi Distinguished Professor of Law at the UCLA School of Law, and founder of the Institute for Advanced Usuli Studies (The Usuli Institute). He is a classically trained Islamic jurist. He is the author of numerous books and articles on Islam and Islamic jurisprudence. Among his books are: *Reasoning with God: Reclaiming Shari'ah in the Modern Age; The Search for Beauty in Islam: A Conference of the Books; Speaking in God's Name: Islamic Law, Authority and Women; And God Knows the Soldiers: The Authoritative and Authoritarian in Islamic Discourses; The Great Theft: Wrestling Islam from the Extremists;* and *Rebellion and Violence in Islamic Law.* He is the recipient of the American Academy of Religion (AAR) 2020 Martin E. Marty Award for the Public Understanding of Religion.

ABOUT THE EDITOR

*D*r. **Josef Linnhoff** holds a PhD in Islamic Studies from the University of Edinburgh, Scotland, U.K. His work has been published in *The Muslim World, Islam and Christian-Muslim Relations,* and *Critical Muslim.* He is editor-in-chief of *Project Illumine: The Light of the Quran,* a multiyear project at The Usuli Institute to publish the first English-language Qur'anic commentary in over forty years. Before joining The Usuli Institute, he worked as a Researcher for BBC Monitoring in London.

Printed in Great Britain
by Amazon

31060045R00198